FORTUNE AND GLORY

Douglas Palmer
Nicholas James & Giles Sparrow

FORTUNE AND GLORY

TALES OF HISTORY'S GREATEST
ARCHAEOLOGICAL ADVENTURERS

Douglas Palmer
Nicholas James & Giles Sparrow

David and Charles

Thanks to Tim Brown for his inspiration and assistance in getting this book off the ground, the team at David & Charles and Val Porter.

A DAVID & CHARLES BOOK
Copyright © David & Charles Limited 2008

David & Charles is an F+W Publications Inc. company
4700 East Galbraith Road
Cincinnati, OH 45236

First published in the UK in 2008
First published in the US in 2008

Text copyright © Douglas Palmer, Nicholas James, Giles Sparrow 2008
Images © (see picture credits, page 272)

Douglas Palmer, Nicholas James, Giles Sparrow have asserted their right to be identified as author of this work in accordance with the Copyright, Designs and Patents Act, 1988.

A catalogue record for this book is available from the British Library.

ISBN-13: 978-0-7153-2959-7 paperback
ISBN-10: 0-7153-2959-6 paperback

Printed in USA by RR Donnelley Co Pte Ltd
for David & Charles
Brunel House, Newton Abbot, Devon

Commissioning Editor: Neil Baber
Editorial Manager: Emily Pitcher
Assistant Editor: Sarah Wedlake
Copy Editor: Val Porter
Designer: Eleanor Stafford
Picture Researcher: Sarah and Roland Smithies
Indexer: Ingrid Lock
Production Controller: Kelly Smith

Visit our website at www.davidandcharles.co.uk

David & Charles books are available from all good bookshops; alternatively you can contact our Orderline on 0870 9908222 or write to us at FREEPOST EX2 110, D&C Direct, Newton Abbot, TQ12 4ZZ (no stamp required UK only); US customers call 800-289-0963 and Canadian customers call 800-840-5220.

CONTENTS

31143007964266
930.1 Palmer
Palmer, Douglas.
Fortune and glory : tales
of history's greatest
archaeological adventures

PROLOGUE

It came to pass that the king's-son, Thutmosis, came, coursing at the time of midday, and he rested in the shadow of this great god. A vision of sleep seized him at the hour (when) the sun was in the zenith, and he found the majesty of this revered god speaking with his own mouth, as a father speaks with his son, saying:

'Behold thou me! See thou me! My son Thutmosis. I am thy father, Horemakhet-Khafre-Re-Atum, who will give to thee my kingdom on earth at the head of the living. Thou shalt wear the white crown and the red crown upon the throne of Keb, the hereditary prince. The land shall be thine in its length and breadth, that which the eye of the All-Lord shines upon. The food of the Two Lands shall be thine, the great tribute of all countries, the duration of a long period of years. My face is thine, my desire is toward thee. Thou shalt be to me a protector, (for) my manner is as I were ailing in all my limbs. The sand of this desert upon which I am, has reached me; turn to me, to have that done which I have desired, knowing that thou art my son, my protector; come hither, behold, I am with thee, I am thy leader.'

When he had finished this speech, this king's-son [awoke]... he understood the words of this god, and he kept silent in his heart. He said: 'Come, let us hasten to our house in the city... and we shall give praise [to]... the statue made for Atum-Horemakhet.'

One morning in early 1818, a 47-year-old Italian sea-captain stood on Egypt's Giza Plateau, face to face with the most famous statue in the world. The Sphinx gazed implacably back, as it had done for millennia, its eyes fixed on a distant and ancient horizon, only its head and shoulders now visible above the shifting sands that had gone uncleared since Roman times.

The Sphinx had proved a magnet to the curious throughout its long existence, and had attracted a thick encrustation of legend and hearsay – not least its association with the monstrous puzzle-setter of Greek myth. The first European to record his visit in detail, the 16th century German traveller Johann Helffrich, believed it represented the goddess Isis, and sketched the statue with prominent breasts. He also perpetuated a myth that the Sphinx was hollow – with a tunnel, he believed, that had allowed ancient priests to hide inside and fool their credulous followers that the goddess herself was speaking. Even at the turn of the nineteenth century, apparently realistic renderings added the artist's own interpolations and extrapolations to the remains, such as elaborate headdresses and jewellery.

The man who now sought audience with the Sphinx came with a different purpose in mind. Captain Giovanni Battista Caviglia was an excavator and treasure hunter as well as a sailor, and was currently in the employ of Henry Salt, the British Consul in nearby Cairo. At Salt's behest, he was determined to expose the Sphinx to the world, digging away the centuries of sand that had long ago overwhelmed its gargantuan, leonine form.

With a team of up to a hundred Arab labourers, Caviglia assaulted the sands of Giza for several months, but his effort was doomed to failure, for the Sphinx's body was far larger than anyone had predicted. When it was eventually freed by dint of massive effort almost a century later, it proved to have a length of 57m (185ft) from forepaws to haunches, and to tower 20m (65ft) above its surroundings: it was, and still is, the largest rock-cut statue in the world.

Caviglia abandoned his efforts in the heat of June, suffering from a severe eye inflammation. But his labours were not in vain; he had successfully exposed the statue's chest and forepaws, revealing the buildings and debris that lay around it. There were fallen fragments of the statue's headdress and beard, a nearby temple apparently dedicated to the statue, and most intriguing of all, a red granite slab or stela, some 3.5m (11ft 10in) high. The upper section of this monument showed an easily interpreted scene of a pharaoh making offerings to the sphinx, while below this was a long inscription in the then-impenetrable hieroglyphic script of the ancient Egyptians.

Caviglia was lucky to live in a time when some of the finest minds in Europe were intent on deciphering the secrets of this ancient language, and the mysteries of Egyptian writing were finally solved a few years later. Before he died in 1845, the Italian captain knew that on that first day before the Sphinx, he had stood in the place of an illustrious predecessor.

The carvings, translated above and already some 32 centuries old when they were rediscovered, told of how the 18th-Dynasty pharaoh Thutmosis IV, when still a junior prince, rested one day beneath the Sphinx whilst on a hunting expedition. As he slept, he heard the voice of the god Horemakhet speaking to him through the Sphinx, promising that he would rise to be pharaoh if only he cleared away the sand that already threatened to overwhelm the God's earthly avatar.

And so, in pursuit of power and prestige, prince Thutmosis was true to his word. The Sphinx was cleared and restored, and Thutmosis did indeed succeed his father Amenhotep II, though he reigned for only ten years. The Dream Stela was placed at the foot of the Sphinx in commemoration of the pharaoh's deal with his god, and later it in turn fell victim to the inevitable tides of history, buried with its guardian until the Italian captain resurrected it.

Though separated by a hundred generations, Thutmosis and Caviglia were both spiritual ancestors of modern archaeologists – each dug in the ground in order to bring past treasures back into the light. But their motivations, principles and operating methods were very different from those of their modern followers. While today's archaeologists are trained professionals, searching for historical evidence that will bring history back to life, these first excavators and explorers were driven by dreams of fortune and glory.

This is a book about the discovery of the past, and the way in which archaeology evolved over little more than a century from mere treasure hunting to a science in its own right. It tells the story of a great age of adventure, when tomb raiders, passionate eccentrics and scholars alike risked their lives and reputations to uncover lost worlds. Such tales are as close as archaeology ever really got to the exploits of fictional explorers such as Tintin, Indiana Jones and Lara Croft, and, just as fiction often reveals a great deal about the preoccupations of the time in which it is written, so these true-life adventures frequently tell us as much about the times of their protagonists as they do about the civilizations whose remains they excavated.

As we shall see, the seeds of true archaeology grew from the European Enlightenment. Until this time, occasional discoveries and unavoidable evidence of ancient relics were treated as mere curios, to be explained away in folktale and legend: Stonehenge and Carnac were the playgrounds of giants, flint axe heads the work of fairies, and even Imperial Rome took on a semi-mythical status.

The Enlightenment was born slowly, the result of a series of blows to old authority inflicted by new discoveries and theories throughout the 17th century. And it was only then, it seems, that people dared to look at the world with their own eyes, describe what they really saw, and form their own theories to explain the evidence. (It's true that they still mistakenly thought Stonehenge was built by the druids who fought Julius Caesar, but at least this was better than giants.)

Growing realization that the past wasn't exactly like the present was paralleled by recognition that the rest of the world was not just like Europe. Investigation into history, both at home and abroad, formed part of the same intellectual 'project' as inquiry into the nature of the forces governing the world, and the collection of anthropological and natural history specimens. The new importance attached to evidence, coupled with a new aesthetic sense, created the antiquarians and collectors of the 18th century, many of whom were proto-archaeologists themselves, while others certainly sponsored them.

But while archaeology was born in the European Enlightenment, it undoubtedly came of age in the era of imperialism, when half the atlas was tinted in the pink of the British Empire, and rival powers vied to extend their spheres of influence through those parts that weren't. Indigenous cultures were often seen as ignorant and backward, awaiting the benevolent influence of European civilization and religion – and if the Europeans happened to benefit from the deal too, then so much the better.

This period of colonization and exploitation of natural resources was undeniably accompanied by a cultural element to empire, but in this post-colonial world it's easy to ignore the fact that it cut both ways. France, Britain and Germany at the height of their imperial ambitions were enthralled and fascinated by the majesty of ancient civilizations, yet they mostly accepted them on their own terms, as peoples indigenous to the lands that had since unfortunately descended from such lofty heights. This realization that any people might rise to glory only to fall back into so-called barbarism was a blow to misguided theorists trying to explain why Europe (and Britain in particular) was historically and scientifically *destined* to rule, but only a few eccentrics such as the British Israelites tried to turn things on their head and claim direct descent from these earlier apogees of civilization.

Throughout the 19th century, great and rising powers sought to accumulate the monuments of earlier civilizations around them for the glorification of their own national image. Depending on one's point of view, this fascination with fallen empires of the past might indicate either a subconscious awareness of the brevity of power, or an amusing and ironic ignorance of the subtext to all these fallen pharaohs and kings. Certainly the poet Shelley had a point to make when, inspired by reports of the ruined Ramesseum and shattered statues at Thebes, he wrote:

'My name is Ozymandias, king of kings:
Look on my works, ye mighty, and despair!'

By the late 19th century, the museums of Europe and the United States were overflowing with treasures accumulated from 'antique lands' around the world – not just from the old world civilizations of the Mediterranean and the Near East, but from as far afield as South-East Asia, South America and sub-Saharan Africa. Some of these finds were the bequests of individual collectors, but an increasing number came from organized academic expeditions, which sometimes went so far as to transport entire buildings back to their homelands.

These days, of course, a lot of nations want their stuff back: the Elgin Marbles are an ongoing source of diplomatic spats between Greece and the United Kingdom, Native American tribes are lobbying for the return of artefacts from prestigious museums, and Egypt is considering copyrighting the Sphinx. The boot is most definitely on the other foot. This sea change began in the aftermath of the World War I, with the dissolution of the old Ottoman Empire government, the gradual loosening of British imperial ties (which would not disappear completely until another war had driven Britain herself to the point of bankruptcy) and the rise of self-government and nationalism. Lest we forget, very little of the material shipped off to western museums was simply stolen: even the worst plunderers described in this book usually operated with the agreement of what were, at the time, legitimate kings, governments and local chieftains.

The nationalization of archaeological treasures, begun by Egypt in the wake of the Tutankhamun discovery of the 1920s, has been understandably important to the self-image and development of many countries, but conversely, the major museums themselves are now international treasures in their own right, visited and appreciated by millions of people from around the world in a continuation of the Enlightenment spirit. Both sides have a point, but hopefully compromises and loan agreements can be reached in at least some cases.

So perhaps we can be lenient with the early treasure seekers on the accusation of imperialism, but how do they stand up from an archaeological point of view? Here, unfortunately, the evidence is often damning. An obsession with artefacts, and particularly with valuable ones, meant that all too often material thought to be worthless was ignored, discarded, or destroyed. Even buildings themselves were frequently damaged in the quest for hidden treasures – like Indiana Jones in the Peruvian jungle, they might have found their (metaphorical) golden idol, but they wrecked the temple in the process. Bas-reliefs were sliced from palace walls, mummies torn open to obtain funeral papyri, and later cities virtually ignored in the search for earlier layers of occupation.

But even in the early days there were hints of a more considered approach struggling toward the surface. The Italian Giovanni Belzoni, sometimes portrayed as tomb-raider-in-chief, was frequently fascinated by the little tableaux of past life he found, even if they profited him nothing. With no formal training, Claudius Rich found the ruins of Babylon and produced a sketch of the city's layout that has stood the test of time remarkably well. And Ephraim Squier's observations in Ohio and Central America proved a good foundation for later researchers.

Perhaps the crucial break came with the decipherment of the ancient languages, and the abrupt shift in the perception of ancient civilizations that this brought with it. The construction of a historical framework in which to place monuments and objects, and the increasing interest in the mundane ephemera of everyday life in the past, brought with them a revolution in techniques that heralded the beginnings of modern archaeology. Auguste Mariette, Flinders Petrie, Robert Koldewey and Hiram Bingham all grew up on tales from the era of the treasure seekers, yet they brought a scientific sensibility to their work, taking more care with the preservation of sites and objects, and above all considering objects in their context and seeking the smallest clues to help date their discoveries.

Even today, though, the archaeologist remains an iconic, romantic figure, in reality as well as fiction. While the old schoolbook view of history as the deeds of great men (with the emphasis very clearly on *men*) has largely been swept away by the rise of social history and an often confusing variety of different perspectives on the forces that shape the story of humanity, a minor echo of the cult of personality remains in archaeology. Television's love affair with archaeology, begun by Mortimer Wheeler after his retirement from 'active service' in the 1950s, is today perpetuated by the National Geographic, Discovery and History channels. Of course, these days the magnification of a few chosen individuals is televisual sleight of hand: the camera stays focused on 'our hero' even as a small army of research students, conservators, finds experts and geophysicists (not to mention volunteers and local labourers) do the majority of the work. But still the image is a powerful and appealing one, recalling memories of a time when things really were that simple, and a young man with a head full of history books and folktales could set off alone in search of archaeological fortune and glory... and very often find it.

INTRODUCTION: CHRONICLES
AND CHRONOLOGIES

Raiding the past for anything that is valuable is itself an age-old pastime and is not necessarily pursued purely for material gain; it has served many other purposes. At the most general level, a curiosity about the reality of the past, rather than some mythical construct, seems to mark a stage in the development of any society. In Britain this was not reached by any significant number of people until the 16th century. Before that time the only available view of Britain's past was provided by just a few chroniclers such as Geoffrey of Monmouth (?1100–1154) whose somewhat fanciful 12th century 'History of the Kings of Britain' included Lear, Cymbeline, Arthur and Merlin.

Geoffrey lacked factual details about what had gone before and cobbled together his fantastical history of Britain by looting or scavenging the past for what scraps of information he could find to produce his history. Consequently, he imagined Britain as being first occupied by Trojans fleeing from the sacked city of Troy and ending with King Arthur's heroic defence of the British realm against the invading Anglo-Saxon hordes. William Caxton's (?1422–1491) 15th century update, which was largely derived from continental sources, can in turn be traced back to Geoffrey of Monmouth's earlier chronicle.

In more recent centuries, the discovery of our own history and prehistory has been a great adventure, an adventure that is far from complete and one that awaits new generations with new techniques, insights, interpretations, determination and perhaps most of all enthusiasm. Our story here tells of many different enthusiasts and adventurers who have raided the depths of history and beyond to the abyss of time. It recounts their hopes and successes, their disappointments and disasters, life stories that have cost some their sanity and some their lives.

Establishing a Chronology
Today, we tend to take for granted the main outline and chronology of human history and that of our extinct ancestors and fossil relatives and forget how it has been arrived at. The prevailing view of the past few thousand years is dominated by a widely accepted worldview of human history and its

chronology with the interplay of different cultures, the coming and going of empires and nation states. Inevitably, peoples across the world view this history from different perspectives depending upon culture, ethnicity, religion, politics and so on but, on the whole, do not disagree about the dating and sequence of major events. Globalization requires common standards of time, dates and chronology. There are still plenty of other calendars used by certain ethnic and religious groups, but they have to live alongside the prevailing western standard based on the Judaeo-Christian calendar.

The extended chronology of prehistory is an even more recent phenomenon, since it has depended upon radically different dating techniques that only evolved in a reliable way from the 1950s onwards and are still diversifying and being refined. Most are based upon naturally occurring radioactivity and require sophisticated measuring equipment; and they can only be used on certain kinds of materials. Nevertheless, we now have a marvellous array of dating techniques, some with high degrees of accuracy and reliability that can be applied to artefacts ranging from organic materials such as bone, wood, skin and fabric to inorganic materials such as stone tools and certain kinds of sediment and rock materials.

Revising our View of Ourselves
The methods and techniques of science have not only revolutionized exploration of the past but have radically altered the way that we look at that past. This applies most particularly to our view of prehistory and the evolution of life, especially the evolution of our own species, *Homo sapiens*. It must not be forgotten that a hundred years ago very little was known about human evolution and that, outside the world of science, few people accepted the evidence supporting Charles Darwin's claim that humans have descended from African apes. Indeed there were still many scientists who still did not accept it in 1900.

Even today, when there is overwhelming genetic, archaeological and anthropological evidence for human evolution, there are many people who do not accept the scientific evidence – mostly because of religious views that demand some kind of divine intervention in the development of humanness. It is somewhat bizarre that we seem to find the existence of some 600 different kinds of extinct dinosaur much more acceptable than the existence of some 20 different kinds of extinct human-related ancestors.

However, 200 years ago there was an almighty struggle and debate, even among scientists, over the question of the creation of Earth, its life, prehistory and events such as the Noachian Flood. The prevailing view of prehistory, even in the developing western world that was beginning to dominate science, technology and global trade, was dominated by the Judaeo-Christian worldview of the bible and especially the Hebraic Old Testament.

Today, it is quite difficult to appreciate the extent to which that worldview permeated culture and society in the Western world. As recently as 1619, the Italian philosopher Lucilio Vanini was burned to death at the stake in Toulouse in France for uttering the heresy that humans might be descended from the apes. Galileo Galilei (1564–1642) had to recant his heretical writings of 1632 under threat of a similar fate, (the Vatican only formally lifted the ban and absolved him in 1992). Luckily for the growth of more free-thinking intellectual development in Britain and other parts of Europe, greater religious, intellectual and social freedom promoted the foundation of societies such as the Royal Society of London (1660), which encouraged the communication and ordering of knowledge along specific methodological lines laid down by Sir Francis Bacon (1561–1626).

Rediscovering and Revising the Past
The modern consensus view is a remarkably new phenomenon and has only been achieved by the combined efforts of many scholars around the world in the last 100 years or so. Before this, there were a number of other perspectives on history, mostly originating from earlier peoples, cultures and empires. They range from theistic to mythical, magical and animalistic views to broader concepts and histories that have dominated particular regions of the world such as those of China, Egypt, Greece, Rome and the Ottoman empire.

The 'rediscovery' of these earlier perspectives by Western scholars has led to their chronologies and histories being questioned, revised and then subsumed into the present worldview. One of the most important scholarly investigations was that of Judaeo-Christian writings: their origin, authorship and chronology. Comparison of texts began to throw up evidence of compilation from different sources and contradictions between versions that made literal interpretation untenable.

Over time, peoples have recorded their own view of their past and that of their neighbours, friends and foes – in many ways from purely oral traditions, passed from generation to generation, to material records carved in stone, set in tablets of clay or written down. All these records have suffered the ravages of time and conflict and have been fragmented and lost to some extent.

The recovery of these records has been an extraordinary endeavour and over the centuries the approaches to them have evolved to a remarkable extent. Most early investigations now seem incredibly crude and destructive. Many were simply searches for objects of value, whether it was the centuries-old occupation of tomb robbing in Egypt, the 'recycling' of the masonry and timbers of historical buildings, early 18th century digging up of Pompeii for gold artefacts or, the 19th century haphazard excavation of cave sites for portable cave art. Unfortunately, it still goes on, especially in war zones, where museums are frequently targeted and looted by desperate people as well as more cynical criminals who do not care about destroying their own history. Most recently, Iraq's National Museum in Baghdad and the magnificent giant statues in Afghanistan have suffered in this way.

Recovering Documents of the Past
We are surrounded by evidence for the past, no matter where we live. There is a huge variety of 'documents' and data in the widest sense, ranging from constructions such as pyramid tombs, monumental carvings and humble dwellings, in various stages of preservation or ruination, to smaller portable artefacts from weapons to jewellery. It is likely that only a small percentage of those that have survived has been recovered from the various processes of burial (both natural and anthropogenic) beneath younger sediments, soils and vegetation. The scope for future discovery of the past is still very great.

Even the most barren desert wastes such as those of the Sahara in North Africa are rich with reminders of the past. These include the relics of recent conflicts in the form of metal armaments (cartridge cases) and human-related remains such as an unposted and intact letter from a combatant in World War II to a relative in Europe. Even more durable are the stone tools and weapons such as flint arrowheads that abound in some places – witness to larger populations of human hunters and the game they hunted in the region thousands of years ago, a view reinforced by the presence of rock art over much of the region. This art depicts a diverse wildlife that could only have survived in a much less arid environment. Deeper geological-scale investigations of deposits, below the present-day desert sands confirm the archaeological view and reveal that the region was indeed wetter, with lakes and rivers that supported abundant game and inevitably the humans whose livelihoods depended upon the animals and plants. Dating of the environmental changes shows that the region became drier as cold glacial conditions took hold at higher latitudes.

The View from the British Isles: the Early Days

Many nations have long-established traditions of historical and prehistorical research that tend to follow similar development over the centuries. Much of Europe has written documentation of some sort dating back over 2000 years to the days of Roman conquest and occupation, though preservation and recovery of this information has been patchy. There are the famous surviving writings such as those of the Roman historian Tacitus (*c*.56–*c*.120 AD) but others are still being uncovered, including the astonishing discovery in 1972 of legionnaires, wooden 'postcards' from the Vindolanda Fortress in Northumberland, dating to around AD 72.

   In England the Venerable Bede (*c*.673–735), who worked in the Tyneside monastery of Jarrow, is often regarded as the 'Father of English history' and wrote a number of histories, including *The Ecclesiastical History of the English People* which he completed in 731. This work is often considered to be the primary source for early English history and includes vivid accounts in which Bede is generally careful to separate hearsay and tradition from more factually based information. It deals with the history of the conquest by the Anglo-Saxons of the Roman province of Britain and its subsequent conversion to Christianity. Material evidence for all this is still being actively recovered but it was partly the preservation of copies of these historical accounts that prompted early investigators to seek out such material evidence.

The Beginnings of Antiquarianism

The search for this past did not happen in any methodical way until conditions were right for such investigations. To begin with a few outstanding individuals, such as John Leland (?1506–52), librarian to Henry VIII, tried to promote antiquarian studies. But, in trying to record and conserve the historical heritage, Leland was in a very difficult position. His 'boss', the king, was responsible for one of the greatest acts of vandalism that has been wrought on the historic fabric of England, when he ordered the dissolution and destruction of the monasteries. Nevertheless, Leland made one of the first antiquarian tours of England (1534–43), noting anything and everything of historical interest and curiosity, with the hope of publishing a great work on 'The History and Antiquities of the Nation'. Poor Leland became increasingly unstable mentally and eventually succumbed to insanity. Nine volumes of *Leland's Itinerary* were published posthumously in 1710, when the 'climate' was more accepting of such endeavours.

There had to be enough literate, scholarly and wealthy persons with enough leisure to spend the necessary time and effort on such investigation. But there were also other more practical factors at work such as the need for accurate and reproducible topographical maps of the country, its centres of population and lines of communication, such as those produced by the cartographer John Speed (1551/2–1629), (interestingly, only the rivers were shown on these early maps because the overland routes had not been mapped and were often too dangerous). For the first time people began to get a sense of place within the land they occupied and, in another sense, were getting a better sense of 'place' within a historical chronology.

This chronology was, however, essentially based upon the information from the Old Testament for its early part. Of the many chronologies produced, that of James Ussher, Bishop of Armagh (1581–1656), is the best known and in it Ussher estimated that some 1,500 years had passed from the Creation to the Flood and another 2,500 years until the birth of Christ. Such a restricted prehistoric timeframe would be questioned and tested by the growing number of naturalists who concerned themselves with the evidence of the rock strata and fossils that make up Earth's surface layers.

The Society of Antiquaries
There was a short-lived Elizabethan society of antiquarians who concerned themselves with the past, its records and artefacts but it was not until 1707 (coincidentally the year in which the kingdom of England and Scotland were formally united by the Act of Union) that the Society of Antiquaries

of London held its first formal meeting – at a tavern in the Strand. At its foundation the Society declared that the its business should be 'limited to the subject of Antiquities: and more particularly, to such things as may Illustrate and Relate to the History of Great Britain'. By 'things' they meant 'Antient Coins, books, sepulchres or other Remains of Antient Workmanship'. The peace and relative prosperity of the recently united nation of Great Britain led to a growing middle class with an interest in the arts and sciences – a development commonly known as the Enlightenment. It also encouraged the foundation of literary and philosophical societies in almost all the cities and major towns around the country and many of these set up museums to house the growing number of artefacts collected and donated by their members.

CHAPTER 1: THE COLLECTORS

The collection of information and illustrations of historic buildings and ruins, such as Hadrian's Wall and Stonehenge, dates back into the early 17th century. There were important pioneers such as John Aubrey (1626–97), who discovered the Avebury monument whilst out hunting in 1649. He drew a measured plan of its circular form for inclusion in his planned book on stone structures called 'Monumenta Britannica' but it was never completed. By the beginning of the 18th century, the growing fashion for the classical antiquity of Italy had led to a renewed interest in more homegrown antiquities. William Stukeley (1687–1765), the First Secretary of the Society of Antiquaries, accurately surveyed the sites of Avebury and Stonehenge using a theodolite and described them as products of a Druidical society that could match that of ancient Rome in sophistication. There was also a growing concern for the preservation of ancient monuments, many of which were at risk from neglect and wilful destruction. Dressed stones were commonly removed for new agricultural buildings.

Hunting for Flints and Fossils
The collection of artefacts began to include primitive objects. For instance, in the 1690s a London apothecary and antiquarian, John Conyers, found a curious piece of flint shaped like an axe-head in a building site excavation in Gray's Inn Road. It was buried in river gravel alongside large bones that were probably those of an extinct mammoth or straight tusked elephant.

It was another well known 17th century antiquarian, Sir William Dugdale (1605–1686), who first drew attention to such flint implements in his book on 'The Antiquities of Warwickshire' (1656) and attributed their manufacture to 'antient Britons' before they 'attained to the knowledge of working iron or brass'. At the time such finds were commonly seen as deposits of the Noachian Flood.

In 1715, John Bagford, a shoemaker and one of the founders of the Society of Antiquaries, recognized that the bones were those of some kind of elephant and suggested that they were the remains of an elephant brought to Britain by invading Roman legionnaires in AD 43 and killed by a native Briton with the flint axe. It was a plausible explanation though with the later discovery of many more flint axes and elephant-like bones from all over the country the idea became less tenable. But not until the mid 19th century did it become clear that such bones were those of extinct elephants and mammoths who had lived in the Ice Age and were occasionally hunted and scavenged by prehistoric extinct human species such as *Homo neanderthalensis*.

The collection of fossils was originally just part and parcel of an interest in curiosities because the true nature of fossils as the remains of once-living creatures was not finally accepted until the latter part of the 17th century. Before this time fossils were commonly part of more general collections that included coins, minerals, crystals and any strangely shaped stones. But by the beginning of the 18th century fossil collections were often more discrete and the study of fossils was one of the earliest specialist subjects, associated with (if anything) biological rather than other antiquarian materials. As a result the study of fossils, along with that of rocks and minerals, was more in the strictly scientific remit of the Royal Society of London than the historical remit of the Society of Antiquaries.

The Enlightenment

With the 18th century growth of foreign trade, including the notorious slave trade, there was an increase in foreign exploration that brought back not only foreign objects of all kinds but also questions about other peoples of the world, their customs, histories and beliefs – a historical and cultural development known as the Enlightenment. How did all these different ethnic groups originate and relate to one another? Needless to say, the prevailing European view was that there was a gradient from the most primitive to the most advanced (and no prizes for guessing who were the most advanced). The classical Greek skull and facial profile were taken as the epitome of beauty and advancement whilst the aboriginal skull and profile of the Papuans were taken as being among the most primitive. All sorts of convoluted and specious arguments were developed to perceive ethnic groups such as black-skinned Africans as people who had once been white but had 'fallen from grace' or 'degenerated' into their present condition. Inevitably it was mostly a cover by so-called Christians to justify slavery.

Faussett and Douglas: The Barrow Diggers

The collection of information and materials that would today be distinguished as belonging within the remit of archaeology was, to begin with, just one of the preoccupations of the antiquarians. Stukeley's investigations of Stonehenge and the barrows (burial mounds) of Wessex proved that such structures predated the period of Roman colonization. The downside of the fashion for barrow digging was that so many sites were haphazardly excavated without proper record and many were just plundered for their potential grave goods, which became eminently saleable. The Reverends Bryan Faussett (1729–76) and James Douglas (1753–1819) were amongst the most indefatigable barrow diggers. Faussett's diaries show that he himself dug out some 700, but at least he provided an excellent standard of detailed description and illustration of the excavations for the time. His remarkable collection of Anglo-Saxon material from Kent, which included more than 400 items of jewellery alone, was finally sold in the 1850s and was left to the City of Liverpool. About a third of the collection was destroyed during the war but, fortunately, the remainder is now safely housed in Liverpool's World Museum. Faussett's diaries were published posthumously as *Inventorium Sepulchrae* in 1856 some 80 years after his death.

Douglas began his adult life as a soldier and military engineer, a discipline that stood him in good stead when he came to record the details of barrows that were disturbed during the remodelling of the defensive earthworks protecting the Medway and Chatham Docks in the Thames Estuary. He mapped the first ground plan of an excavated tumulus and it was published in his 1793 book *Nenia Britannica*, which was a general systematic history of the funerary customs of 'Ancient Britons', beautifully illustrated with aquatint plates. But its pioneering significance was not appreciated until after his death. The excavation of barrows and mounds continued throughout the 18th and into the early 19th century, to such an extent that the antiquarians' preoccupation with the dead was often lampooned by cartoonists such as Thomas Rowlandson (1757–1827).

William Hamilton and 'Shopping' for Antiquities in Europe

There were other British antiquarian collectors who extended their activities to continental Europe and beyond. The many wealthy people who made the

Grand Tour from Northern Europe southwards across the Alps into Italy and Greece, the Middle East and North Africa brought back all manner of new ideas, interests and mementoes of their journeys from books, paintings and other portable objects to less readily portable ones that had to be shipped home.

The fashion for the recovery of the past became a pandemic with kings, emperors and popes becoming involved. When the ruined town of Pompeii was discovered in 1738, the King and Queen of Naples treated it as a personal treasure trove that could be dug into whenever they needed money or statues for their gardens. The British Ambassador of the time, Sir William Hamilton (1730–1803), complained about the destruction of 'many curious monuments' in an account of the excavations he sent to the Society of Antiquaries.

Although an aristocrat, Hamilton was not wealthy and had acquired a young and beautiful 'trophy' wife, Emma, who had been his nephew's mistress. Emma required 'high maintenance'; consequently Hamilton was always in need of money and supplemented his income as a diplomat by buying and selling antiquities. He was an avaricious collector who shipped loads of Greek vases, including the famous 'Portland Vase', and other antiquities back to Britain to sell to his wealthy friends. He was a member of the influential and highly selective Society of 'Dilettanti', founded as a London dining club in 1734, whose aim was to promote classical art and Italian opera and which was instrumental in establishing the Royal Academy of Arts in 1768. Behind the scenes its members also dabbled in erotica with Hamilton privately publishing an illustrated account of the worship of Priapus and the use of erotically charged votive objects in Naples.

At least one of Hamilton's collections was lost at sea in a shipwreck but another was bought by the British Museum for 8,000 guineas, a great deal of money in those days. Hamilton did publish beautifully illustrated books of his activities and acquisitions which were enormously influential, especially as Josiah Wedgwood used them as patterns for his fashionable 'Etruscan ware' made in his new pottery factories from 1769.

Something of a Renaissance man, Hamilton was also interested in geology and made some of the first accurate observations of the volcanic eruptions of Vesuvius (1776–7) and Etna, which he communicated to the Royal Society along with specially commissioned paintings. It was during his time as plenipotentiary in Naples (1764–1800) that Hamilton and Emma met Admiral Horatio Nelson in 1793. Following Nelson's famous victory in the Battle of the Nile (1798), he and Lady Emma became lovers.

Lord Elgin's Marbles

Not satisfied with easily portable objects such as vases, British and other European collectors had larger ambitions such as outstanding carved friezes on the Acropolis. Now known as the Elgin Marbles, they were purchased from the colonial Turkish authorities by Thomas Bruce, seventh Earl of Elgin (1766–1841). A French aristocrat, the Comte de Choiseul-Gouffier, had been after them for some time and in 1784 had instructed Fauvel, his Athens agent, to 'take everything you can. Do not neglect any opportunity for looting all that is lootable in Athens and the environs. Spare neither the living nor the dead'. Fauvel was still trying to persuade the occupying Turkish authorities to let him remove the friezes in 1798, when Lord Elgin arrived as British Ambassador. Elgin had planned to have the sculptures moulded and cast in plaster but, following the defeat of Napoleon's forces in Egypt in 1799, he persuaded the Turkish authorities to let him have the actual carvings. They were shipped back to England between 1803 and 1812 and sold to the nation in 1816.

Britain was not alone in its wholesale acquisition of antiquities. The Napoleonic forces were notorious for their looting of anything of value or potential interest back in Paris and the capital's museums were soon filled to overflowing. Their ambitions extended to fossils, one of the most famous of which is the 'Beast of Maastricht' – *Mosasaurus*. The giant metre-long jaws of this strange extinct marine reptile were first discovered in the 1780s in the underground chalk workings that perforated the hills around Maastricht. The fossil was the object of great interest because it was not clear what kind of animal the jaws belonged to – a crocodile or whale.

After an acrimonious local lawsuit the fossil was claimed by a local priest, Canon Godin, who housed it in a small museum in the grounds of his chateau. When the Napoleonic forces besieged Maastricht in 1795, the fossil was removed for safe keeping but to no avail. The story has it that the French general Pichegru offered 600 bottles of wine, no doubt looted from elsewhere, as reward for information as to its whereabouts. Inevitably, the French soon had the fossil and shipped it off to Paris – to the delight of French scholars such as Faujas de Saint-Fond (1742–1819), who described it as a kind of giant crocodile. His younger colleague Georges Cuvier (1769–1832) disagreed: he recognized features that suggested a closer relationship to the lizards and redefined *Mosasaurus* as an extinct giant marine reptile related to the monitor lizards. The specimen is still in the National Museum of Natural History in Paris and the Dutch have to make do with a plaster cast.

From Antiquities to '-ologies'
The various '-ologies' such as archaeology, palaeontology and anthropology as separate and discrete academic subjects did not emerge until the 19th century. By this time such studies, researches and associated field investigations had become increasingly methodical, scientific and professionalized. Participation by amateurs continued, especially within archaeology, but gradually more and more university- and museum-based professionals took over. The subjects eventually became academic studies in their own right with departments established in the new 'redbrick' universities of the late 19th century. Most of the adventures in this book, and the explorers who undertook them, belong to the past two centuries, since science and professionalism took hold, but the enthusiasms and ambitions that drove them are much the same as those of the earlier historic adventurers into the 'terra incognita' of the past.

CHAPTER 2: PRE-HISTORY AND DISCOVERING LIFE BEFORE THE FLOOD

'… to confirm the evidence of natural religion; and show the facts developed by it are consistent with the accounts of the creation and deluge recorded in the Mosaic writings …' (William Buckland, 1819)

A huge number of investigators have made significant contributions to our story but we are telling the tales of just a select number of outstanding individuals. Their names are prominent and interesting for a variety of reasons that are not always to do with intellect but range from ambition, force of character and opportunism to luck, mingled with curiosity and intellect. More often than not these individuals have built on extensive groundwork by many others, either with or without acknowledgment.

Following the revolutionary fervour of the late 18th century, the first decades of the 19th century saw further momentous changes in economy, politics, science, culture and society as the Industrial Revolution and its ramifications spread throughout the Western world. Humanity's 'egocentric' view of itself and its position in the world was about to change forever. From being one step below the angels in the Christian hierarchy we descended to being the evolutionary 'kissing cousins' of the great apes. But it took over a hundred years for the prevailing orthodoxy finally to give way under the growing mountain of evidence revealed by the new sciences of geology, biology and archaeology.

One of the main paradoxes of the Old Testament account of the creation of humankind and its subsequent history involved the Noachian Flood. A number of questions taxed those who believed in the literal truth of the story. For instance, how big would Noah's ark have been to accommodate a male and female of all living beings? What happened to the remains of all those beings and organisms that were drowned by the waters of the Flood?

By an extraordinary coincidence of geological reality and biblical history the Flood story became pivotal in much of the struggle over the understanding of prehistory and Earth's recent geological history. One investigator in particular epitomized the rearguard reaction of those who had an unshakable belief in the Old Testament accounts, not just as historical documents but often as the word of God as well. William Buckland (1784–1856) was intimately involved with three major scientific controversies – over the antiquity of humankind, over the nature and reality of the Flood and over the recognition of a completely extinct and major group of animals that lived in the remote past: the dinosaurs.

William Buckland Fights the Good Fight

The Reverend William Buckland was one of the rising stars of the natural sciences in early 19th century Britain. He had all the advantages of class and connections, for his uncle was a Fellow at Oxford and helped to steer William's educational progress through Winchester from 1798 and Corpus Christi, Oxford from 1801. But he was also academically gifted, being awarded a Fellowship in his Oxford College in 1808; he was made Professor of mineralogy in 1813, at the age of 29, when he also joined the Geological Society of London. His active lobbying for recognition of the new science of geology resulted in his appointment as Reader in geology in 1819. His inaugural lecture as Reader was entitled 'The Connexion of Geology with Religion Explained' for, as Buckland saw it, one of the prime objectives of geology was 'to confirm the evidence of natural religion; and show the facts developed by it are consistent with the accounts of the creation and deluge recorded in the Mosaic writings'.

Like most Oxbridge academics of the time, Buckland was ordained into the established Church of England. And, like other academics, he could only retain his College fellowship as long as he remained a bachelor. He resigned his Fellowship in 1825 to take up a living as a vicar in Hampshire, but before he could do so he was appointed Canon of Christchurch in Oxford. This very well endowed post was a reward for his academic distinction; it allowed him to continue his geological researches and teaching in Oxford without too much distraction for ecclesiastical duties and it made it possible for him to get married.

By the end of the year he had met Mary Morland, a collector of fossils and an accomplished illustrator. The story goes that whilst travelling by coach in Dorset, Buckland was reading the latest of Cuvier's books and noticed that his lady companion was reading the same work and so they fell into conversation. The penny eventually dropped for Buckland and he declared, 'You must be

Miss Morland, to whom I am about to deliver a letter of introduction.' Sharing Buckland's love of natural history, she was not put out by his obsessions and collecting mania and in due course they were married and took a geological honeymoon for the best part of a year in Europe, much of the time being accompanied by his ex-student Charles Lyell. Mary was of great assistance to Buckland by illustrating his books and papers as well as bearing nine children of which only five survived to adulthood. Another story claims that she also helped him to analyse some fossil footprints by rolling out raw soft pastry on a table and allowing their pet tortoise to walk across it so that Buckland could analyse a typical set of reptilian footprints.

Buckland eventually rose in the Church hierarchy to become Dean of Westminster in 1845, and so became one of the most senior ecclesiastics in London. Although he had many advantages to begin with, his very successful career, combining religion and science, would be achieved largely through force of his charismatic if somewhat eccentric personality plus innate ability and a distinct tendency to showmanship. Later on, with age and success he became pompous, somewhat overfond of his own rhetoric and as a result a caricature of himself. Within a few years of becoming Dean he was beginning to show increasingly erratic and irrational behaviour with violent mood swings that alarmed his family and friends. He had always been eccentric and, to begin with, his family thought that he was just fooling. But he began to scratch himself and beat his head as if to alleviate some terrible internal torment. His wife sought the advice of friends as the frequency of the bouts increased and by 1851 he had been committed to a lunatic asylum in south London. As more of his friends heard of his committal they suggested various different cures over a period of years, but none were of any good. His dementia increased and only the Bible was of any interest to him until he finally died in 1856.

One of his Oxford colleagues remarked that, in his prime, 'Dr Buckland's wonderful conversational powers were as incommunicable as the bouquet of a bottle of champagne' and his glowing commendation continued: '… it was at the feast of reason and the flow of social and intellectual intercourse that Buckland shone. A merrier man within the limit of becoming mirth I never spent an hour's talk withal. Nothing came amiss with him from the creation of the world, to the latest news in town … in build, look and manner he was a thorough English gentleman, and was appreciated within every circle'. But he was also, in many ways, lucky to be the right man in the right place at the right time.

The Theological Geologists
From boyhood at Axminster in Dorset, Buckland had been fascinated by rocks and fossils. It was an interest encouraged by his father, the Reverend Charles Buckland, who was an Anglican priest. Axminster is just inland from Lyme and Buckland later reminisced that the famous fossil-rich cliffs 'were my geological school ... they stared me in the face, they wooed me and caressed me, saying at every turn, Pray, Pray, be a geologist!' Geology was rapidly becoming one of the foremost sciences of the day; it was also a science whose major issues and discoveries could readily be understood by an increasingly literate public.

Buckland became one of the leading lights of the so-called 'theological geologists' who were convinced that the study of rocks, strata and fossils and how they were formed would reveal the truth of the Judaeo-Christian Creation story and that of the Flood. By the 1800s, it was generally acknowledged by the growing scientific community of geologists that the hugely thick piles of fossiliferous strata that form our rocky landscapes cannot have been formed by any single 'universal flood' but must have been the product of many such flood events over an inconceivable period of geological time.

These strata were in the process of being mapped as the Industrial Revolution demanded an expanded canal and rail network. There was a growing demand for all sorts of rock and mineral materials from brick clays to dimension stone, coal and iron ore. One particular British engineer and surveyor, William Smith (1769–1839), was pioneering new techniques of geological mapping by using fossils to characterize successive strata. More academically minded geologists were busy grouping and subdividing strata into formally named geological intervals, such as the coal-rich Carboniferous that was actively exploited in order to fuel the Industrial Revolution. The coal strata had been described in 1808 by the Belgian geologist Jean Baptiste Julien d'Omalius d'Halloy (1783–1875). The term Carboniferous period was first used by the British geologists the Reverend William Conybeare (1787–1857) and William Phillips (1775–1828) in their 1822 book *Outlines of the Geology of England and Wales*. Conybeare was dean of Llandaff Cathedral, a close friend of

Buckland's and another theological geologist.

It was also generally recognized that above the solid rock foundation to much of the landscape of northwestern Europe and North America lay a patchy veneer of sands, gravels and muds that were sometimes full of shells and bones that were often very large. Unlike most fossils in rock strata, these bones were often very well preserved and not flattened or broken. Over many centuries such bones had been ploughed up from fields and washed out of river banks and were a great puzzle to naturalists and collectors.

Some of the earliest finds dated back to classical times and were taken as proof of the existence of the gods and giants of the worlds of ancient Egypt, Greece and Rome. In mediaeval times, even in Christian Europe, they were still seen as evidence for giants living in the remote past. But gradually many were recognized as the skeletal remains of extinct species of large mammals such as elephants, bears, lions, rhinoceros and so on.

The Relics of the Flood

The problem was: how and why were the remains of such exotic tropical animals found scattered over the high latitude landscapes of northern Europe and North America? Some antiquarians had argued that the elephant-like bones were perhaps the remains of military elephants brought to Britain by the Romans. But to Buckland and his theologically minded associates there was a clear and simple answer: they were 'Reliquae Diluvianae' ('Relics of the Flood'), as he named his book of 1823 – remains of animals drowned in the Flood and carried from their original homes by the flood waters as they spread from Noah's homeland over the globe. Buckland realized that some of the best deposits of such bones and consequently potential evidence for the 'Diluvial' theory were to be found in the unexplored caves that riddle the limestone terrains of the British landscape.

Cave floor deposits are generally protected from the ravages of weathering and erosion that disturb and eventually destroy most surface deposits. Buckland postulated that they should likewise protect any flood deposits and any skeletal remains caught up within them. Like many of his contemporary scientists, Buckland espoused the relatively new, so-called Baconian methodology of science, which required observation, experimentation and deduction as opposed to the largely library-bound practices of earlier academic learning. He, like the new breed of young geologists, who saw themselves as a 'fellowship' or 'brethren of the hammer', was an energetic and indefatigable 'field man', traveller and explorer who delighted in taking his students out of the academic cloisters into the numerous quarries and rock excavations of the hills around Oxford. He was famous for his elaborate garb: a great-coat, muffler, top hat, umbrella, blue bag containing hammers all topped off by his academic gown.

Kirkdale Cave and the Pope of Bones

In the 1820s quarrymen working the Carboniferous limestone in Yorkshire discovered the entrance to what became known as Kirkdale cave. On breaking into the interior they had discovered bones that were so numerous that they used them as 'hardcore' to 'metal' muddy cart tracks. On hearing about the abundance of bones, Buckland set about exploring the underground system of caves and connecting passages. He had previously visited the Bavarian cave of Burggaillenreuth that had been excavated by the German priest Johann Friedrich Esper in 1771.

Esper had found human bones buried in cave floor deposits beneath those of extinct mammals such as giant cave bears. From the evidence he had to consider whether they were contemporaneous and posed the question: 'Did they belong to a Druid or to an Ante-diluvian or to a Mortal Man of more recent times?' Despite his findings, Esper could not bring himself to such a controversial conclusion and wrote 'I dare not, however, suppose without adequate reason that these remains are of the same age as other animal petrifications. They must have come together with the others by chance.'

The latter conclusion was supported by none other than Georges Cuvier (1769-1822), the pre-eminent French anatomist, nicknamed the 'Pope of Bones' presumably by those who were ignorant of the fact that he was a French protestant. Cuvier was an international star of science at the time and his opinions, generally accepted without question even by the British. He firmly believed that the Creation of mankind had been so recent that there would be no fossil remains and he went out of his way to debunk any claims of Diluvial or Ante-diluvial humans to be found anywhere.

Cuvier's opinions were so pervasive that they even penetrated the thoughts and writings of some of the greatest poets of the time. Byron's preface to his drama 'Cain', published in 1821, demonstrates his clear understanding of Cuvierian catastrophism: 'The reader will perceive that the author has partly adopted in this poem the notion of Cuvier, that the world has been destroyed several times before the creation of man. This speculation, derived from the different strata and bones of enormous and unknown animals found in them, is not contrary to the mosaic account, but rather confirms it; as no human bones have yet been discovered in those strata, although those of many known animals are found near the remains of the unknown.'

Likewise Buckland did not expect to find any human remains but from a slightly different basis. He reasoned that they would only be found in and around the Garden of Eden. As it turned out, he did not find any human remains in Kirkdale but he did find a huge number of bones. Buckland sent drawings of the bones to Cuvier as the universally acknowledged expert and he recognized over 20 species of mammal. A strange mixture they turned out to be: they included a few deer that were native to Britain mixed with extinct elephant-related species, horses, big lion-like cats, bears, rhinoceros, hippopotamus and hyena, from which Buckland concluded that they must have lived in Ante-Diluvian times under a tropical climate.

Mark of the Hyena
Buckland was an acute observer and could see that many of the bones were extremely well preserved and unlikely to have been transported very far by flood waters. So he made a significant intellectual leap and considered the possibility that the animals had actually lived in the neighbourhood of the cave around 6,000 years ago. According to Buckland, it was only in the recesses of the cave that their bones survived; outside, the Flood waters had swept them all away. More interestingly, he went much further in his interpretation of the remains. He had noted that many of the bones, like those of the elephants, were so large that the parent animal could not have entered the cave whilst alive but that individual bones dismembered from the carcasses must have been brought in by some agent – but what agent?

Buckland had also noted that many of the bones were broken and covered with chew marks like those made by powerfully jawed dog. Amongst the remains were many hyena bones and Buckland was well aware of the ability of this animal to crack open bones in pursuit of the nutritious marrow. Luckily for Buckland, a live South African hyena came to Oxford with a circus and he took the opportunity of feeding various bones to it and then examining what it regurgitated and what it defecated. He went further and imported another hyena which he intended to dissect but grew so attached to that it survived as a family 'pet' for the next 25 years. The Buckland household became famous for its bizarre menagerie, which also included a bear and monkey.

Legend has it that dinner at the Bucklands' was a curious affair often accompanied by crunching noises from under the table as 'Billy' the hyena chomped his way through one of the guinea pigs that also frequented the dining room. The chewed bony products of the hyena's efforts all became evidence for Buckland's reconstruction of life and death in Kirkdale cave. As Buckland wrote to a friend 'Billy has performed admirably on shins of beef, leaving precisely those parts which are left at Kirkdale and devouring those that are wanting ... So wonderfully alike were these bones in their fracture ... that it is impossible to say which bone had been cracked by Billy and which by the hyenas of Kirkdale!'

He argued from the chewed bones and over 300 hyena canines (indicating the original presence of at least 75 hyenas) and by his experimental evidence from living animals, that Antediluvial hyenas had lived in the caves and dragged individual bones from larger animals into the protection of their cave to consume without disturbance from other predators and scavengers. This was pioneering work that earned him the Royal Society's prestigious award, the Copley gold medal, and guaranteed the success of his book *Reliquiae Diluvianae*. Even so, there was a storm of criticism from Christians who were more fundamentalist than Buckland and who abhorred any deviation from texts of the Old Testament account. By this time Buckland had already moved on to another cave excavation in the Carboniferous limestone of South Wales.

The Red Lady of Paviland

Today, the coastal location of Goat's Hole cave in Paviland, a few miles west of Swansea, means that it is only accessible from the sea or by a perilous descent from the cliff above. Nevertheless, Buckland recovered many animal bones, but this time the remains were accompanied by artefacts made from bone and ivory along with stone tools – and, most importantly, a human skeleton, complete except unfortunately for the skull. The skeleton was that of a modern-looking, slenderly built human, 1.7m (5ft 6in) tall, who Buckland concluded was female and he nicknamed her the 'Red Lady of Paviland'. He described and illustrated how the cadaver had been laid in a shallow grave dug into the cave floor deposits. Seashells, perforated as for a necklace, carved mammoth-ivory bracelets and long thin ivory wands were placed in the grave and all covered with a dusting of red ochre.

As Buckland acknowledged, the body had evidently been buried with some ceremony. However, the power of his religious belief was so great that he could not contemplate the reality of what he had – one of the first findings of a human skeleton that was contemporary with extinct 'Diluvial' animals. Instead, Buckland produced a convoluted argument in which he claimed that the young woman was from one of the Welsh Celtic tribes that lived in the region during the Roman occupation. How she died was not clear but her kinsfolk decided to bury her discreetly in the cave, where they happened to find some mammoth ivory that they then carved and placed in the grave.

MacEnery and Kent's Cavern
Buckland was not the only scientist to take up the exploration of 'ossiferous' caves. In 1825, Father John MacEnery (1796–1841), an Irish Catholic priest who was chaplain to a family living at Torre Abbey, began excavating Kent's Cavern developed in Devonian age limestones at Wellswood (now part of Torquay) in Devon. MacEnery broke through the most recent flowstone covering to the floor and dug out teeth and bones of rhinoceros, sabre-toothed cat, bear and hyena, along with stone tools and some human remains. As he wrote: 'They were the first fossil teeth I had ever seen, and as I laid my hands on them, relics of extinct races and witnesses of an order of things which passed away with them, I shrank back involuntarily. Though not insensible to the excitement attending new discoveries, I am not ashamed to own that in the presence of these remains I felt more awe than joy.'

MacEnery communicated his findings to Buckland, who came to look for himself and published some of MacEnery's findings that seemed to support his own conclusions from Kirkdale. When MacEnery dared to suggest that the association of the human and animal remains might demonstrate their contemporaneity, Buckland dismissed the proposition out of hand and again used his 'ancient Celt' hypothesis in which the Celts had dug oven pits through the stalagmite floor and left some of their tools mixed with the bones below. Poor MacEnery was so discouraged by Buckland's dismissal of his findings and conclusions that he never published them, writing that it was 'painful to dissent from so high authority, and more particularly so from my concurrence generally in his views of the phenomena of these caves'. Luckily his manuscript survived his early death and was eventually published 18 years later in 1859 through the intervention of William Pengelly (1812–94), a largely self-taught Cornish-born amateur of the antiquarian tradition. Pengelly had established a successful private school in Torquay and helped to found the local Natural History Society in 1844.

The Evidence Stacks up for Pengelly
From 1858–9 Pengelly excavated another West Country cave in Devonian age limestone, that of Brixham, a fishing village just 8km south of Kent's Cavern. The pristine cave was initially explored by its owner, John Philp. He was a typical Victorian entrepreneur and realized that there was money to be made from public interest in the contemporary publicity attached to 'Ossiferous Caves'. He advertised it as a 'Great Natural Curiosity' full of the bones and teeth of 'Hyenas, Tigers, Bears' that would be 'exhibited for a short time only, by Mr Philp, who has just disposed of it to a well-known scientific gentleman'. The charge for adult admission was sixpence, and fourpence for children.

Pengelly had realized the great potential of the cave and tried to get Philp to sell it to the Torquay Natural History Society but Philp demanded the exorbitant price of £100, much more than the society could afford at the time. Fortunately Pengelly had become well connected with some of the most important independent scientists of the day and persuaded Hugh Falconer (1808–65) to look over the cave site. In turn Falconer was able to persuade the Royal Society and the Geological Society of London to sponsor the excavations.

The dig was carried out by Pengelly with such care and precise recording that his work was instrumental in helping to break through the conceptual barriers defended by Buckland and the other theological geologists. Again luckily, the flowstone covering to the cave floor deposits had effectively sealed them as a time capsule against more recent ravages of weathering and human intrusion. Pengelly was one of the first to develop and employ the now classic system of grid excavation and three-dimensional recording in which every object can be mapped in plan and within the sequence of layered deposits. A large number of animal bones, including those of hyena and rhinoceros, were recovered and intimately associated with them were a number of stone tools, just as MacEnery had found in Kent's Cavern. Pengelly and Falconer presented their results at a meeting of the British Association for the Advancement of Science, held in Leeds in September 1858. Amongst the scientists who were now convinced that humans had lived alongside extinct 'Ante-Diluvial' animals was Charles Lyell, one of the most influential geologists of the era.

Lyell's great book *Principles of Geology*, first published between 1831and 1833, had been through numerous editions and was assiduously read by Charles Darwin during his voyage on the *Beagle*. Lyell was fairly cautious and tended to sit on the fence over controversial subjects until there was overwhelming evidence to support one side or the other. He had visited some Belgian caves, beside the River Meuse near Liège, that had been excavated since 1825 by Philippe Charles Schmerling (1791-1836), a Belgian doctor, who abandoned medicine for prehistory and became a professor at the University of Liege. Schmerling spent several years exploring over 40 caves and recovered the remains of 60 animal species, including cave bear, mammoth and rhinoceros, as well as human remains, stone tools and bone artefacts. At Engis, a child's skull was found next to a mammoth tooth. (It is now known that this child's skull is actually that of a Neanderthal and, as such, the first Neanderthal ever found. But this was not recognized until 1936, because the most obvious Neanderthal feature – the prominent bony brow ridge – is not yet fully developed and was overlooked.)

Schmerling published a record of his findings in 1833 and commented that 'there can be no doubt that the human bones were buried at the same time and by the same causes as the other extinct species'. Furthermore, 'even if we had not found human bones in circumstances strongly supporting the assumption that they belonged to the antediluvian period, proof would have been furnished by the worked bones and shaped flints'.

Despite seeing the evidence for himself Lyell had not been convinced but finally had to admit in his usual convoluted lawyer's prose that Schmerling's specimens were found 'under circumstances far more difficult to get over than any I have previously heard of'. Such was the weight of Lyell's opinion that, once convinced, he could help to sway others.

The success of the Brixham excavation was such that Pengelly returned to Kent's Cavern in 1864 and carried out more extensive work there with his new techniques right through until 1879, in the course of which he confirmed MacEnery's conclusions. He also set the record straight by publishing MacEnery's notes on the original excavation. Buckland and the other theological geologists were forced to give way in the face of the overwhelming evidence. It was not the only important argument on which they were to be defeated – the Flood theory was also overturned by revolutionary new ideas and evidence from the Continent.

Louis Agassiz Turns the Flood Waters to Ice

Buckland, along with many other natural philosophers of previous centuries had argued that the Diluvial sands, gravels and muds that plastered so much of the landscape of Northern Europe had been deposited by the waters of the Noachian Flood or Deluge as it was known.

But scientifically the days of the Flood were numbered. European geologists were intrigued by the phenomenon of alpine glaciation and its influence on the landscape. There were pioneers such as the Swiss pastor, Bernhard Kuhn, who first suggested in 1787 that in the past Alpine glaciers must have extended far beyond their present extent. He took as his evidence the numerous massive boulders found scattered over the landscapes around the Alps and especially across the North German Plain to the Baltic.

Known as 'erratics', such boulders were also being found in the British Isles. However, it was the Swiss scientist Jean de Charpentier who first accurately mapped the former extent of the Rhône glacier from the distribution of 'erratics'. He argued that the scratches and grooves on the surfaces of the boulders were similar to those produced by the action of existing glaciers and different from the rounding action on boulders carried by flood waters. Charpentier had met and encouraged a young fellow countryman by the name of Louis Agassiz (1807–73) who managed to combine a very active research programme into fossil fish with a field study of glaciers which he shared with a German contemporary, Karl Friedrich Schimper (1803–67).

By the end of the 1830s, Schimper, in a series of lectures given in Munich, developed his concept of a great Ice Age (*Eiszeit*) in the recent past. He even wrote an ode:

Ice of the Past! Of an Age when frost
In its stern clasp held the lands of the South.
Dressed with its mantle of desolation white
Mountains and forests, fair valleys and lakes!

In 1837, Agassiz formulated his own *Eiszeit* theory without giving much in the way of acknowledgment to the previous work of Schimper or Charpentier and then developed his ideas in a beautifully illustrated book, *Etudes sur les glaciers* which was privately published in 1840. He claimed that following the accumulation of Earth's ancient geological formations, repeated falls in temperature resulted in the growth of an enormous ice sheet that extended over the greater part of Europe and across the Mediterranean to the Atlas Mountains of North Africa and across northern Asia and northern North America. Like Buckland, Agassiz was an excellent speaker and intrepid self-publicist and rarely missed an opportunity to give a lecture on his ideas.

Buckland already knew Agassiz from when he visited Oxford to study the fossil fish in the Ashmolean Museum collections which were under Buckland's care. The Oxford Diluvialist first heard Agassiz lecture on his new theory in Freiburg in 1838. Following the lecture, Buckland and his wife travelled south to Neuchatel with Agassiz and a wealthy amateur naturalist by the name of Charles Lucien Bonaparte, Prince of Canino and brother of the deposed Emperor. Agassiz demonstrated the abundant evidence in the Alps for the action of glacial ice and its products, especially those that were sufficiently unique to be indicative of glaciation, even in the absence of glacial ice. Buckland was not so easily swayed; again his ideological background influenced him so strongly that he could not appreciate what he was seeing for what it was truly worth.

Agassiz was not so easily put off by Buckland's intransigence. In 1840 he travelled all the way to Glasgow to address the annual meeting of the British Association for the Advancement of Science on his glacial theory. Once again he strove to prove that 'at a certain epoch all of the north of Europe and also the north of Asia and America were covered by a mass of ice'. But his audience of British geologists were unimpressed and, whilst Buckland remained unusually silent, Lyell was particularly vociferous in attacking the idea, which was not surprising as he had a vested interest in an alternative theory. By 1840, polar exploration had amply demonstrated the power of sea ice to transport rock debris, called 'drift', by flotation in icebergs over very great distances.

The idea, known as the 'Drift theory' had been proposed by Lyell back in the 1830s and seemed to be supported by the discovery of well preserved modern-looking marine seashells stranded high up on mountain slopes in parts of North Wales and Scotland. It seemed easier to imagine that the distribution of the scattered erratic boulders of the British Isles resulted from carriage by icebergs than accept the idea of a vast ice sheet and glaciers covering the whole country. Following the Glasgow meeting, Buckland took Agassiz along with another rising star of British geology, Roderick Murchison, on a field trip to examine the 'Drift' in Scotland and the north of England.

Agassiz soon found ample opportunity to point out other glacial features of the landscape, such as ice-scratched rock surfaces and trails of moraine debris that were identical to those Buckland had seen in the Alps – features that were not associated with sea ice. This time Buckland was converted and he set about bringing Lyell round. Murchison was not so easy to convince, particularly as he was a well known advocate of the 'Drift' theory and a very stubborn man, concerned about 'losing face'. By mid-October Buckland was able to enthuse to Agassiz: 'Lyell has adopted your theory in toto!!! On my showing him a beautiful cluster of moraines within two miles of his father's house, he instantly accepted it, as solving a host of difficulties which have all his life embarrassed him.' A month later Agassiz, Buckland and Lyell each presented papers at the Geological Society in London on the evidence for glaciation in Britain.

Murchison still demurred and protested at the way Buckland now viewed all Diluvium as glacial moraine. He asked somewhat facetiously whether London's Highgate Hill 'will be regarded as the seat of a glacier, and Hyde Park and Belgrave Square will be the scene of its influences?' But the glacialist 'party' was able to respond well to more serious objections with chapter and verse from British localities. As an observer recorded, 'with a look and tone of triumph [Buckland] pronounced upon his opponents who dared to question the orthodoxy of the scratches and grooves, and polished surfaces of the glacial mountains (when they should come to be d—d the pains of eternal itch without the privilege of scratching!)'.

The remarkable volte face by Buckland did not go unnoticed by the London press who regularly covered the energetic debates in the Geological Society. The Oxford professor was lampooned in a cartoon, entitled 'The Rectilinear Course of these grooves corresponds with the motions of an IMMENSE BODY the momentum of which does not allow it to change its course upon Slight Resistance'. Buckland is regaled in his characteristic field clothing (called Costume of the Glacier), encumbered with his large collecting bag, hammers and a roll of 'maps of ancient glaciers' standing on 'prodigious glacial scratches' with a couple of rock specimens, one labelled 'scratched by a glacier thirty three thousand three hundred and thirty three years before creation' and the other 'scratched by a cart wheel on Waterloo Bridge the day before yesterday'.

A year later, in 1841, a justifiably aggrieved Charpentier published his evidence for widespread glaciation in his 'Essai sur les Glaciers', in which he meticulously gave credit to earlier observers, especially those Swiss non-academics, such as Jean-Pierre Perraudin, a chamois hunter from Chamonix, who had noticed icescratched rock as long ago as 1815 and had correctly concluded that they were evidence for glaciers having filled now empty valleys, leaving behind boulders and moraine when they melted away. Charpentier also correctly argued that before glaciation the Alps had been uplifted and developed river valleys that were then exploited and deepened by the glaciers.

Encouraged by Lyell, Agassiz took up an invitation to lecture on the Eiszeit theory in North America. He recorded that as soon as his ship docked in Halifax, Nova Scotia, on its way to New York, he 'sprang on shore, and started at a brisk pace for the heights above the landing … I was met by the familiar signs, the polished surfaces, the furrow and scratches, the line engravings of the glacier…and I became convinced … that here also this great agent had been at work.'

A year later Agassiz accepted a professorship at Harvard where he was to remain for the rest of his life. He visited South America and continued his enthusiasm for the *Eiszeit* to such an extent that in 1865 Lyell remarked that Agassiz 'has gone wild about glaciers … the whole of the great [Amazon] valley, down to its mouth was filled with ice' and yet 'he does not pretend to have met with a single glaciated pebble or polished rock'.

In less than 20 years the magnificent edifice of 'diluvialism' based on a universal Flood as described in the Old Testament had completely crumbled away. The foundations of Buckland's theological geology and all his hopes of using geology to vindicate the truth and wisdom of the Bible were slowly but surely disappearing. But the idea of the special creation of humankind was still being desperately adhered to, not just by Buckland but by a much wider section of the geological community.

Humankind's Changing Status
Whilst Britain had its remarkable and informative cave deposits, some more spectacular evidence was found on the continent. In 1837 a French director of customs at Abbeville, Jacques Boucher de Crevecoeur de Perthes (1788–1868), was finding fossil animal bones and associated stone tools that were initially dredged during the excavation of the Somme canal. Then he turned his attention to the same deposits of ancient river terrace gravels exposed in quarries near Abbeville. Finally, after some nine years of collecting, he had amassed over a thousand worked flint handaxes and in 1847 published *Antiquites celtiques et antediluviennes*, a monumental three-volume work describing and illustrating the finds. A well educated amateur from a wealthy family, Boucher de Perthes claimed that the bones and tools were buried together within the ancient river deposits and, like Schmerling in Belgium and MacEnery in Devon had done before, concluded that humans had been contemporaries of the great antediluvian beasts which, in Abbeville, included straight-tusked elephant, mammoth, rhinoceros, bison and ox. As he wrote, 'in spite of their imperfection, these rude stones prove the existence of man as surely as a whole Louvre would have done'.

The succession of stone tools showed that there was an early primitive culture of flaked stone tools followed later by a more advanced one that produced polished stone tools. But Boucher de Perthes was also very much a man of his times and adopted a somewhat romantic literary style with rhetorical flights of fantasy and imagination. Unfortunately his enthusiasm tended to run away with him at times and amongst many genuine stone tools he also illustrated a number that merely had odd natural shapes. Other scientists easily spotted these and tended to dismiss the whole work.

One of his critics was the French geologist Jerome Rigollet, who set about his own excavations in the gravel pits of Saint-Acheul to show just how wrong Boucher de Perthes was. But Rigollet ended up finding the same association of stone tools with extinct animal remains and in 1854 he published carefully measured excavation sections in his *Memoires sur les Instruments en Silex trouvees a Saint-Acheul*. Even so, it still took a few years to convince the growing community of scientists interested in the early history of humankind in relation to the 'Ice Age'.

Meanwhile pioneering British scientists, such as Charles Lyell, Hugh Falconer, Joseph Prestwich (1812–96) and John Evans (1823–1908), had grasped the reality of the British finds. In 1859, Falconer, Prestwich and Evans visited Abbeville and Saint-Acheul. Evans found his imagination stretched to 'think of their finding flint axes and arrow heads at Abbeville in conjunction with bones of Elephants and Rhinoceroses 40 ft below the surface of a bed of drift … I can hardly believe it'. But believe it they did and on returning to England Prestwich soon reported their findings to the Royal Society with a paper 'On the Occurrence of Flint Implements associated with the Remains of Extinct Species in beds of a late Geological Period at Amiens and Abbeville and in England at Hoxne'. Evans added a discussion of the stone tools and supported the idea, writing that 'this much appears to be established beyond doubt, that in a period of antiquity remote beyond any of which we have hitherto found traces, this portion of the globe was peopled by Man'.

A Clearer Vision
The full importance of Paviland and Kent's Cavern could not be appreciated at the time. It is now known that the Buckland's Red Lady of Paviland was not a 'she' but a 'he', around 25 years old, and a member of the Cro-Magnon people who first entered Europe some 40,000 years ago. This particular individual and his clan have now been radiocarbon dated to around 26,350 ± 550 years old, but in Buckland's day there was no means of dating such remains. In retrospect it can be seen that Paviland is one of the richest and most important prehistoric sites in the British Isles and the only known

ceremonial burial of Early Upper Palaeolithic (Gravettian) age. Dating of the artefacts spreads beyond that of the burial, with some stone tools as old as 28,000–30,000 years whilst a bone spatula is around 23,670 years old, suggesting intermittent occupation over a considerable period. But that occupation was terminated 23,000 years ago when the climate descended into the very cold conditions of a glacial maximum as glaciers crept southwards from the upland regions of Snowdonia and the Scottish Highlands. As the volume of ice increased, sea levels fell and as a result Paviland was about 1km inland across a flat coastal plain that was used by migrating herds of animals such as horse, deer, wild cattle (aurochs) and elephant. The cave would have provided an ideal vantage point from where the movement of game could be watched by Cro-Magnon hunters. Britain was abandoned by humans and not recolonized for another 10,000 years at the end of the last glacial.

As for Pengelly's finds at Kent's Cavern, the cave deposits here are now known to be one of the most important Pleistocene 'Ice Age' records in Britain. The oldest animal remains are mostly those of cave bears with some sabre-tooth cat fossils – animals that lived in a temperate climate that existed between 300,000 and 4000,000 years ago – and are associated with crude stone handaxes and flakes, with a few choppers and cleavers of Lower Palaeolithic (Acheulian) type. Originally Pengelly recovered some 116 stone tools from this layer but only 29 survive.

Above this, the next fossiliferous layer contained abundant remains of spotted hyena, woolly rhinoceros and horse, along with some giant deer, mammoth and brown bear remains and around a thousand Middle Palaeolithic artefacts (of which only 33 can be traced today). Several different tool types belonging to the Mousterian industry dated to around 28,000 years ago have been recognized. Additionally the upper part of this layer includes more diverse types of advanced tools belonging to an Early Upper Palaeolithic industry, particularly associated with the giant deer and brown bear, and these are dated to between 12,000 and 14,000 years ago. Finally the uppermost layer contained 16 kinds of Upper Palaeolithic tool types, including needles, awls and harpoon points made from bone from around 8,000 years ago.

In 1926 a human jaw fragment with heavily worn teeth was found at Kent's Cavern – dated to between 30,000 and 40,000 years ago, when Neanderthals and Cro-Magnon people could have been in contact with one another.

Altogether, it is now known that the cavern records the remarkable vicissitudes of climate and occupation of the British Isles through a significant part of the Pleistocene 'Ice Age'. Buckland and his fellow theological geologists were spectacularly wrong in their assessment of the evidence and there is an important lesson to be learned about the intrusion of religious-based prejudice into science.

With the benefit of historical hindsight, it can be seen that the late 1850s marked the beginning of the end for the final bastion of the theologically based 'special creation' version of humanity's origins. Ever since the beginning of that century there had been mounting evidence showing that human antiquity was much greater than previously thought, with humans living alongside animals such as the giant cave bear, mammoth and woolly rhinoceros. And it was recognized that their extinction had occurred since the end of an 'ice age' rather than a 'Diluvial' flood event. In his later years of intellectual and emotional torment, Buckland had seen all his cherished hopes dashed by the new evidence of the science to which he had devoted his life. He had hoped to establish theological geology and a material basis for the history of life and its creation as outlined in the Bible, but it was not to be. The 'flood' tide had indeed turned, the 'ice age' was accepted along with the existence of 'antediluvian' humans. But no sooner had this ground been gained than another battlefront opened up as the theologically minded prepared to defend a new position. Was it possible that extinct species of humans had existed in the remote past?

CHAPTER 3: HUMAN REMAINS

' ... *light will be thrown on the origin of man and his history* ... '
(Charles Darwin, 1859)

Over more than two centuries, many intrepid investigators have searched for the fossil 'roots' of the human family tree. Of these, two examples stand out to illustrate what is needed in terms of inspiration and determination to uncover the very sparse and fragmentary fossil evidence for our prehistoric ancestors and relatives. Right at the end of the 19th century, Eugene Dubois was sure that humanity had evolved in southeast Asia and set out to prove it. Nearly 50 years later Louis and Mary Leakey were equally sure that Africa was the home to humankind.

New Theories and Human Evolution
The idea of evolution and the evolutionary 'descent' of humans from animal ancestors was not a new idea in the mid 19th century but it was not respectable and was roundly condemned by religious leaders of all faiths and most scientists of the time. Charles Darwin (1809–82) was all too aware of the widespread and vehement hostility to the idea. His wife Emma was a very sincere Christian and he knew that she would be dismayed by his ideas. As a result all that he said about it in *The Origin of Species* (published in 1859) was a prediction that 'light would be thrown on the origin of man and his history'. By 1871 and the publication of *The Descent of Man* he had added that 'it is somewhat more predictable that our early progenitors lived on the African continent than elsewhere' because that is where our nearest living relatives, the higher apes, live. Even then, most scientists regarded the whole question of the place of humans in relation to the apes as being far from settled. Many still argued that mankind held a 'special position', including Alfred Russell Wallace, Darwin's co-author of the so-called 'Darwinian' evolutionary theory.

Some biologists, such as Thomas Henry Huxley (1825–95) embraced the new Darwin–Wallace theory. Huxley showed that there were no essential differences of anatomy or embryology between humans and apes and he argued that the 'structural differences which separate Man from the Gorilla and the Chimpanzee are not so great as those which separate the Gorilla from the lower apes'. The controversial but charismatic German evolutionist Ernst Haeckel (1834–1919) went so far as to argue that the origins of Man were based upon the acquisition of speech, the ability to walk upright and an enlargement of the brain. Consequently, according to Haeckel, mankind evolved from the primates sometime in the Tertiary period. He postulated that there was an intermediary or 'missing link', which he called the *Pithecanthropi* (ape-men) or '*alali*' (speechless beings) and even claimed that they must have lived somewhere between Africa and the Philippines on a sunken landmass that he called 'Lemuria'.

The very eminent French anatomist Georges Cuvier (1769–1832) had been silent on the subject of Man's origin. But he had claimed that 'there were no human fossil bones', by which he meant that none had been discovered at the time (the early 19th century).

He took the trouble to expose certain claimed discoveries, especially in the case of Johann Jacob Scheuchzer (1672–1733), as false. Scheuchzer, a Swiss naturalist and physician had seized upon the discovery of a human-like fossil skeleton from Oeningen in Switzerland as 'relics of the race of man drowned in the Flood'. He illustrated the fossil and called it *Homo diluvii testis*, meaning 'a man, a witness to the Deluge and Divine Messenger', who had been drowned in 2306 BC. In 1809 Cuvier demonstrated that the skeleton was actually that of a giant salamander: the flattened fossil is still preserved in the Tyler Museum at Haarlem, in The Netherlands.

In the first few decades of the 19th century, a number of archaeological and palaeontological finds were made that began to turn the tide and suggest that 'man' did have a prehistory and had coexisted with extinct animals of the Ice Age.

Human-related fossil remains and stone tools associated with the bones of extinct animals were found in a number of European sites, especially in some cave deposits. In retrospect, the most important of these was made in 1856 in the Neander Valley near Dusseldorf. Named as *Homo neanderthalensis* in 1863, the new species was the first extinct human relative to be distinguished as such, but by the 1880s it was still not fully accepted. Even the 1868 discovery of the more human-like 'Cro-Magnon Man' at Les Eyzies in the Dordogne did little to stimulate new debate about the human evolution. Late in the 1880s the understanding of human evolutionary relationships was about to be revolutionised but in a very unpredictable and unlikely direction.

Eugene Dubois and the Search for the Missing Link

On 29 October 1887, the life trajectory of Eugene Dubois (1858-1940) was irrevocably redirected. The bright and ambitious young Dutch anatomist abandoned his promising academic career and uprooted his family from a comfortable existence in Amsterdam to set sail on the steamship *Prinses Amalia* for the Dutch East Indies and the life of an army medic. Why he did this is not entirely clear. He certainly felt stifled, both personally and academically, in Amsterdam; he intensely disliked teaching and was not entirely enthralled by his chosen profession of anatomy. But he was interested in research and in trying to make a name for himself.

Despite being brought up in a devout Catholic family, Dubois was a dedicated evolutionist and already deeply interested in the debate about human origins; he was well aware of the state of knowledge at that time. Perhaps he had fallen for Haeckel's ideas about a Southeast Asian origin for humankind rather than the African origin that Darwin had proposed.

The idea had been bolstered in a much more material way by the 1878 discovery of a fossil ape in the Siwalik Hills of what is today the borderland between northern Pakistan and India. Initially the new fossil was named as *Palaeopithecus sivalensis*; it was changed to *Anthropopithecus sivalensis* in 1891 and it is today known as *Sivapithecus sivalensis*. The Asian location and age of the bones seemed to support Haeckel's claim of a late Tertiary age and oriental origin for our ancestors. Anyway, from then on, Dubois' devoted his life to finding the so-called 'missing link' between humans and apes. But where to begin? Haeckel's speculative Lemuria was out of reach beneath the waves and Asia was a rather dauntingly large region for one man to search.

The Dutch East Indies

Dubois knew that, of all the Dutch controlled islands of the Southeast Asian archipelago, Sumatra was riddled with unexplored limestone caves of the kind that provided so many of the European finds of fossil bones. There was even a mountain range called Boekit Ngalau Sariboe meaning 'the mountains of a thousand caves'.

It was 11 December by the time Dubois and his family arrived at the

Sumatran town of Padang to take up his hospital duties and he soon managed to get a transfer inland to an army convalescent hospital at Pajakombo, where the duties were much lighter and left him time to begin his real purpose – to find the 'missing link'. By any objective criteria, it was a crazy quest and finding the proverbial needle in a haystack would have been easier. In this case the 'needle' was a fossil one and nobody knew where it was buried, or whether it was buried intact or not. But Dubois was very determined and confident that he was on the right track.

By August 1888 he was already uncovering a wealth of animal fossils, including those of elephant and rhinoceros, and publishing the finds. This success helped hin to gain support from the Dutch colonial government and he was allowed to devote most of his time to his research; he was even assigned two young officers from the engineering corps as field assistants plus some 50 forced labourers to help with the excavations. At that time such official recognition and support was virtually unheard of except for quasi-military 'geographical' expeditions by other colonial nations. But after a year's work in difficult conditions not much else had been achieved and Dubois decided to move his search to the neighbouring island of Java.

One of the reasons for the move was a mining engineer's discovery of a human-like fossil skull in a rock shelter close to the village of Wadjak in East Java on 24 October 1888. The skull had been forwarded to Dubois who declared: 'I am virtually certain that the first discovered representative of the primordial people of Java has now been discovered.' But it was not what he was searching for as it looked too modern. He did not get around to describing it in detail for another 30 years but its discovery rejuvenated his determination and, not surprisingly, he first searched the caves around Wadjak though to no avail. By this time, it was already known that the best animal fossils on the island were to be found elsewhere and in different geological circumstances and in due course Dubois turned his attention to these other sites.

Eureka!
Through the early 1890s his teams excavated sites in the Kendeng Hills and along the banks of the Solo River. Numerous animal fossils were recovered, including those of *Stegodon* (an extinct elephant relative), whose presence indicated that at least they were dealing with deposits of the right age. The

ancient river sands and gravels along the bank of the river Solo at Trinil could only be worked during the dry season, when the river levels were low. Many tons of sediment were sieved and searched and eventually, in October 1891, there was a 'eureka' moment: they turned up a human-like skullcap – the brain's roof bones. Against all odds, they had indeed found the proverbial 'needle in the haystack'. Dubois himself was not on site to enjoy the moment and as a result the details of the exact situation and location of the find were not recorded with much accuracy. Nevertheless, he was certain that 'he' had found the bones of Haeckel's putative *Pithecanthropus alalus*.

The skullcap was very different from that of any living human and was distinguished by a very prominent bony brow ridge that projected like a visor above the eyes. The forehead sloped back and had a shallow dome over quite a large brain cavity. Dubois noticed that the sutures that 'knitted' the skull roof bones together were fully developed, indicating adult growth. Unfortunately all the lower part of the skull, facial bones and jaw were missing. Dubois could see that it was very different from the skull roof of both the southeast Asian orangutan and the African gorilla. Rather than adopt Haeckel's name, he initially decided to use the recently published genus name of the Siwalik fossil ape, *Anthropopithecus*, since it translated as 'man-ape', suggesting a closer affinity with humans than apes.

Just over six months later, the Trinil excavation team found another fossil: an almost complete thigh bone. Although he had little basis for it, Dubois assumed that the remains all belonged to the same individual. The legbone was robust and quite modern in appearance, certainly without any critical difference to that of modern humans. Dubois correctly concluded that this individual stood and could walk upright and added the species name '*erectus*' to the new find.

Pithecanthropus erectus – *the Missing Link*
Not until August 1894 was his description and illustration of the finds published. Dubois had originally intended a larger work on all the fossils from Java but he decided that his 'missing link' was of such importance that the results of its investigation should be 'rushed' into print and the news broadcast to the wider world. He reverted to Haeckel's *Pithecanthropus* name but added his own species name '*erectus*', so the new human relative became known as

Pithecanthropus erectus. Dubois calculated that the brain size was around 984cc, more than double that of a chimpanzee but less than that of adult modern humans (which range between 1100 and 1400cc). From the size and strength of the thigh bone, he estimated that the body weight was similar to that of modern humans and that the individual had stood some 1.7m tall, a stature similar to that of modern Europeans at the end of the 19th century.

Altogether, for Dubois, *Pithecanthropus erectus* is the transitional form which, according to the theory of evolution, must have existed between Man and the anthropoids; he is Man's ancestor'. Accordingly the human family tree developed from *Anthropopithecus sivalensis* – *Pithecanthropus erectus* – *Homo sapiens*. To Dubois the Neanderthals were already humans who 'stood at a level of morphological development no lower than that of the modern races of mankind'. Furthermore, his Java fossil proved that 'our ancestors' first step on the road to becoming human must have been the acquisition of the upright position ... and consequently the factual evidence is provided that ... the East Indies was the cradle of humankind'. From the accompanying animal fossils he gave a relative age of late Pliocene or early Pleistocene, making it younger than the much more primitive Siwalik ape fossil which was late Miocene or Pliocene in age.

During 1895 Dubois managed to get the scientific description and conclusions of his find published in academic journals in Holland, Germany, France and Britain. All he had to do was wait for the accolades. Little did he realize what disappointment and anguish lay before him.

Doubts and Anguish
The new member of the human family tree did not go unnoticed: over the next five years until the end of the century some 80 scientific articles were published that discussed Dubois's remarkable Java find. Opinion varied enormously and ranged from the utterly dismissive and condemnatory to the congratulatory but overall there was a generally critical and unaccepting tone. Dubois was surprised to find that instead of being hailed as a great discoverer and 'hero' of science he was being questioned and doubted – something that his pride found very hard to accept.

One of the main criticisms focused on Dubois's claim that the bones belonged to a single individual, though they had been found separately in both time and space. Taken individually, his claims for the separate skeletal elements were further torn apart: the skullcap was merely that of a large gibbon whilst the thigh bone was that of a modern human and so on. Initially Dubois's reports had been in Dutch but he was well aware of the limitations this imposed on reaching a wider scientific readership and made sure that accounts were also published in German with the result that French and English critiques soon became available. Some argued with his dismissal of the Neanderthals from the 'equation' and raised the possibility that the form of the skull and small brain size resulted from a rare genetic disorder known as microcephalism.

One of the few outright compliments came from the American palaeontologist Othniel C Marsh (see next chapter) who supported Dubois's conclusions and regarded the find as the most important discovery since that of Neanderthal 'Man'. Dubois did have high hopes of significant support from one eminent European biologist, Ernst Haeckel, and he got it. Haeckel immediately incorporated Dubois's find into his writings: in 1895 he observed that, of known primate fossils, 'some of these are certainly of great importance, especially the skullcap of the Pliocene *Pithecanthropus erectus* of Java (1894), which really seems to represent the "missing link" so eagerly sought for, in the train of transitional forms'.

Dubois was faced with a number of problems. Out in Java, he was isolated from European science and its practitioners. He was a virtual unknown who had suddenly come up with an extraordinary find and claim. Nobody else had seen the specimens or knew the circumstances in which the find had been made; they only had Dubois's word for it all. Why should they believe him? Dubois realized that he had to return to Europe with his specimens to mount a campaign of persuasion and by August 1895 he was back in The Netherlands. The following month, the third International Congress of Zoology in Leiden gave him the opportunity to display his fossils and explain their significance to an international audience that included many eminent scientists. He described the context of the find in more detail, provided more information about the accompanying animal fossils and tried to answer some of the specific criticisms about his interpretation of the bones. It was all quite well received but did not quell the general dissension as he had hoped.

Still hopeful of drumming up some heavyweight support, Dubois wrote to

Haeckel on Christmas day 1895: 'I should like to tell you how happy I am to be able to express my gratitude for the influence which you … have exerted on the whole course of my life.' The following year he embarked upon an international campaign of persuasion and publicity and lectured about the find in Brussels, Paris, London, Edinburgh, Dublin, Berlin and Jena. In 1889 he was appointed to a professorship in Amsterdam which secured his future but not much satisfaction.

For the first time he provided a reconstruction of the skull. He continually refined his analyses and measurements, especially his estimate of the brain capacity, and in doing so pioneered techniques for such analysis from fragmentary material. Then in 1900 he produced an upright standing life-size reconstruction of his 'man-ape' for the World Exhibition in Paris. It had a very human-like body, with a more ape-like head and face. One hand held a fragment of deer antler and suggested that *P. erectus* was capable of using tools. It was good publicity but had little effect on scientific opinion, which remained very divided with few outright supporters, even though the latter included eminent scientists such as Haeckel, O C Marsh, Otto Jaekel, and Arthur Keith in Britain.

In 1907 and 1908 there were expeditions to the Trinil find-spot in Java to try to uncover more fossils, but without any luck. Little did they know that if Dubois had taken the trouble to unpack and catalogue the numerous boxes of animal fossils from the site they would have found more *P. erectus* material. Thanks to Marsh's support of Dubois's claims, a well funded American expedition under Roy Chapman Andrews was sent to Central Asia to look for more Asian evidence of an oriental origin for humankind. It did not find any but did not come away empty handed (see next chapter).

Although Dubois eventually received many formal honours for his work such as diplomas and honorary degrees, there was still no general acceptance of his claims. Suspicious by nature he tended to see conspiracy, especially anti-evolutionary Catholic plots, and malice in any objection to his work. He stopped showing the fossils to fellow scientists and constantly prevaricated over his description of the other Javanese fossils. Meanwhile European students of human evolution became embroiled in much more local arguments over the status of the Neanderthals and the disastrous farrago of the so-called Piltdown Man, discovered in southern England in 1912. Then the whole region descended into the prolonged slaughter and stalemate of World War I and much of Europe's non-military science was on hold.

Eventually, after the Armistice in 1918 and the end of hostilities, the Royal Dutch Academy of Science was forced to intervene in Dubois's affairs: he had to allow his collection of Java fossils to be unpacked and catalogued and he had to provide casts of the fossils to those who wished to examine them, such as Henry Fairfield Osborn. Amongst the collection there were found to be four more human-related bones, including a fragment of another legbone, proving that there were the remains of more than one individual preserved at Trinil. Dubois lived on as an increasingly cantankerous and embittered old man until 1940 and died as the Hitler's forces invaded Holland. His 'Java Man' has stood the test of time, and 'Peking Man' is evidently so closely related that it is now regarded as the same species – and that this species is so closely related to our genus that it is now called *Homo erectus* and is one of the most important of our extinct human relatives. The *H. erectus* people were the first to leave Africa around 1.8 million years ago and spread as far as Asia.

Raymond Dart's Southern Ape in Africa
In a curious reprise of a Dubois-like story, it was another army medic who was to make the next breakthrough in understanding the human family tree. Raymond Dart (1893–1988) was an Australian doctor who survived service in World War I and following his discharge wanted to pursue palaeoanthropological-related anatomical studies in London. Fellow Australian Grafton Elliott Smith (1871–1937) had just been appointed professor of anatomy at University College in London and agreed to take Dart on as a student and assistant along with a Canadian by the name of Davidson Black (1884–1934). Black left in 1920 to become professor of anatomy in China's Peking Union Medical College and three years later Dart moved to South Africa to become professor of anatomy at the University of Witswaterand.

Dismayed at the lack of teaching material, Dart encouraged his students to bring in anything that might be useful to the teaching of human anatomy and in 1924 he received a box of fossils that would eventually revolutionize the way we look at human evolution. Apparently Dart was about to leave home to attend a wedding when the box arrived but he could not resist a quick look.

He was amazed to see the partially exposed bones of a tiny face peering at him from amongst the rocks. The specimens came from the limestone quarries of Taung, southwest of Johannesburg.

After many hours of painstaking excavation Dart exposed a remarkable sight: the beautifully preserved facial bones and jaw of a child-like ape. To him the canine teeth were smaller than those of living apes and therefore more advanced in the human direction. Although the back of the skull was missing there was another stone that fitted exactly the space where the brain had been. It was a natural endocast, or rock infill, of the brain cavity and Dart considered that its surface form was also more human than ape-like. Furthermore, his analysis of the position and orientation of the opening at the base of the skull for the spinal cord suggested to Dart that this little ape-like being, perhaps no more than 7 years old (later revised to 3 years old), could stand and walk upright rather than habitually knuckle-walk like chimps.

Dart gave the little fossil human relative a new genus and species name *Australopithecus africanus*, meaning 'southern ape from Africa'. In 1925, Dart managed to get his description and conclusions published in the prestigious international science journal *Nature* which is published in London. But, yet again like Dubois, Dart was out of the European academic 'network' and despite his connection with such an eminent anatomist as Elliot Smith, his find was not taken seriously – it was merely a fossil chimp or some such ape. It was thought that its brain was too small and it was in the wrong place to be anything to do with human evolution.

Dart decided to take the skull to London and show it to people who mattered such as Elliot Smith and Sir Arthur Keith, in the hope that it would help to persuade them of its significance. Dart's bad luck was that his arrival in London in 1926 coincided with the announcement of the discovery of 'Peking Man' (*Sianthropus pekinensis*) in China by Elliot Smith's Canadian student Davidson Black. Dart and the little Taung 'baby' *Australopithicus africanus* were completely overshadowed and got nowhere.

A Doughty Ally
At least Dart had one ardent supporter in Robert Broom (1866–1951), another expatriate doctor and indefatigable palaeontologist living in South Africa. Broom was a very independently minded Scot of remarkable industry

who had carved out a name for himself by uncovering many new and important ancient reptile fossils in the vast Karoo Highlands of South Africa. In later years Dart liked to recount how Broom, upon hearing of the find, had 'burst into my laboratory unannounced. Ignoring me and my staff, he strode over to the bench where the skull reposed and dropped to his knees "in adoration of our ancestor" '.

Although he was already 60 years old Broom set out to find more supporting evidence for African ancestors in the human family tree. It took ten years of field exploration, especially in and around the limestone quarries and caves of the Sterkfontein area north of Johannesburg. Eventually he found another wonderfully preserved skull but it was very different from the Taung 'child'. Broom's new skull had a very broad, heavily boned and forward projecting face with prominent brow ridges and receding forehead. Whilst the brain was small and ape sized, the teeth were more human like and the position of the foramen magnum suggested an upright-walking individual. Initially, Broom called it *Australopithecus transvaalensis* but then thought it sufficiently different from the Taung find to warrant a new genus, *Plesianthropus transvaalensis* – meaning the 'near ape from Transvaal' and nicknamed 'Mrs Ples'.

In 1938 Broom found another ape-like skull, which he placed in yet another genus, *Paranthropus robustus*, and more fossils over the next decade culminating in a partial skeleton which confirmed Dart's claim that these small brained and small statured ape-like beings walked upright. Such was the volume of finds – they amounted to remains from some 30 separate individuals – that eventually the eminent British palaeontologist Wilfred le Gros Clark decided to visit South Africa to see what was going on. He made a detailed study and report concluding that Dart and Broom 'had been entirely correct in all essential details'. The human family tree did have significant members who had lived in Africa. So where was our evolutionary 'Eden': Asia or Africa?

A Chinese Home for Humanity?
Like many other limestone caves and quarries, those of Dragon's Bone Hill or Choukoutien near Peking (today's Beijing) turned out to contain the buried bones of a great variety of recently extinct animals when they were first excavated in the early decades of the 20th century. For centuries bones and

teeth had been excavated for traditional medicine and sold in markets before they came to the attention of European scientists, who eventually traced the source to Choukoutien. It was an Austrian Otto Zdansky who found the first human-related teeth and this stimulated a new round of serious excavations by Swedish palaeontologists who uncovered a few more teeth and jaw fragments. In 1926, they were described by the Canadian anatomist Davidson Black as belonging to another new genus and species in the human family tree – *Sinanthropus pekinensis* or 'Peking Man'. It was the publication of this new find in *Nature* that overshadowed Dart's arrival in London with the Taung skull.

Black had persuaded the American Rockefeller Foundation to sponsor several seasons of excavation. Thousands of tons of rock were removed in the search for fossil bones and although some 1,500 cases were filled and shipped back to the United States they only found a few more human-related teeth. But at the end of the 1929 season Black's colleague, the Chinese palaeontologist W C Pei, found the first skull. It had a prominent bony browridge and a brain size of around 1000cc. Dubois's Java 'Man' was also sidelined although there were marked anatomical similarities between the finds.

Black died in 1934 but the work was carried on by a French Jesuit priest and anthropologist Teilhard du Chardin and the German Franz Weidenreich. Over the next few years another 14 skulls, 11 jawbones and some 147 teeth, along with lots of stone tools and more animal bones, were recovered from the Dragon's Bone Hill, an astonishing haul, especially as some of the skulls were beautifully preserved. But all excavation work ground to a halt as Japan invaded China in 1936 and the foreign scientists beat a hasty retreat. The human-related fossils were all boxed up and dispatched to Dr Roy Chapman Andrews at the American Museum of Natural History in New York. The problem is that only one box ever arrived and it only contained casts. Nobody knows what happened to the rest and it is one of the biggest tragedies in anthropological history that such important and magnificent specimens were lost to science. Fortunately the casts, made by Chinese technicians, were superb.

Louis Leakey and the Africans

By the 1930s, the endeavours of just a few medically trained scientists such as Eugene Dubois, Raymond Dart, Robert Broom and Davidson Black had transformed the human family tree. The most advanced fossils were those of the European *Homo sapiens*-like Cro-Magnon people, along with the Neanderthals (*Homo neanderthalensis*). Then there were the Asian fossils of Java and 'Peking Man', which turned out to have similarities to the Neanderthals but had distinctly smaller brains.

Finally there were the even more primitive and ape-like beings of South Africa, the australopithecines and paranthropines with their very ape-like skulls, brains and small stature but who nevertheless stood and walked upright and had some more advanced human-like features such as their teeth. But were these African finds just fossil apes or part of the human family tree? The academic world was deeply divided upon the subject but there was a young man who thought he knew the answer and was just as determined as Dubois and the others to prove himself right. His name was Louis Leakey.

One man and his family initiated a revolution in our view of the human family tree and the role of Africa in our ancestry, just as Darwin predicted. Louis Seymour Bazett Leakey (1903-72) was the Kenya-born son of English missionaries. Whilst his parents were converting native Kenyans to Christianity, their son was brought up amongst the Kikuyu people, learned their language, was initiated into the tribe at the age of 13 and saw himself as a 'white African'. He had little or no money and no official job, until 1945, when he was appointed curator of the Coryndon (now National) Museum in Nairobi. Nevertheless, after some 30 years of searching, Louis and his second wife Mary eventually managed to find some fossils that help to fill the yawning gap between Dart's australopithecines and the Asian fossil human relatives.

Louis Leakey was a charismatic enthusiast and also a controversial figure. He was proud, self-confident in many ways and yet shy; he could easily rub people up the wrong way but he could also charm when he wanted to, especially potential donors to his research funds. And he was what the Irish would call a 'bit of a chancer'. Entering the University of Cambridge in 1922, he found a handy loophole in the University regulations and was able to persuade them to accept Kikuyu as one of his two modern languages. He even produced a testimonial as to his proficiency in the language from Chief

Koinage, signed with a thumbprint, leaving them with the problem of finding somebody who could teach him.

A Dinosaur Diversion

Leakey's first brush with controversy arose from a chance meeting in Germany with palaeontologist Hans Reck, who had been a member of a dinosaur-hunting expedition to Tendaguru in German East Africa (then Tanganyika and now Tanzania) from 1907–19. By an extraordinary coincidence, Leakey had also been dinosaur hunting in the same region with a British expedition in 1924 and so they had a lot in common. He probably told Reck that he was much more interested in human evolution than that of the dinosaurs and Reck told Leakey that he had also discovered a fossil human skeleton buried in strata at a place then called Oldoway (now known as Olduvai), a long way from Tendaguru in the north of the country. Knowing that Olduvai was accessible from Kenya, Leakey was intrigued and said 'half jokingly, half seriously', that 'one day he must come and join me, and that we would visit Oldoway together'. Six years later it actually happened.

Leakey graduated in 1926 with a double first in anthropology and archaeology and was awarded a research fellowship by his college, St John's. He promptly set up his first anthropological expedition to Africa. By July 1928 he had met and married his first wife, fellow Cambridge graduate Frida Avern, and took her with him to Africa. Following the search habits of the time, Leakey first chose to investigate a Kenyan cave site near Elmenteita in the centre of the great East African Rift Valley. The results were encouraging with lots of stone axes of a kind (Acheulian) previously unknown in Africa. They rounded off a successful expedition by taking a 3,000-mile 'trip' down to Johannesburg, a cross-country journey that took six weeks, to attend the 1929 annual meeting of the British Association for the Advancement of Science.

It was well worth it; Leakey met many of the foremost anthropologists of the day including Raymond Dart, whom he did not like and with whose identification of *Australopithecus africanus* he did not agree. He did like Gertrude Caton-Thompson and her startling new interpretation of the great Zimbabwe ruins, which she regarded as the work of native Africans rather than some unknown northern race. Leakey's description of his cave excavation was well received and he found, somewhat to his dismay, that a considerable number of the scientists wanted to see the site for themselves. Consequently, he had to scurry back as soon as the meeting ended in order to prepare for their arrival. But it all went very well and as a result he was awarded another two-year research fellowship at St John's back in Cambridge.

A Nebraska 'Pig in a Poke'

By 1929, the anthropological world was still trying to decide where the human family originated and, if anything, Asia was the favoured 'Eden' rather than Africa, despite Dart's South African finds. The water was further muddied by the curious affair of the Nebraska pig. In 1922, a single fossil tooth found amongst fossiliferous deposits of Pliocene age in Nebraska led to a media frenzy over another so-called 'missing link' – Nebraska Man.

Experts who examined the worn tooth, including Grafton Elliott Smith, verified that it was of human-related origin. Duly named *Hesperopithecus haroldcooki*, it was reconstructed and illustrated in popular journals such as the *Illustrated London News*, which carried the caption – 'The Earliest Man Tracked By A Tooth: An "Astounding Discovery" Of Human Remains In Pliocene Strata – A Prehistoric Columbus Who Reached America By Land? An Artist's Vision of Hesperopithecus (The Ape-Man Of The Western World) And Contemporary Animals'.

The find figured as evidence in the notorious trial of John Scopes for violating Tennessee State law against teaching Darwinian evolution in public schools. Perhaps evolutionary 'Eden' was in North America or at least the find supported an Asian origin if the Nebraska 'people' had migrated into North America, across the narrow Bering Strait? But in 1927 a re-examination of the original site revealed more remains including similar teeth but this time still in a jawbone, which was clearly that of a pig rather than a human relative. As an omnivorous mammal, the cheek teeth of a pig are not that dissimilar to human teeth but when well preserved they can be clearly distinguished.

Back to Africa and Olduvai Gorge

Home in England, Leakey found a very well placed supporter in Sir Arthur Keith who was conservator in the Hunterian Museum attached to the Royal College of Surgeons in London and was a world renowned expert in all matters anthropological. Keith was greatly impressed by this unusual fast talking enthusiast, who thirsted after anthropological knowledge and expertise in order to pursue his anthropological exploration of Africa. As a result Keith gave Leakey all the assistance and support that he could in the preparation and description of his cave material. When finally written up in 1930 the results earned Leakey a University of Cambridge doctorate. Then with the help of several grants he organized another, more elaborate African expedition to Olduvai and Kanjera by Lake Victoria in southwest Kenya, where there were fossiliferous strata that seemed promising. He set out in June 1931; Frida and their baby daughter were to join him later in the year.

Scientific exploration of Olduvai Gorge had been first carried out in 1911 by a German entomologist, Professor Wilhelm Kattwinkel, who was searching for insect vectors responsible for transmitting sleeping sickness. Whilst there he had also collected fossil bone material from the strata eroding out of the gorge sides. Back in Berlin, the bones caused something of a stir when it was realized that they belonged to an extinct diminutive three-toed horse, previously unknown from Africa and which had survived there much longer than its European relatives. As a result, a further expedition to the Gorge was mounted by the Germans in 1913 with the palaeontologist Hans Reck.

Now, in September 1931, Reck was returning to Olduvai with Leakey and his team of scientists and African support staff. Stone tools literally littered the Gorge and Reck was soon able to relocate the site where he had found the skeleton 18 years previously. Indeed the four wooden pegs he had left still marked the spot. Although the skeleton had turned out to be that of a modern human, *Homo sapiens*, Reck argued that it had been excavated from within one of the stratified layers of the Gorge side (known as Bed II in Reck's scheme, which ran from the oldest Bed I to the youngest, V, at the top).

To begin with Leakey was sceptical but when Reck showed him the excavation site, he was converted to the idea that it was as old as Bed II and therefore the oldest specimen of *Homo sapiens* not just in Africa but perhaps also in the wider world. They immediately drafted a paper to *Nature* making the claim and suggesting that it was perhaps as much as half a million years old. Leakey had only been at Olduvai for a week and was already staking his claim to scientific fame.

He rushed back to Nairobi and alerted the newspapers (including the London *Times*) to the discovery. Frida arrived in October with the baby but was reluctant to take their daughter to the camp as Leakey wanted and so began her difficulties of wanting to be with her husband but not wanting to put the child at risk out in the bush. Leakey returned to Olduvai without Frida and found that so many animal fossils were being recovered that they had to cart them back to Nairobi every week.

They included the remains of strange extinct elephant-like animals known as *Deinotherium* whose tusks grew out from the lower jaw and curved downwards somewhat like the teeth on a mechanical digger. Stone tools were often found scattered amongst the bones, suggesting that they had been used to butcher the animal carcasses. The style of the tools clearly changed from the most primitive in Bed I to more sophisticated forms higher up. But where were the remains of the beings who had made the tools? Were they the same as represented by Reck's *Homo sapiens* skeleton? Leakey doubted it and thought that there must have been more primitive beings around, if they could only find the evidence. None had been found by the end of November when Leakey headed back to Nairobi.

Leakey's palaeontologist Arthur Hopwood from the British Museum in London had doubts about the contemporaneity of Reck's skeleton with the rest of the animal fossils, many of which Hopwood had personally collected. Back in London Hopwood heard that John Solomon, a geologist who had been on the 1928 expedition to Elmenteita, had developed a new technique for the comparative mineral analysis of sediment samples. Hopwood sent a sample of the Bed II sediment to Solomon, who compared it with sediment associated with Reck's skeleton. Hopwood was not surprised to hear that they were very different and so could not be of the same age. But Leakey did not like evidence that went against his ideas and was furious and rubbished the usefulness of the test. To his dismay even Arthur Keith, who initially had supported his ideas, now began to question them. In response Leakey blustered and fumed that he would just go and find another skeleton to prove his ideas right.

Kanjera and Kanam

March 1932 saw Leakey setting up camp at Kanjera, near Lake Victoria, where they soon found fossil fragments of the same kind of animals from the Olduvai strata and also bits of human skulls, but by this time he knew that he had to find the remains *in situ* – as an integral fossil within stratified sediment. One day Leakey, palaeontologist Donald McInnes and Frances Kenrick (a friend of Frida's) visited the nearby site of Kanam where they soon found more fossiliferous deposits.

Again, they contained *Deinotherium* and near the top of a gully they found a very weathered human-like jawbone with teeth. Leakey was convinced they came from the bedded sediment that contained the animal fossils and asked Frances Kenrick to take some photos of the site, whilst he arranged to mark it with four iron pegs set in concrete. He wrote to Hopwood that it was 'definitely in situ in this horizon … with a pre-chellean tool was a fragment of a human (sapiens) mandible. At Kanjera too where at first I only got parts of 3 human skulls washing out of the equivalent of Bed II at Oldoway I know have bits of No 3 actually in situ. So Oldoway man has an is situ compeer from Kanjera to hold his hand!!' As before he sent off another paper about his new finds to *Nature*, arguing the case for the antiquity of *Homo sapiens* in Africa.

Back in England further tests had shown that Reck's skeleton was much younger than the fossils found nearby. Leakey was dismayed but still determined to prove that this time the human-related fossils were the 'real thing' and so he returned to England and Cambridge in late November 1932. Once back in Cambridge, Frida used the remainder of her own money to buy a house so that she could settle down with her daughter and husband when he was not in Africa. Leakey was still not prepared to abandon his belief in the antiquity of Reck's skeleton, much to the dismay of his supporters, who thought that he was just being unnecessarily pig-headed and unscientific.

Sir Arthur Keith suggested that a committee of the Royal Anthropological Society should review the evidence for Leakey's claims. Twenty-six scientists duly met in Cambridge on 18 March 1933 with Leakey in attendance with his fossils and stone tools. To Leakey's huge relief it all went well: they reported the Kanam jaw to be 'a most startling discovery' and went on to congratulate Dr Leakey 'on the exceptional significance of his discoveries, and expressed the hope that he may be enabled to undertake further researches, seeing that there is no field of archaeological enquiry which offers greater prospects for the future'. With an accolade like that his future prospects looked very bright.

There was one small shadow, cast by the eminent geologist Percy Boswell, the professor of Geology at Imperial College in London. Boswell was a meticulous field geologist and sedimentologist and was not happy with the field evidence that Leakey had presented for the location of the Kanam jaw because there was no proper field map or section of the strata at the site, only a few black-and-white photos.

But the Leakey star was in ascendance, the Kanam jaw was exhibited in the British Museum and at the Royal Society and Frida was pregnant again. Leakey was commissioned to write a popular book about his ideas on human evolution and invited to give lectures on the subject. One of these was at the Royal Anthropological Institute in London after which a dinner was given in his honour. Gertrude Caton-Thompson of Zimbabwe fame was there with a young protégé, one Mary Nicol, daughter of Erskine Nicol (a well known landscape painter, especially of Egyptian scenes and peoples). Mary's mother was Cecilia Frere, who had studied painting in Florence and was a direct descendent of the antiquarian John Frere (1740–1807), who in 1797 had been the first to recognize a stone tool found among animal bones as the work of ancient humans living, as he described it, at 'a very remote period indeed, even byond that of the present world'.

Although not formally trained in archaeology, Mary was a great enthusiast for the subject and an excellent artist and illustrator. Seated next to Leakey she found him fascinating and he found himself a replacement illustrator, since Frida could no longer act as his unpaid assistant. Gertrude had actually set them up to be seated next to one another since she knew that Leakey was looking for another illustrator. Little did she realize what she had inadvertently set in motion. They corresponded and within a few months they met again at the Leicester meeting of the British Association for the Advancement of Science at which Leakey gave a lecture. And that was the beginning of the end for his marriage to Frida. Their son Colin was born in December and a month later Leakey confessed to Frida that he had fallen in love with Mary and was taking her to Africa, which was what he proceeded to do.

Cambridge was then a small market town on the edge of the East Anglian Fens that just happened, for historic reasons, to have at its centre, a world famous university which dominated the town and much of its life. Even in the 1930s, the University was in many ways a very conservative and Christian place although a significant minority of its academics were politically, socially and morally very different in their habits from the prevailing majority.

You could, more or less do what you wanted and believe what you wanted provided you did not disturb the status quo too much. Leakey had always sailed close to the wind and now he had overdone it well and truly. Cambridge and his college frowned upon his affair with Mary and upon his treatment of his wife Frida. He was lucky that he had Africa to escape to but he had not yet dared tell his parents what had happened.

An African Home for Homo: the Kanam Fiasco
By November 1934 Leakey was back in Kenya and returned to Kanjera. Before leaving for Africa, he had increased the stakes on his reputation by distinguishing both the fossil jaw from Kanam and the Kanjera skull fragments as belonging to a new species *Homo kanamensis*. He had also extrapolated from these new finds to claim that their antiquity indicated that modern humans had originated in Africa. He got the support of Elliot Smith and Sir Arthur Smith Woodward, who had believed his claim for the antiquity of the finds.

But Leakey got a shock when he went back to Kanam: his carefully placed iron pegs were nowhere to be seen and he had no map. Being made of iron, the stakes had proved irresistible to locals who could make excellent harpoons out of them. The terrain of dry gullies was very monotonous; all he had to guide him back to the location was a photo taken by Frida's friend Frances and it was no help. To make matters worse, when he got to the Kanjera site, he could not find the exact locations there either. Worse still, Professor Boswell was arriving in a week, as an emissary of the Royal Society to check the field relationships of the finds.

As an editorial in *Nature* announced: 'Notwithstanding the close and expert scrutiny to which Dr L.S.B. Leakey's evidence for the early occurrence of man in Kenya has been subjected, the far-reaching effect of the conclusions to which it leads make it eminently desirable that no means of verifying and substantiating the data should be neglected.' Boswell was a precise and fastidious geologist whose field maps were famous for their detail and accuracy, he did not like sloppiness and had already been alerted to Leakey's mode of working. He had been particularly critical of the relative dating of Reck's Olduvai skeleton and as a sedimentologist supported Solomon's comparative and ultimately negative test of the sediment matrix.

Shortly after his arrival, Leakey told Boswell of the problem with the missing stakes but reassured him that he was sure of the location. He also hoped to divert Boswell by showing him the sites so that he would not be too critical when the time came to examine them in detail. But Boswell was not easily diverted and was anxious to get to the crux of the matter. Also he was not impressed by the way Leakey's enthusiasm kept taking him off at tangents.

It was nearly two months before Boswell managed to get Leakey to Kanjera and when the location photo was produced it became evident that it did not depict the site but a small cliff some distance away. Then Boswell wanted to check Kanam in detail and when they arrived Leakey's surveyor had already found that the photo of that site was also that of another site some distance away. Boswell was getting annoyed despite Leakey's plaintive pleas that they were just honest mistakes. When Boswell quizzed him about who had made the Kanjera find, Leakey had to admit that it was one of his Kikuyu field assistants. This annoyed Boswell even more, since he did not regard such helpers as scientists, despite Leakey's protestations that they were as good as any scientist (in this he was quite right, in fact most of the best finds of human-related fossils in Africa have been made by such men).

Leakey suddenly realized that he had used one of the so-called site photos as a frontispiece in a book that was in press. It was imperative that it should be removed and he drove off immediately to cable Oxford University Press about the necessary change. Boswell had had enough and packed his bags: as far as he was concerned he had spent two months on a wild goose chase. He was back in London by the end of January 1935 in time for the publication of Leakey's book *The Stone Age Races of Kenya* in which the Kanam and Kanjera finds were described, and the book was getting some very favourable reviews.

Boswell not only wrote up a very unfavourable report to the Royal Society but also wrote another version for *Nature* and was openly critical of Leakey and his fieldwork without explaining any of the extenuating circumstances. The news quickly spread through the small gossipy world of academic palaeoanthropology and even got into the the *New York Times*, which reported 'Oldest Fragment of Man Disputed – British Professor Reports He Found in Africa No Support for Leakey Discovery Claim'.

In Britain and Cambridge in particular there were those who were only too glad to see the brash young Leakey taken down a peg or two and his supporters were dismayed that he should have let them down by his impetuousness and somewhat less than meticulous field work. But the damage was done and Louis' support and potential for research funds from Cambridge and Britain were running out. The good news was that Mary Nicol had left England and was due to arrive in Tanganyika.

When Mary arrived, Leakey whisked her off to Olduvai via the Ngorongoro Crater and the Serengeti. As an introduction to Africa it could not have been better; the view down into the Serengeti plain with its wildlife from the rim of the old volcano was entrancing. Mary was plunged into business as usual at Olduvai. She soon proved her worth as an excavator and was not in the least put off by the primitive rigours of camp life and long hours in the heat looking for fossils day after day. There was also an abundance of animal fossils and stone tools and Mary even managed to find a couple of human-like skull fragments, but they were the only ones uncovered by the team during the whole three-month field season, much to Leakey's disappointment.

By the end of September 1935, Leakey and Mary were back in England and penniless. He had still not told his parents about Mary and they had to earn a hand-to-mouth existence with Leakey finding book contracts and getting fees for lecturing – both of which he was very good at and so they managed. He still had some supporters who pointed him in the direction of some funds that would be available for projects in social anthropology, especially studies of the Kikuyu people with whom he was familiar with and who accepted him. He was prepared to do anything to get back to Africa and carry on the work. he and Mary married on Christmas Eve 1936 and by the end of January they were on their way back to Kenya for good.

Whilst her husband got down to writing his study of the Kikuyu people, Mary settled into her own archaeological excavation of a Stone Age burial site, all of which was of more interest to the Colonial authorities than looking for more ancient human ancestors and relatives. Leakey hoped that he would persuade them to set up a Bureau of Archaeology but it was not to be: Italy had invaded Ethiopia in 1936, annexed it in 1937 and formed an alliance with Germany and the Kenyan white settlers were beginning to feel vulnerable. But in an indirect way the situation provided a financial relief to the Leakeys because Louis was hired and paid as a civilian intelligence officer. Whilst

Mary at least was able to carry on her archaeological work, Louis's excavation programme had to go on hold. Then in 1940, their son Jonathan was born.

Plenty of Stones but No Bones

Two years later, in 1942, the Leakey couple were back in the field and managed to find a handaxe site at Olorgesailie that Leakey had been looking for since 1929. It was truly spectacular with hundreds of large and beautifully preserved handaxes just lying around on the surface. But there were no fossil remains of the people who had made the tools. Nevertheless, Leakey was intrigued, especially when round stones were found amongst the worked tools. Louis' imagination went into overdrive and he envisaged a campsite where the original inhabitants butchered the game they had hunted and brought down (especially baboons whose bones were numerous at the site) using the round stones as projectile bolas. He duly sent off an article to the London *Times* describing his reconstruction of the scene. The stone artefacts were left *in situ* as they found them and today the site is an open-air public museum. The stone tools are now known to be some 800,000 years old but few support Leakey's interpretation; instead the rounded stones are seen as hammer stones used to manufacture the handaxes.

By the end of the hostilities of World War II, Leakey needed to find a new job. He had been working for some time as the honorary and unpaid curator of the Coryndon Museum in Nairobi, although he and his growing family did have use of a rather rundown curator's house. Eventually in November 1945, he was given a paid post with an annual salary of a mere £750 and a better house. The following year they paid a visit back to postwar England and he tried to re-establish his contacts in European palaeoanthropology and promote his idea for a Pan African Congress of Prehistory to be held in Nairobi. Luckily he got the positive responses he needed and, armed with supportive letters from eminent scientists like Wilfred le Gros Clark and the French expert on cave art Abbé Henri Breuil, he was also able to get the essential support, especially financial, from Kenya's colonial governor. He was beginning to find his feet again and his talent for talking people round. A natural communicator, he even made his first appearance on British television. All the signs were looking good for 'his' Congress meeting.

By October 1946 the Leakeys were back in Nairobi and three months later in January 1947 the delegates arrived; there were lectures, dinners, field trips. For the first time in years people from all over were able to discuss their ideas and ambitions, all thanks to Louis Leakey's inspiration, and they were greatly impressed by the quality of Mary's excavations, especially at Olorgesailie. It was all so successful that they agreed to meet again every four years. Wilfred le Gros Clark was there and announced his support for Raymond Dart's and Robert Broom's finds in southern Africa and proclaimed that the australopithecines were 'man in the making'. Le Gros Clark was such a respected and cautious scientist that everyone at last took notice and Sir Arthur Keith wrote a *mea culpa* to *Nature* ' I am now convinced ... that Prof. Dart was right and that I was wrong, the Australopithecinae are in or near the line which culminated in the human form.'

Africa was ascendent in the search for the roots of the human family tree. Luckily, Le Gros Clark had been impressed by Leakey's enthusiasm and on his return to London put in a good word for him with the Royal Society. There was another agenda as well: the international bone wars in Africa were about to begin as the Americans awoke to the scientific possibilities of the Great Continent. Hopes of further finds in Asia had all but dried up and there was the postwar expansion of the American universities with plenty of research funds just waiting to be used. Indeed Leakey was informed that a 20-strong American expedition, led by Wendell Phillips, with US$150,000, trucks and an airplane would be arriving in Kenya in July, though fortunately for Leakey they were delayed and did not turn up until March 1948. He gave them a choice of sites to investigate and they chose an unexplored area west of Lake Rudolf (now Lake Turkana) in northern Kenya.

News of the anthropological 'arms race' had reached the national press. It was a wake-up call for British scientists interested in African anthropology. British businessman Charles Boise offered financial help and Leakey managed to get £1,000 from him, the Kenya government provided an additional £1,500 and the Royal Society promptly awarded him a grant of £1,500 for the investigation of the ancient Miocene age deposits of Rusinga Island in Lake Victoria. The richness of fossils was well known to Leakey from previous visits dating back to 1935 and most importantly he knew that there were primitive ape fossils, especially one called *Proconsul*, to be found that had potential significance for the early evolution of primates and the human lineage.

In September 1948, Mary Leakey 'struck gold' on Rusinga. First the jaw then the facial bones of a Proconsul skull were uncovered and it was by far the best fossil find they made. Much of the skull consisted of tiny fragments of bone but Mary painstakingly collected them all and glued them back together. To Louis the brow region of the skull looked more human than that of Dart's australopithecines and he cabled le Gros Clark 'we got the best primate find of our lifetime'. As soon as possible he sent photos of the skull Sir Arthur Keith, who was suitably impressed and told him that the find was attracting considerable interest in Britain.

So Mary and the skull were dispatched to London and when she flew in on 29 October 29 1948 she was amazed and taken aback to be greeted by a clamouring press and television reporters. *Proconsul* and Mary Leakey were front page news. When Le Gros Clark had a chance to have a close look at the skull he realized that he did not agree with Louis Leakey, who, like the proverbial leopard, had not changed his spots; he still had a dangerous tendency to be overenthusiastic. The skull showed more of a link between the monkeys and the apes, rather than between the apes and humans. It was not what the press wanted to hear either and they gave Mary and le Gros Clark a hard time trying to get them to use the magic words 'missing link', but at least it was publicity and that meant money.

For the next ten years the Kenya government provided the Leakeys with an annual grant of £1,500 for field work and research. They continued work at Rusinga, discovering more fossil apes, and gradually were able to reconstruct a remarkable view of what the animal and plant life had been in this part of Africa during early Miocene times, which we now know to have been some 18 million years ago.

Back to Olduvai
It was not until 1951 that the Leakeys managed to return to Olduvai. Louis was determined that they would find what he had always wanted – a significant new human-related fossil. He wanted something that would bridge the gap between the ape-like australopithecines and the much more human-like Asian fossils of Peking and Java which by this time were amalgamated in Dubois's species '*erectus*' and our own genus *Homo*. Their earlier work had sorted out the succession of strata, the fossils and stone tools. They had helped

to elucidate the evolutionary lineages of some of the mammal groups but still the remains of the toolmakers eluded them. They thought that their best bet was to concentrate on the Bed II deposits of the Gorge sequence, especially those sites within the Bed II deposits that had yielded the most abundant of the stone handaxes belonging to the African equivalent of the European Acheulian industry.

Continued work produced plenty more animal fossils and stone tools but it was not until 1958 that there was even a glimmer of human-related fossils and that came in the form of many fragments belonging to a single tooth. An untrained excavator had inadvertently smashed it to pieces but Mary collected them and put them all back together to emerge as what Louis called a 'really gigantic human milk tooth' in an article he promptly wrote for the *Illustrated London News*. He included a scale drawing of 'this giant baby', which he said was some three years old. Today the tooth is recognized as that of an australopithecine. After such frugal results for so much work the Leakeys decided in 1959 to turn their attention to the older Bed I deposits which contained the most primitive stone tools, referred to by Louis as the Oldowan industry.

Our Man
The day after they arrived at Olduvai in June 1959, one of the African field assistants spotted a massive human-like molar tooth, surrounded by stone tools and animal bones and they decided to excavate the site. One morning Louis was not well and Mary went out for a walk and general search around with her two dalmatians. By midday, with the sun reaching its zenith, she was heading back to camp when she spotted a bit of bone projecting from the strata. Carefully scraping some of the sediment, she realized that it was not just the usual tiny fragment; there was more bone with teeth still in place. Rarely was Mary really excited but on this occasion she was and rushed back to camp to arouse Louis from his sick bed. Reportedly she shook him awake with cries of 'I've got him, I've got him. Him, the man! Our man, the one we've been looking for.'

When Louis got to the site he was very excited, especially when he could see what might be more than just a bit of jaw. But he could also see that the teeth were again very large and unhuman-like, so it was not really what he was hoping for. Nevertheless, it was an important find and he was determined to make the best of it in true Leakey style. Was it an australopithecine or something else? The former had already been discovered by Dart and Broom but perhaps it was something equally fascinating, especially something more in the human line.

Examining the teeth in the upper jaw along with the bony roof to the mouth (the palate) and the skull fragments, he concluded that it was not an offshoot australopithecine but definitely more in the human line, even though he already knew that other experts would disagree with him. He thought of calling it *Titanohomo mirabilis*, meaning 'wonderful giant-man'. At last he had what he had spent so many years looking for – or so he thought. When finally excavated in the beginning of August, they found that they had most of the skull although the upper part was in pieces, but as usual Mary worked her wonders of reconstruction. Only the lower jaw was missing.

Dear Boy

They nicknamed their find 'Dear Boy' and Louis immediately wrote a description for the magazine *Nature*, in which he claimed there were enough differences between the new skull and those of the australopithecines to warrant placing it in a new genus and species called *Zinjanthropus boisei*, meaning 'man from east Africa', with the species name honouring his faithful financial backer Charles Boise. As luck would have it the fourth Pan African Congress on Prehistory was due to open at Leopoldville (now Kinshasa) in the Congo and would provide a splendid opportunity for Louis to drop heavy hints about their find. He could not publicize it openly, because his *Nature* paper had not been published, indeed he took everyone aside discreetly to show off the skull, telling them they were the first to see it and then swearing them to secrecy.

The skull did indeed look magnificent with its broad heavy-boned flat face that sloped forward and had a massive bony brow ridge, no forehead, small brain with a distinct bony ridge (for muscle attachment) over the skullcap and massive cheek teeth. The Leakeys had travelled to the Congo via South Africa, where they took the opportunity to look at Dart and Broom's wonderful collection of skulls.Louis could not deny that 'Dear Boy' resembled Dart's australopithecines, but he had more difficulty when he saw Broom's australopithecine finds because these included some very like 'Dear Boy' that Broom called *Paranthropus crassidens*, meaning 'large-toothed robust equal of man'. Undeterred Louis stuck to his new genus, despite having all the similarities pointed out to him. Rumours of the find filtered back to England, where le Gros Clark was dismayed to hear that Louis might be embarking on another of his impetuous forays.

When they got back to Nairobi, Louis held a press conference to announce their finding of 'the connecting link between the South African near-men ... and true men as we know them', the nearest he could come without using the hackneyed 'missing link' phrase. 'Dear Boy' became a huge international news story and Louis was in demand, first in London, then in America for a month during which he was to give 66 lectures at 16 universities. Whilst he thrived on the publicity, Mary did not and so he went by himself even though she had found the skull. He was a natural communicator and charmer whose enthusiasm soon brought in more donors for his research.

Most important of all was his lucky meeting with Dr Melville Bell Grosvenor, then president of the National Geographic Society. It was a meeting of like minds and the president made sure that the society's grant committee awarded the Leakeys a bumper US$20,000, by far the largest single sum they ever attracted, and it was to finance their activities for several years.

With their new-found solvency, the Leakeys planned a more extensive excavation, beginning in 1960, at the *Zinjanthropus* site at Olduvai and Mary was to be in charge since Louis still had to fulfil his curatorial duties at the Coryndon Museum back in Nairobi. Under Mary's supervision everything was more organized and systematic and she set up a more permanent camp on the northern flank of the Gorge more or less opposite the 'Dear Boy' site. They felt confident that if they excavated more they would be bound, sooner or later, to find the elusive 'missing link' between the australopithecines and decidedly human relatives such as *Homo erectus*.

To expose a suitably large surface of strata they had to cut into the gorge side and remove some 6m (20ft) of younger strata. By the time they had finished they had exposed, mapped and removed some 21 successively older layers and sieved several hundred tonnes of sediment to get to the layer they were really interested in. They had previously found a leg bone near the *Zinjanthropus* skull Louis thought may have belonged to 'Dear Boy' (if it did, he was small despite the massive bony skull and teeth). The surface they exposed was about 36×36m (about a third of an acre) and on it lay over 3,000 scattered fossil bones, nearly 2,500 large stone tools and thousands of small bone fragments, stone flakes and chips. Almost all of them were mapped in place and recorded. Mary noticed that there were some patterns to the distributions of the various pieces, especially one distinctly oval area in which there were many broken animal bones, small stone flakes and tools and some distance away there was another collection but of heavier mostly unbroken bones and larger stone tools. Mary realized that they may have uncovered an original *in situ* ground surface that had been occupied by 'Dear Boy' and his relatives nearly 2 million years ago.

Mary pictured a lakeside setting to which these beings returned year after year to butcher the carcasses of any animals they could kill or scavenge. They stripped the meat from the bones and smashed open the long bones for their nutritious marrow. It was the first time such an ancient living surface had been mapped in sufficient detail to reveal the behaviour of our ancient relatives, suggesting that they must have been cooperating in a small band. Meanwhile the Leakey's eldest son, the teenage Jonathan, had found the jawbone of a sabre-toothed cat lying on the surface of the ground some 100m from the excavation and his father encouraged him to sieve the site in the hope that he might find more of the skull or skeleton. He did find more – a toe bone and tooth – but they did not belong to the sabre-tooth and Mary encouraged Jonathan to do a proper excavation of the site.

Johnny's Child

Within one small area they uncovered 14 other bones, all part of a foot. These formed the first discovery of a fossil foot, bones of such an ancient human relative. Louis hurried down from Nairobi and they found small bits of skull, some finger bones and a collar bone. The thinness of the skull fragments was tantalizing and suggested to Louis that they did not belong to 'Dear Boy' but perhaps were the remains of the 'other' being that he suspected had lived alongside *Zinjanthropus*. A month later Jonathan found some more significant skull fragments – roof bones – and as Mary immediately spotted they did not have the typical australopithecine bony sagittal crest (as it is called) this was looking more in the human line. But Jonathan had not finished: on 2

November he found a lower jaw with 13 teeth still in place, and they were clearly smaller than those of *Zinjanthropus*. Known to the Leakey family as 'Johnny's child', it turned out to be one of the most contentious finds in 20th century palaeoanthropology and questioned the whole basis of the definition of our family genus, *Homo*.

Handyman

In an effort to find more of Johnny's child, Mary organized a more extended excavation and tonnes more sediment were carefully removed and sieved without anything further turning up (eventually the site was closed down in 1962). Meanwhile Louis was embarking on yet another campaign to promote the find as something really special. He had already heard from Peter Davis, an anatomist, who thought that the foot bones were clearly that of an upright-walking fully bipedal individual. Louis realized that he did not have the expertise to deal with the detailed analysis that would be required to turn these patchy remains into what he wanted. He recruited Peter Davis and Michael Day from Britain to help with the hand and foot bones; and for the skull material Philip Tobias and John Napier, whose unenviable task was to reconstruct the brain size from the separate skull roof bones.

This very difficult task was crucial, a generally accepted 'glass floor' to humanness and membership of the genus *Homo* was a minimum adult brain size of 750cc. This had largely been determined by Sir Arthur Keith and was known as Keith's cerebral rubicon. He had calculated it as the midway point between the largest gorilla brain (around 400cc) and the smallest modern human brain (around 1100cc). Firstly the roof bones had to be correctly realigned to give an accurate curvature for the original skull roof and then there had to be a lot of very careful measurement, explanation and comparison of other cranial remains to produce a reasonable argument that would be accepted by other experts. The analysis took over a year, much to Louis's continuing frustration. What was worse was their preliminary conclusion: that the brain was between 600 and 700cc (and finally between 675 and 680cc), definitely on the wrong side of the line. It was not a member of *Homo*.

Meanwhile analysis of the footbones was more comforting as they were certainly from a bipedal animal and the hand looked as if it might have had a fully opposable thumb, giving a precise grip and therefore humanlike. Perhaps this was the real toolmaker instead of *Zinjanthropus*. Louis decided that it was and so, in 1964, in yet another paper to *Nature*, he and his co-authors, named his new species 'habilis', suggested by Raymond Dart and meaning 'apt' or 'fit', referring to its potential for tool making. Then Louis made a bold decision: come what may he was going to shoehorn his new species into *Homo*, even if meant moving Keith's rubicon and thus revolutionizing the definition of humanness. Accordingly he lowered the critical brain size, not just by 50 cc, not by 100cc but by 150cc to 600cc, to make sure 'his' *Homo habilis* was well above the glass floor for his redefined human family.

Needless to say he stirred an academic hornets' nest which erupted in a flurry of angry activity and criticism against the still maverick and cavalier Louis Leakey. His most faithful academic supporter, Le Gros Clark (by then Sir Wilfred), was particularly dismayed because of the redefinition of *Homo*. Others argued that there was no proof that the hand and foot bones belonged to the skull and so the whole edifice was built on supposition. Academic opinion is still divided between those who agree with naming *habilis* as a member of *Homo* and those who place it back within the australopithecines. Another crushed skull, found at Olduvai in 1968, was thought to be that of a 'habiline' and its brain size was a mere 612cc, perilously close to Louis's redrawn line in the sand.

Louis Leakey died in London in 1972 whilst Mary and their second son Richard continued the good work back in Africa. Within just a few years, Richard found more human-related fossils than his father had done in a lifetime. Mary continued to make spectacular finds, especially the 3.6 million-year-old footprints at Laetoli in Tanzania, proving beyond doubt that the little australopithecines did walk upright almost like modern humans. Mary died in 1996 but Richard's wife, Maeve Leakey, is now one of the major investigators of our human ancestry. The Leakeys are still very much involved in the family business.

A Perspective on the Human Family Tree

Today our view of human evolution has expanded enormously with some 20 different extinct species within the human family tree, ranging in age from the 6-million-year-old ape-like *Sahelanthropus chadensis* to the recently discovered dwarf species *Homo floresisiensis* which may have survived on the Indonesian island of Flores until 18,000 years ago. But still there is an intense debate about the relationship of the African australopithecines which, though bipedal, were quite chimp-like in size and form, to the earliest members of the genus Homo with more modern, human-like stature. The Leakeys' *Homo habilis* is now a better known species and its brain size ranges from about 520–680cc ie below the revised Leakey cerebral rubicon.

Dubois' *Homo erectus* is now known to have had a much wider distribution from Asia into Georgia (in southeast Europe) and Africa with considerable variation in its brain size, especially in Africa and Georgia (from 600cc to just over 1000cc). The new Georgian finds are particularly important because they make dividing line between the australopithecines and *Homo* much less clear. The numerous and well preserved remains from Georgia show considerable variation and range into the australopithecine field in terms of brain size. The skeletons also show some more primitive australopithecine features, such as a lack of torsion in the arm bones so that the palms face forwards and more primitive and movable shoulder blades.

As so often with prehistory, the more that is found the more complex the story becomes. There is still plenty of scope for future generations to explore the unknown frontiers of the human family tree.

CHAPTER 4: DINOSAUR HUNTERS

'... the combinations of such characters ... altogether peculiar among Reptiles
... will, it is presumed, be deemed sufficient ground for establishing a distinct
tribe or suborder of Saurian Reptiles for which I would propose the name of
'Dinosauria'. (Richard Owen, 1842)*

The name 'dinosaur' (from the Greek deinos, terrible, and sauros, lizard)
was not invented until 1842 when Richard Owen, a ruthlessly ambitious
English anatomist, first coined the word for a particular group of fossil reptiles
that had already been found, though not by him. Owen's extinct 'terrible
lizards' included just three genera at the time: Megalosaurus, Iguanodon and
Hylaeosaurus (today there are some 547 known genera and around 600
species). They were known from just a few scattered fossil bones all found in
water-laid deposits in southern England.

This is the story of the discovery and recognition of these first dinosaurian
reptiles and the men who described the fossil bones and tried to work out from
their very fragmentary remains what the beasts had originally looked like. The
two main characters, William Buckland and Gideon Mantell, were very
different men but both ended as tragic figures.

Puzzling bones in the Ashmolean Museum
Megalosaurus was the first gigantic saurian reptile to be named and described
and, in retrospect, it was the also first dinosaur. The man who named it in
1824 was the Reverend Dr William Buckland (the theological geologist whose
story has been told in the Pre-history chapter) but this very first dinosaur to be
described had a complex and curious gestation. It was only known from some
isolated bones found at various times over the previous century in limestone
strata of the region around Oxford and eventually lodged in the Ashmolean
Museum.

When Buckland was appointed Reader in Geology at the University of
Oxford in 1818, he also became director of the Ashmolean Museum, and so
the fossil bones it contained came under his care. One of the fossils was
a thigh bone and looked remarkably mammalian, so much so that in 1677
Dr Robert Plot, the first Keeper of the Ashmolean, had drawn the conclusion

that it had 'exactly the figure of the lower most part of the Thigh-bone of a Man' but since the bone was of a size similar to the thigh bone of an elephant, the original owner had to be of gigantic proportions.

However, 1818 was also the year in which the French anatomist Georges Cuvier was at last able to visit the museum, since the Napoleonic War had ended. Cuvier was shown the more puzzling fossils in the collections in the hope that his long experience would throw some light on what they truly were. Cuvier was familiar with a wide range of living and fossil vertebrates, especially fossil mammals from the Tertiary strata around Paris, and quickly realized that the thigh bone more probably belonged to a reptile. He also took the opportunity to examine a large fragment of jawbone nearly 30cm (1ft) long in which there were several partly erupted teeth along with a large, recurved and blade-shaped mature tooth that had a serrated cutting edge. Again Cuvier pronounced that it belonged to a reptile and predicted that, like all other reptiles, it would have been egg-laying and have had a scaly skin. And so the matter was to rest for several years whilst Buckland was engaged on matters that were more pressing at the time.

Mantell's Giant Lizard

The discovery and naming of *Iguanodon* and *Hylaeosaurus*, which turned out to be the second and third dinosaurs to be discovered, were the result of the ambition and obsession of one man, Gideon Mantell (1790–1852). The son of a nonconformist bootmaker and tradesman from Lewes in Sussex, England, Mantell was a bright child, quick to learn and determined to better himself which was quite a difficult task in the highly stratified social structure of early 19th century England. He had a particular interest in fossils ever since he had first found them in the banks of the River Ouse. In 1811, following a medical apprenticeship in London, he qualified as a physician with membership of the Royal College of Surgeons and returned to Lewes.

Whilst in London, Mantell was lucky to have met and won the support and encouragement of James Parkinson (1755–1824), the doctor who first recognized the degenerative disease now known as Parkinson's disease. Parkinson was a remarkable man, a free-thinker and reformer who also published a well received three-volume book on fossils called *Organic Remains of a Former World* between 1804 and 1811. His geological knowledge and expertise were invaluable to Mantell who was otherwise self-taught in geological matters.

Even more important for Mantell's future geological prospects was George Bellas Greenhough (1778–1855) who, like Parkinson, was a founder member in 1807 of the Geological Society of London, which effectively became the metropolitan headquarters of geology in the British Isles. Greenhough was a wealthy, well connected member of Parliament who devoted much of his time to geology and was engaged with William Buckland in compiling a geological map of the British Isles. He recognized that Mantell, with his growing knowledge of Sussex geology, could be very useful for his project.

During the second decade of the 19th century when Mantell was establishing himself as a doctor, one of his patients was a prosperous businessman, George Woodhouse. His attractive daughter Mary seemed to share Mantell's interest in fossils and they were soon married in 1816, with her father's permission since she was still legally a minor. After their marriage Mary continued to help Mantell in his growing enthusiasm for fossil hunting and worked at her drawing skills for their illustration. At the same time Mantell was building an excellent reputation as a successful deliverer of babies, some two or three hundred a year and with a very low mortality rate for the time.

Even the birth of their first child in 1818 did not lessen Mantell's geological ambitions. He could see that he was a pioneer in unravelling the sequence of strata in the region, mapping their distribution and describing the fossils to be found within them. By 1819 he had an imposing house in the centre of Lewes and was busy filling its rooms with his ever-growing collection of fossils that began to attract more and more visitors as his reputation spread. People also began to send him fossils that they had found and in 1820 he received a package from Cuckfield containing, as he noted in his diary, '..a fine fragment of an enormous bone, several vertebrae and some teeth'.

Mantell's immediate assumption was that with such a size (by far the largest fossil bone he had ever seen) they must belong to one of the recently discovered fossil 'seamonsters', the only large vertebrates known at the time from these particular strata of southern England. The fossils of large marine reptiles (ichthyosaurs and plesiosaurs) were among the first remains of clearly extinct animals to be found and they entered public awarenenss long before the dinosaurs. Some of the best preserved and earliest fossil skeletons were found in Jurassic strata from around Whitby in Yorkshire and Lyme Regis in Dorset in the early decades of the 19th century. The ichthyosaurs were dolphin-shaped fast-swimming animals whilst the plesiosaurs were slower swimming forms with long necks and small heads: both were predatory carnivores.

Mantell lost no time in visiting the working stone quarry where the bone had been found near a small village called Whiteman's Green a dozen miles from Lewes. It was the first of many visits and he even made joint family excursions – 'my brother drove the ladies in his chaise and I rode on horseback'. Along with more bits of bone he began to find fossil plants that he could not identify from any published records, though some of them looked a bit like the stems of tropical palmtrees.

The more he studied the bones and teeth and contemplated their association with the remains of land plants, the more he began to doubt their relationship to the *Ichthyosaurus* that had been described and illustrated by the Reverend Dr William Conybeare in 1821. Then another tooth fragment was found which threw doubt on the crocodile idea. There is a story, subsequently repeated by Mantell, that it was found by his wife whilst she was waiting for him as he attended a patient but he contradicted this by saying that he found it. More importantly, the fragment did not have the typical conical shape characteristic of the meat-eating crocodile teeth. Instead, it had strongly ridged sides and a large flat grinding surface on top and was much more like the tooth of some plant-eating animal – perhaps it belonged to some giant mammal or plant-eating lizard? An extraordinary feature was the size of some of the fossil fragments such as a part of a limb bone 75cm (50in) long and 60cm (25in) in circumference, a rib that was 55cm (21in) long and bits of backbones 12cm (5in) long.

Mantell compared 'the large bones of the Sussex lizard with those of the elephant' and concluded that 'there seems reason to suppose that the former must have more than equalled the latter in bulk and have exceeded thirty feet in length!' Moreover, he realized that 'this species exceeded in magnitude every animal of the lizard tribe hitherto discovered, either in a recent or a fossilised state'. Because of his relative isolation from the inner network of palaeontologists. Mantell was aware that William Buckland had the fossil remains of another giant 'lizard' from older strata at Stonesfield in Oxfordshire.

Whilst Buckland was otherwise engaged trying to prove the geological reality of the Noachian Flood, back in Paris Georges Cuvier had not forgotten the bones he had seen in the Ashmolean. In September 1820, he got his Irish assistant Joseph Pentland (1797–1873) to ask Buckland: 'Will you send your Stonesfield reptile, or will you publish it yourself?' Buckland prevaricated and it was another four years before he finally got around to describing it.

The Struggle for Recognition
Mantell continued his investigations and acquired new geological acquaintances such as Charles Lyell (1797–1875), an Oxford-trained barrister and student of Buckland's, through whom he got to hear of Buckland's giant Oxford reptile and Cuvier's interest in the fossil, which was being talked of as a 40-foot-long meat-eating monster. Although its greater size seemed to outshine Mantell's find, the good news was that he was not alone in claiming that such gigantic monsters has once roamed Earth's landscapes; as a carnivore, it was clearly different from his plant-eating beast. But Mantell was still struggling to become part of the recognized cognoscenti of the geological world. He thought that if he could publish a book full of geological novelty and information he might become accepted and even elected to the fellowship of the Geological Society of London. But publishing any such book, essentially required printed maps and other illustrations, especially those of fossils, was almost prohibitively expensive and the book needed to be pre-sold to private subscribers to help to recover the costs, let alone make any profit.

Nevertheless, in May 1822 Mantell published his *Fossils of the South Downs* with drawings by his wife Mary. It included a brief discussion of his unnamed giant reptile and even made comparison with what was known of Buckland's unnamed Stonesfield monster. Even after the income from sales was deducted, the publication cost Mantell £300 – which was £300 more than he could afford and it was his brother-in-law George Woodhouse who underwrote the debt. Soon after the book's publication, Mantell took some of his reptile fossils to a Geological Society meeting at which Buckland was present in his role as vice-president of the Society. When he showed them around to the august experts of the day, he was dismayed to hear his fossils dismissed out of hand as most likely the remains of some mammal from a Diluvial deposit. Part of the problem was that they did not believe Mantell's relative dating of the strata in which they were found.

Mantell recruited Lyell to help him in trying to resolve the problem by resurveying the geology of the region. Lyell agreed with Mantell that the Wealden strata in which the bones and teeth had been found were Cretaceous in age rather younger Tertiary deposits. Mantell submitted his findings to the Geological Society but again he, the provincial outsider, was snubbed and it was over three years before his letter was published. In 1823, Lyell offered another possible avenue of recognition as he was going to Paris to see Cuvier and other French geologists. He would take the fossils with him and ask the great Cuvier's opinion. It was at one of Cuvier's regular Saturday soirées on 23 June 1823 that Lyell unwrapped one of Mantell's fossil teeth for presentation, only to be told without hesitation that it was merely a worn rhinoceros incisor.

When Mantell received the bad news by letter from Lyell he felt that all his ambitions had finally come to nothing. By this time his wife was getting increasingly restive about his obsession with the fossils that were gradually taking over their house and the way that he was beginning to neglect his practice in favour of the pursuit of geology, which paid nothing and only seemed to lead to disappointment. But he still believed in the importance and uniqueness of his fossil and was determined to persist. Little did he realize what sacrifices he would have to make to fulfil his dream.

News of the strange bones from Sussex appeared in a winter 1823 issue of *The Gentleman's Magazine* which was widely circulated. It may well be that it was this report, and the realization that a Sussex doctor might upstage him, that prompted Buckland to renew his interest in the Ashmolean fossils he had shown to Cuvier. It certainly prompted Buckland to inform Cuvier at last that he would indeed be describing the new reptile. And so Buckland set about it in some haste and had his description ready for the beginning of 1824 and the February meeting of the Geological Society. The same meeting was due to have Buckland's close friend, the Rev Dr Conybeare, read his account of a remarkable new marine reptile, *Plesiosaurus*, so it would be a long meeting and would be bound to draw quite a crowd of members and visitors.

Buckland Announces the Megalosaurus

Amongst the visitors was Gideon Mantell, listening in rapt attention as Buckland explained why he thought that the few scrappy fragments of bone and teeth from Stonesfield belonged to some ancient and extinct lizard despite the fact that the bits of limb and backbone had certain mammalian characteristics. The true nature of the beast was betrayed by jawbone and teeth that were so distinctly reptilian. Furthermore, he argued the fact that since the remains had been found together with so many fossils of sea-dwelling creatures suggested that the beast was 'probably an amphibious animal'. As to its size, Cuvier had suggested that, scaling up from lizard bones, the 25cm (10in) circumference of the thigh bone indicated an animal some 12m (40ft) long, but Buckland was more tentative since 'we cannot safely attribute exactly the same proportions to the recent and extinct species'. Yet with Conybeare's assistance he thought that the unprecedented size of the beast warranted the name *Megalosaurus*, meaning 'giant lizard'.

Mantell was all too well aware that if Buckland's *Megalosaurus* was truly 40ft long then his own beast with its much bigger thigh bone must have been substantially bigger, perhaps even twice as long. At the end of his talk, following the tradition of the Society the meeting was thrown open to the audience for questions or other relevant information. Mantell took the opportunity to inform Buckland of his find and his interpretation of the nature of the animal, adding with a touch of one-up-manship the possibility that it had been twice the size of Buckland's *Megalosaurus*. There are no records of how Buckland replied, if he did at all, but it is known that within two weeks Dr Buckland had taken the express coach from Oxford to Lewes to see Mantell's specimens for himself. He stayed over and the next day Mantell took him to see the quarries in which the bones had been found.

Back in Oxford, Buckland hurriedly set about preparing his manuscript for publication and added to it information about Mantell's find. The Society's publication committee spotted the addition and, despite the fact that he was president, told Buckland that 'it is not correct practice, and one repeatedly prohibited to other authors to be putting in the last words on the eve of publication; and as President, you are required to stand by and see fair play to all parties concerned in authorship'. However, he did still manage to squeeze in some essential information about Mantell's fossils, including an estimate of its possible size revised down to 'sixty to seventy feet' and moreover concluded that it was not a new reptile but another specimen of his *Megalosaurus*, albeit bigger. Buckland still regarded the Sussex teeth as those of some much younger mammal.

Cuvier Changes his Mind

A month or two later, Mantell felt that his only chance would be to get a second opinion out of Cuvier. To improve the case he made drawings of all the teeth that he had which included different stages of growth and wear, and he sent some specimens. Buckland also wrote to Cuvier about Mantell's teeth and suggested that they might be from some kind of fish. This time Cuvier was prepared to give a more considered opinion and Mantell had his reply by the 20 June 1824. For once it was good news: Cuvier recognized that they belonged to some kind of new animal. Although they might superficially look like certain fish teeth, as Buckland suggested, they were more likely to belong to some new kind of plant-eating reptile. What was essential was to find some teeth that were still attached to a jawbone.

For Mantell, the one accessible place that contained a really good comparative collection of bones and teeth of both living and fossil animals was the Hunterian Collection of the Royal College of Surgeons in London. Mantell knew William Clift, the very able Curator who had spent the best part of a lifetime cataloguing the 10,000 or more specimens collected by the late John Hunter and bought by the Government after his death in 1793. In early September Mantell visited the museum and, with Clift's help, searched through looking for any specimen that had similar distinctively shaped teeth but without luck until the assistant curator Samuel Stutchbury intervened. He had just prepared a specimen, newly arrived from Barbados, and thought that it might be the kind of thing they were looking for.

Mantell's Iguanodon

Despite the enormous difference in size, when they compared the tiny teeth of the iguana lizard with the 20 times bigger fossil teeth, they were all struck by the remarkable similarity of shape and form. Both were leaf shaped with a serrated edge and ridged sides. And being typically reptilian, the immature unerupted teeth could be seen within the jaw bone and immediately below the fully formed mature ones. Clift provided Mantell with an exquisitely accurate drawing of the iguana's lower jaw that clearly showed the form of the teeth, a drawing that Mantell was to use in the paper he now felt able to write. He wrote to Cuvier in November to inform him of the similarities between the living and fossil reptiles and remarking that he was thinking of calling the animal *Iguana-saurus*. Conybeare pointed out that his proposed name was effectively tautological and that he would be better calling it *Iguanodon*, meaning 'having teeth like iguana' or *Iguanoides* meaning 'like iguana': Mantell chose the former.

Luckily, Cuvier had changed his mind and was sufficiently impressed by the series of teeth to comment upon Mantell's remarkable new fossil *Iguanodon* in a new edition of his *Recherches sur les Ossemens Fossiles*. He even admitted his former mistake and explained how it had come about. As Cuvier's books were widely circulated throughout Europe, this public acknowledgment by the eminent Frenchman immediately opened previously closed doors for Mantell. Buckland urged him to attend the next meeting of the Geological Society, inviting him to join the inner circle dining club, and before long he was elected as a fellow. An even more prestigious opening was to the Royal Society. Since the early 1820s Mantell had been corresponding on palaeontological matters with Davies Gilbert, an MP and fellow of the Royal Society, and it so happened that by 1825 Gilbert was vice-president and was prepared to present Mantell's account of his discovery to the Society. By the end of the year, the 35-year-old Gideon Mantell, son of a bootmaker from a provincial town, was also admitted to fellowship of the Royal Society. Success was his at last; all the toil and burning of candles late into the night had been worthwhile.

Gideon Mantell versus Richard Owen

Scientific and social recognition did nothing to satisfy Mantell's enthusiasm and ambition for fossils and geology but rejuvenated it, to the despair of his wife Mary. His third child, Hannah, who was to become his favourite, had been born in 1822 and here he was embarking upon another book about the fossiliferous strata of the Weald. He also wanted to find more complete remains of his *Iguanodon* to get a better idea of what it had looked like. He already had a conical bone which he suspected might have been part of a horn on its nose. And there were other fragments that suggested the presence of yet more giant beasts that had lived alongside *Iguanodon*.

Mantell's *Illustrations of the Geology of Sussex* was eventually published in January 1827 but, despite his newfound scientific respectability, he had failed to raise many subscriptions and only 150 copies were printed. Even these were slow in selling and in the end only 50 did sell.

In August that year Mantell's fourth child, a boy, was born and his wife despaired of her husband's obsession with rocks and fossils. By Christmas she had left him and returned to her family for several weeks. But her husband did not give up his passion and Mary returned to try to make the best she could of it all. Her husband was seemingly oblivious to the problem and proceeded to make it worse when Charles Lyell advised him to concentrate on a detailed study of the fossil saurians. The doctor took on a young assistant who bought a share in his medical practice, giving him even more time to devote to his fossils. He wrote off for more specimens and plaster casts of those already described and they duly arrived by the cartload to fill up every nook and cranny in a family home that was becoming more and more like a museum, much to Mary's distress. A new room was built on to house the specimens and Mantell prepared a catalogue with the intention of opening the collection to the public in September 1829. The constant stream of visitors made the growing domestic disquiet worse and the situation gradually deteriorated over the next few years.

A New Reptile from a Forest – Hylaeosaurus
In 1832 Mantell was informed of more bone fragments found in a quarry in Tilgate Forest and managed to recover some 50 pieces that had inadvertently been blasted apart by the quarrymen. Of course he brought them home. When he eventually managed to put the pieces back together, he had a slab of hard rock over 1.35m (4.5ft) long. Many long evening and night-time hours were spent chiselling away the hard rocky matrix to reveal the bones. For the first time he had some bones that were still joined together as part of the skeleton and he could see that there were several neck and backbones, ribs and several spines each some 37cm (15in) long, plus the shoulder blade and part of the breastbone (sternum) and strange bony plates that looked as if they reinforced the skin as an armour plating. Did he have yet another kind of giant reptile?

The more he studied it, the surer he was that he had found a new kind of armoured reptile. He called it *Hylaeosaurus* meaning 'forest reptile'. This time when he told his newfound acquaintances in the Geological Society of his discovery he had no problem in communicating his results at the next suitable meeting. The specimen had been far too big to bring to the meeting so he exhibited a lifesize painting. All was apparently well received but little did Mantell realize that sitting in the audience was a young man, Richard Owen, whose ruthless ambition and deviousness would blight the rest of Mantell's palaeontological ambitions.

Richard Owen Steals the Limelight

Richard Owen (1804–92) came from Lancaster and had been at school with William Whewell, who went to Cambridge University and eventually became Master of Trinity College, whilst Owen had to struggle through a medical apprenticeship from the age of 16, in much the same way as Mantell had done. After several years of drudgery money was found to send Owen to study medicine at Edinburgh University, where he flourished and was recommended to try his luck as a surgeon in London rather than bother completing the university course. Owen arrived in the metropolis in 1825 and was taken on as an assistant to William Clift at the Hunterian Museum of the Royal College of Surgeon. This was the same Clift who, the previous year, had been so helpful to Mantell. Owen was indefatigable in making himself indispensable to Clift and was soon courting his only daughter Caroline.

Owen was a very skilled anatomist and his ambition was to become the English Cuvier. Consequently he took advantage of his position to gain access to the cadavers of any animals from London's Zoological Gardens that died. Dissecting them gave Owen detailed knowledge that few could exceed and certainly not a provincial doctor such as Gideon Mantell.

The Mantellian Museum

By 1833 Mantell thought that he could afford a move to the much more fashionable seaside town of Brighton with its Royal Pavilion and patronage. By the end of the year he was renting an elegant house near the sea and moved in with his family and all his fossils. The bones and stones were soon rehoused in expensive new cabinets and the Mantellian Museum opened its doors to the public. Mantell gave public lectures that were well reviewed by the local paper. Within weeks the new museum was being visited by over a thousand people.

His growing reputation as a fossil collector brought in new specimens and news of new finds, especially a letter from a quarry owner in Kent whose workmen had uncovered some large bones. Mr Bensted, the owner, had also spread the news of the find far and wide so that it appeared in the London papers. By June 1834 Mantell had managed to see the fossil and recognized it as part of 'the lower extremities of the *Iguanodon*'. There were 15 connected backbones, ribs, the pelvis, several limb bones, toe bones and the very characteristic teeth. It was at the time the most complete skeleton of one of the new large terrestrial reptiles known and Mantell wanted it. But Bensted was a sharp business man and he wanted to make as much money as he could from its sale. Luckily for Mantell, some of his rich and well placed supporters got together and managed to buy the specimen. Within weeks the slab, known as the 'Mantell-piece', was in Brighton and Mantell was spending every spare moment chiselling away to reveal as many bones as possible.

Again, Mantell tried to estimate the animal's original size, using the living lizard-shaped iguana as a base-line. The 76cm (30in) long shoulder blade was 20 times bigger than that of an iguana, suggesting that the fossil reptile might have been as much as 30m (100ft) long. Mantell could see that the fossil foot bones were very large and robust and actually very different in form from those of an iguana. But still Mantell sketched a reconstruction of the animal as a lizard with a long tail and its legs sticking out sideways from the body. A curious conical bone about 11.5cm (4.5in), he imagined to be a blunt nose horn as is seen on some iguanas.

The following year (1835), Mantell's great achievement was recognized by the Geological Society when they gave him their highest award, the Wollaston, medal for 'the discovery of two genera of fossil reptiles, *Iguanodon* and *Hylaeosaurus*'. Mantell was the second recipient of this fine medal (made of palladium) the first being William Smith, the surveyor, canal engineer and pioneer geological mapmaker. At last it seemed as if there was true recognition of his labours and sacrifices and the future looked bright. But it was not.

Richard Owen was rising through the ranks. He had been appointed Professor of Comparative Anatomy at St Bartholomew's Hospital and Fellow of the Royal Society with the result that Caroline Clift's mother finally dropped her objections to their marriage. In 1836 a special post of Hunterian Professor was created for Owen at the Royal College of Surgeons: he was becoming recognized as the most able anatomist of the day. Not satisfied with this he was looking for new challenges and realized that the newly discovered giant fossil reptiles were ripe for the picking. Owen was not a palaeontologist, he new little or nothing about rock strata and had never looked for fossils himself but he was a much better trained anatomist than the likes of Mantell or even William Buckland. When the British Association for the Advancement of Science decided to appoint someone to 'Report on the present state of knowledge of the Fossil Reptiles of Great Britain', it was neither Buckland nor Mantell that they chose for the job but the young rising star of anatomy' Richard Owen.

Failure in Brighton

Despite the success of the new Mantellian Museum in Brighton, it did not bring in any money, and despite the richer clientele of the seaside resort, Mantell's medical practice did not grow as he had expected. If anything, his increasing fame as a fossil man seemed to put off potential patients from seeing him as a medical doctor. The rent for the new house was high and Mantell had to sell some of his stocks and shares; it seemed as if he would have to dispose of his collection, which by then housed some 30,000 specimens. The house was turned into the public Sussex Scientific Institution and Mantellian Museum with a paid curator, George Richardson.

Mantell's family had to go into lodgings. This really was the final straw for his wife Mary and they separated. Mantell's standing as a fossil man and public lecturer did not diminish; he was earning some money and was preparing yet another book, to be called *The Wonders of Geology*, based on his lectures, but the Institution was not contributing and it became clear that only the sale of the collection would resolve the financial problems. After several false hopes, it was finally agreed in November 1838 that the collection would be sold to the British Museum for £4,087, which was a lot of money in those days but Mantell had probably spent more than that on buying many of the specimens over the years. Nevertheless, it avoided bankruptcy and gave him the chance of a new start in London. Mary did not go with him.

Ironically, *The Wonders of Geology* was very successful and sold a thousand copies within a month of publcation. The frontispiece was a dramatic reconstruction, derived from a painting by the eminent artist and illustrator John Martin and showing a gloomy gothic landscape with giant lizard-like reptiles locked in a fight to the death – this really was Tennyson's 'Nature, red in tooth and claw, / Dragons of the prime, / That tare each other in their slime …' (In Memoriam, 1833).

By spring 1839, Mantell was setting up a new medical practice in Clapham but his older children had grown up and had left home. There was just his beloved daughter Hannah and she was seriously afflicted by hip bone infection; there was nothing he could do for her and she died in the autumn of that year. Mantell was alone and did not even have his fossil collection to console him.

Owen Classifies the Fossil Reptiles
Richard Owen, presenting the first part of his reptile survey (which covered the marine reptiles) to the Birmingham meeting of the British Association for the Advancement of Science used the opportunity to attack emerging ideas about evolution, stating that 'there is no evidence whatsoever that one species has succeeded or been the result of the transmutation of a former species'. The Association's hierarchy was sufficiently pleased with the result to grant him £200 to continue the study to cover fossil turtles, crocodiles and the new giant 'lizards'. The indefatigable Owen duly set off around the country to see as many specimens as possible in public and private collections. Most important of all, by this time he had open access to Mantell's collection in the British Museum.

It was August 1841 before Owen had completed his reptilian survey for the British Association meeting at Plymouth and on the second day of the month he read his report. It was 'an account of the remains of the Crocodilian, Lacertian, Pterodactylian, Chelonian, Ophidian and Batrachian reptiles' and it lasted for 2½ hours (speakers and audiences had much greater stamina in those days). The Association immediately voted another £500 to assist in the engraving of the illustrations and for another report.

Gideon Mantell read about Owen's report in the *Literary Gazette*, which carried a detailed account. It must have been dismaying for him to discover the extent to which Owen had taken over his fossil reptiles.

Owen classified the saurians (lizard-like reptiles) into four groups: the 'Enaliosauria' (ichthyosaurs and plesiosaurs), the Crocodilian Sauria, the pterodactylians (the extinct flying reptiles) and finally the 'Lacertians', the 'very singular and very gigantic species which have now utterly perished' (*Iguanodon, Hylaeosaurus* and *Megalosaurus*). At this stage his report was not very controversial but then he went on to detail the most important features of these fossils as if he had been the first to discover them. He had seen some newly discovered *Iguanodon* limb bones that were even bigger than Mantell's and using Mantell's crude method of scaling, he suggested that the animal would have been some 63m (200ft) long, which seemed preposterous. Owen also attacked those attempts to compare living and fossil reptiles such as Mantell had made between the iguana and his *Iguanodon*. Furthermore he stated that, unlike most living reptiles, these giant fossil forms did not have their limbs sprawling out on either side but rather they were tucked in under the body, the better to support their immense weight. Owen saw these fossil forms as more advanced than living reptiles, a concept that he was to develop in his subsequent battle against Darwin and the evolutionists. A further consequence was that any simple scaling up, from the dimensions and form of living reptiles to extinct ones, would be misleading.

Mantell must have felt that his position as the foremost interpreter of fossil reptiles was being undermined by Owen. But a much more catastrophic misfortune befell Mantell a couple of months later: he was thrown on to the road from an out-of-control horsedrawn carriage. Dragged along for some distance, he seriously damaged his spine and could no longer walk. He had heard of new fossil finds that he dearly longed to see. It was impossible for him to do so – but Owen could.

At the time Owen was busy improving his report for publication and whilst doing so seems to have had his 'eureka' moment. He saw that there were certain features of the extinct Lacertians that seemed to set them apart from other reptiles. The mammal-like nature of their limb bones had been noticed before but Owen realized how they related to differences in the pelvis as well. He had been able to examine yet another important *Iguanodon* fossil which preserved the fused vertebrae of the animal's sacrum and he could see that it was very like the sacrum of *Megalosaurus*. Here was a fundamental anatomical feature that was common to both a plant-eating and a carnivorous reptile.

By contrast the crocodiles, marine ichthyosaurs, plesiosaurs and flying reptiles had very different pelvic structures.

Richard Owen 'Invents' the Dinosauria

Owen concluded the new material for his report in typically convoluted scientific language: 'the combinations of such characters, some, as the sacral ones, altogether peculiar among Reptiles, others borrowed, as it were, from groups now distinct from each other, and all manifested by creatures far surpassing in size the largest of existing reptiles, will, it is presumed, be deemed sufficient ground for establishing a distinct tribe or suborder of Saurian Reptiles for which I would propose the name of "Dinosauria".'

The 'terrible lizards' were 'born' when the report was finally published in 1842. Owen variously downplayed and ignored much of Mantell's contribution to the early understanding of these reptiles but made much of Mantell's mistakes. Our image of the geological past was changed forever and the extraordinary phenomenon of the dinosaurs was launched upon the world. Not that they were an instant success, but Owen was. He became the English Cuvier, received by Prince Albert, granted a Civil List pension of £200 a year and had his portrait hung alongside that of Cuvier in the home of the Prime Minister, Sir Robert Peel.

Mantell's Last Chance at Crystal Palace

Mantell never fully recovered from his fall in 1841 and his medical practice suffered. However he managed to write another successful book *Medals of Creation*, published in 1844, and that sold well. He continued to work on more finds, most importantly in the late 1840s another new dinosaur, which he called *Pelorosaurus*, which was based on a large legbone and four backbones. As the first of the large plant-eating sauropods to be named. Despite all of Owen's efforts to blackball him, Mantell was awarded the Royal Society's Royal Medal in 1849. Three years later he was given a golden opportunity to recover more of his lost status as the 'elder statesman' of fossil reptiles. In 1851, the Crystal Palace company was planning to relocate Paxton's fabulous glass building for the Great Exhibition of 1851 to a new permanent site in southeast London surrounded by 200 acres of lake and parklands. The idea was to construct a geological theme park – the first of its kind in the world,

1. *The Reverend Dr Buckland was frequently lampooned for his eccentricities. Here he is regaled in field mode complete with academic gown for tackling the problems of glacial geology. The subtext refers to his 'volte face' on the question of the Flood vs glaciation.*

2. *Jean Louis Rodolphe Agassiz (1807–73), a Swiss-born expert on fossil fish and student of glaciers, was first to point out the evidence for glaciation of the British landscape. He emigrated to America, took up a professorship at Harvard and became a vehement opponent of Darwin's theory of evolution.*

3. Georges Léopold Chrétien Frédérich Dagobert, the Baron Cuvier (1769–1832) portrayed as a bemedalled 'hero' of post revolutionary French science. A pioneer of comparative anatomy, palaeontology and geological mapping, he was internationally recognized and revered, even by the British, as 'the' authority on vertebrates.

4. The discovery of metre-long fossil jaws in underground chalk workings at Maastricht became a 'cause célèbre' in the 18th century. Named as Mosasaurus by Cuvier in 1809, there was a fierce debate over what kind of animal they belonged to and whether or not it was extinct.

5. *African remains of our human relatives were first found and named as* Australopithecus africanus *in 1925 by the Australian anatomist Raymond Dart (1893–1988). Here, the original face, lower jaw and natural stone cast of the brain are reconstructed as a complete skull.*

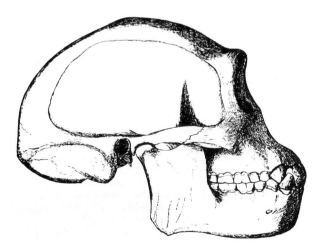

6. *Not lacking in imagination, Eugene Dubois (1858–1940) reconstructed the entire skull of his 'Java Man' just from the skull cap, his knowledge of the few other available ape and fossil skulls and his intuition. Originally named* Pithecanthropus erectus, *it is now known as* Homo erectus.

7. Mary and Louis Leakey getting down to the back-breaking business of looking for fossil remains of extinct human relatives. Most fossils first appear as tiny fragments of bone or teeth; very rarely are complete jaws, larger pieces of skull or other parts of the skeleton preserved.

8. Rarely seen without his homberg and rifle, the dapper Roy Chapman Andrews (1884–1960) was not an expert palaeontologist but was very good at raising funds and running expeditions to remote places, which were staffed with experts who knew what they were doing.

9. *Roy Chapman Andrews led several expeditions of the American Museum of Natural History into Central Asia in the 1920s looking for human origins. They did not find any but they did come away with dinosaur eggs, nests and tons of bones.*

10. The ruthlessly ambitious anatomist Richard Owen (1804–92) never missed a trick to do down his competitors. One of the first to realize that some fossil reptiles had distinctive anatomical features, he quickly grasped the opportunity to be the first to name them as the Dinosauria in 1842.

11. Gideon Mantell struggled to combine his obsession with fossils, his geological ambitions and his profession as a physician. In the end fossils and geology won (and his family and profession suffered) but he is remembered as the man who described some of the first dinosaurs ever to be discovered.

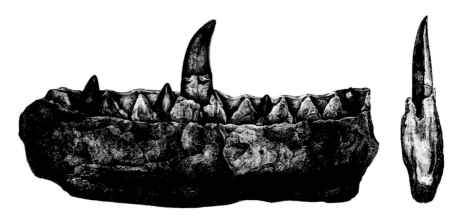

12. This fossil fragment of a jawbone (30cm long) and still 'armed' with some sharply serrated and blade-shaped teeth, was first described as a giant reptilian carnivore by William Buckland in 1824 and named Megalosaurus. It was one of the extinct reptiles recognized as a dinosaur by Owen in 1842.

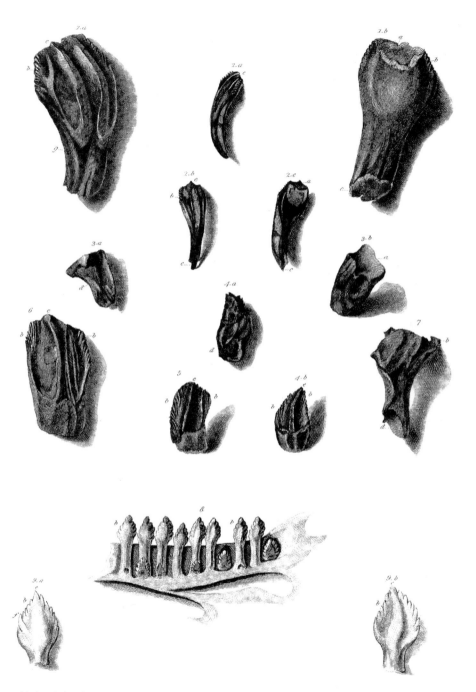

13. In 1825 Gideon Mantell described the newly discovered teeth of a giant plant-eating reptile. He named it Iguanodon *because of the similarity of the teeth with those of the living iguana and, by comparing their size, estimated the extinct reptile to be 60ft in length.*

14. An exotic figure even without his Arab dress, Italian-born strongman and engineer Giovanni Belzoni retrieved many Egyptian treasures that now reside in the British Museum. Despite his early celebrity, later archaeologists saw him as little better than a tomb robber.

15. Scottish painter David Roberts (1796–1864) captured the spirit of Egypt and the Holy Land in a series of paintings and illustrations published in the 1840s. His magnificent portrayal of Abu Simbel shows the temple, first entered by Belzoni in 1817, still half-buried in sand.

16. *The densely-packed inscriptions of the Rosetta Stone record an unimportant taxation decree of the late Greek-Egyptian ruler, Ptolemy V Epiphanes. However, the stone's true significance lies in its parallel hieroglyphic, demotic, and Greek texts, which allowed Champollion and others to decode ancient Egyptian writings for the first time.*

17. Henry Salt, British Consul in Cairo, made this sketch of the Sphinx during Caviglia's 1816 attempt to excavate the great statue from its sandy resting place. The remains of the 'Sphinx Temple' and the Dream Stela of Tuthmosis IV can be seen between the enormous forepaws.

18. Flinders Petrie, shown here in later life, established many of the principles of modern archaeology during his early work for the Egypt Exploration Fund. Many other archaeologists got their first experience on his famously abstemious digs.

19. In 1798 Napoleon's invasion force won the only major land engagement of their Egyptian campaign when they took on a 60,000-strong Mamluk army within sight of the pyramids. Before the battle, Napoleon encouraged his troops with a reminder that 'from the summit of these pyramids, forty centuries look down upon you.'

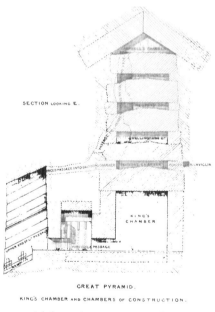

20. The 'explosive' Colonel Richard William Howard Vyse inflicted enormous damage on the Egyptian pyramids with his indiscriminate use of blasting to open up passageways and look for hidden treasure chambers. He did, however, produce the first accurate illustrations of the Great Pyramid's internal construction.

21. Howard Carter pauses in his work to peer out from behind the dividing wall that separated Tutankhamun's antechamber from the tomb itself. An unperturbed Lord Caernarvon looks on with interest.

22. A small sample of Carter's 'wonderful things' – the gold-encrusted grave goods of the boy king, Tutankhamun. After more than a century of exploration in the Valley of the Kings, Carter's discovery was an unexpected triumph, though it heralded the end of freelance archaeology in Egypt.

23. *Arthur Evans in 1936, examining the model of a bull's head from his dig at Knossos. His discovery of the skulls of oxen years before had led him to suspect that for the ancient Minoans, the bull was a symbol of the earth. It is also depicted in some of the site's famous wall paintings.*

24. *One of Arthur Evans' reconstructions at Knossos: part of his attempt to bring the ancient Minoan palace to life for the visiting public. He also reconstructed some of the lavishly decorated interiors. Today, these reconstructions are controversial.*

25. *A portrait of Heinrich Schliemann, taken about the time that he began digging for Troy. Note the absence of smile lines; he was conceited, very self-centred and few warmed to him. He worked intensely but his health was never robust.*

26. *The mound that Schliemann selected as the site of Troy overlooks the Dardanelles. Schliemann had immense sections of it cut out in his search (expecting to find the ancient city at the bottom) but Wilhelm Dörpfeld showed him that he had cut through the level of Homer's period in the middle layers.*

27. *'Grave Circle A' at Mycenae, where Schliemann discovered the tomb that he attributed to Homer's murdered King Agamemnon. When the surrounding ledge was first uncovered, Schliemann interpreted it as a bench for citizens to meet and chat.*

28. Masks covered some of the corpses that Schliemann exposed at Mycenae and this one of gold is one of the most famous. In view of Schliemann's general reputation, at least one sceptic suspects that the mask is a forgery that he planted there. We now know that the mask is far earlier than the date assumed by Schliemann.

29. Schliemann claimed that one of the corpses found in the Grave Circle at Mycenae was so well preserved that, at first, the eyes could be seen. He ordered his artist to record the find even as the features decayed on exposure.

illustrating the procession of life through the ages, illustrated by lifesize models. Mantell was asked to superintend its construction, which would take at least a year, but by this time he was having to take all the painkillers he could manage – in other words opium and brandy – to relieve the agony from his damaged and deformed spine. He was dying and he knew it and had to decline the offer. The President of the Royal Society granted him a civil list pension of £100 a year but it was all too late. In November 1852 he fell again, took an overdose of narcotic and died. With terrible irony his deformed spine was removed and found its way, as a pathological curiosity, into Owen's domain in the Hunterian Museum.

Inevitably the job of arranging the exhibit for the new Crystal Palace fell to Owen, basking in the royal patronage of Prince Albert. He arranged for a sculptor, Benjamin Waterhouse Hawkins, to construct lifesized models of *Megalosaurus*, *Iguanodon*, *Hylaeosaurus* and some of the marine and flying reptiles. When opened in 1854, the dinosaur park attracted huge crowds and was an enormous popular success, so much so that there were plans to repeat the exhibit in New York's Central Park, but they fell foul of city politics and came to nothing. Owen went on to become the first superintendent of natural history in the British Museum (1856–83), tutor to the Royal family (1860–4) and was knighted in 1884. To be fair, he did make significant contributions to the study of fossil vertebrates and biology in general, even though he also became an implacable opponent of Darwin and Wallace's theory of evolution. And investigations would continue into the extinct reptiles of Owen's 'new suborder Dinosauria'. Buckland's *Megalosaurus* had been named on the basis of very fragmentary material and even today little more is known about the genus, since no more skeletal material was found at Stonesfield, where the first finds had been made. The Stonesfield strata are no longer available for exploitation and so it is unlikely that any more bones will be found. As for Mantell's *Iguanodon*, this plant-eating ornithopod dinosaur is now very well known thanks to the discovery of many complete skeletons, especially from Bernissart in Belgium. But the 'horn' that Mantell had placed on its nose is actually a big bony spike on its thumb.

Roy Chapman Andrews Takes the Search to Mongolia

Following the first discovery of the fragmentary remains of giant reptiles in southern England in the first decades of the 19th century and their recognition as dinosaurs in 1842, the search for new and better preserved dinosaurs moved elsewhere, especially to North America. The latter half of the century saw momentous discoveries, especially in the dry badlands of the American Midwest where there were vast areas of well exposed strata of the right Mesozoic age that had originally been laid down in terrestrial environments where the dinosaurs actually lived. The establishment of the great public, university and private museums, many of which were well endowed, led to intense competition between them (know as the 'Great Bone War') for dinosaur fossils – the bigger and the more complete the better– as dinomania gripped the public imagination.

The leading dinosaur experts, men like Edward Drinker Cope (1840–97) and Othniel Charles Marsh (1831–99), were aggressively big 'egos' and became great rivals. Cope was an intrepid fossil hunter, especially out in the Indian territories of the American West, and always rushed to publish descriptions of new finds that he made – nearly 1,500 articles altogether. Inevitably he often made mistakes and leapt to incorrect conclusions that frequently led to acrimonious disputes with his great rival O C Marsh, who was equally ruthless and unscrupulous when it came to dinosaurs. Marsh was very wealthy and had the particular advantage of being the super-rich George Peabody's nephew. Peabody offered Yale University US$150,000 towards establishing a museum and his nephew was promptly appointed professor and director.

Marsh and Cope paid little attention to one another's work and often gave different names to the same dinosaur, a confusion that took decades for later generations of palaeontologists to sort out. In 1890 Cope accused Marsh of plagiarism and their dispute became very public, with rival newspapers taking sides. Cope had to sell his collection to the American Museum of Natural History in New York for just US$32,000 and ended his life surrounded by fossils and papers but virtually no furniture. Between the two of them, Cope and Marsh named over 1,700 new fossil genera and packed several major American museums with wonderful dinosaur skeletons. Many of their taxonomic creations have not stood the test of time but some very spectacular ones have, such as *Allosaurus*, *Stegosaurus*, *Diplodocus*, *Apatosaurus* and *Camarasaurus*.

By the beginning of the 20th century, new ambitions and new technologies were opening up the possibilities of exploration well beyond the home territories of the advanced scientific nations of the Western world. Motorized transport in particular made it possible to quadruple the distance travelled in a day, at least over some terrains, and to increase the amount of 'booty' that could be recovered from exceedingly remote places.

As far as the discovery of ancient fossil life was concerned, whether it was that of the human past or extinct reptiles, the really promising and virtually unexplored regions seemed to be the vast continents of Asia and Africa, to which priority was given over South America, although the archaeological promise of the latter was recognized and was actively being explored. On the whole, the fossil riches of Australia were still unappreciated. There was so much to do and so many possibilities that choices had to be made.

Making such a palaeontological choice required a balance between the greatest possible prize, the 'do-able' in terms of logistics and cost, and evidence that the chosen site had the right kind of rocks of the right age. It was well known from the North American experience that for dinosaur hunting, semi-arid badlands where there was little or no vegetation or soil and plenty of bare rock outcrops were a much better bet than highly vegetated and populated terrains. Much of northern and southern Africa and Central Asia had these conditions, though much of southern Africa could be discounted because the rocks were too old for dinosaurs.

Henry Fairfield Osborn's Asian Ambitions

The choice between northern Africa and Central Asia depended upon theory as much as anything else. Curiously the great dinosaur discoveries of Central Asia were the by-product of the search for human fossil ancestors and in the early 20th century it seemed that Asia might be a better bet than Africa for finding such fossils. One man who was a strong advocate of this theory was Henry Fairfield Osborn (1857–1935) who became president of the American Museum of Natural History in 1908.

Born in the mid 19th century, Osborn proudly proclaimed that he had 'studied with Huxley, and once met Darwin'. Famously egocentric, combative and autocratic, he even published a book listing his academic articles, books and speeches, illustrated with pictures of his medals and other awards. But he was also talented as a palaeontologist and evolutionist. When he took over the museum in 1908 it did not have a single dinosaur skeleton, but Osborn soon hired the famous dinosaur 'hunter' Barnum Brown and bought up collections to boost the museum's emerging role as a world-class repository of dinosaur fossils. He also hired the artist Charles R Knight who pioneered the large scale illustration of prehistory through his meticulous reconstructions of huge prehistoric murals that illustrated the animals, plants and environments that were represented by the museum's fossil collections. For the first time, the best skeletal material was mounted in lifelike poses as if the animals were living in the Knight panoramas.

But Osborn was also a eugenicist and believer in racial purity who opposed 'the massive influx of Asian and southern and eastern European immigrants' into the States on the grounds that they 'threatened the existence of the Nordic race that had founded this country'. He wrote a laudatory preface to Madison Grants notorious 1916 racialist creed 'The Passing of the Great Race' in which Grant argued that 'miscegenation' between races resulted in a degeneration of the superior breed.

Not surprisingly, Osborn was an outspoken advocate of the brain-first theory of human evolution, which postulated that expansion of the brain was a prerequisite to the evolution of an intelligent ape that then became bipedal before evolving into the human form. In contrast, the bipedal theory suggested that bipedalism came first, followed by brain expansion to give an intelligent ape that then evolved into the human form. The latter approach was the Darwin–Huxley African Ape-man theory, whilst the former theory was supported by most European anthropologists in the early 20th century – men such as Sir Arthur Keith, Grafton Elliot Smith and Henry Fairfield Osborn.

Osborn was one of the few international experts who supported Eugene Dubois in his ideas about the evolutionary position and role of his Java Man (*Pithecanthropus erectus*, later known as *Homo erectus*), discovered in 1891. By 1900 he had published his ideas about Asia as the centre for the dispersal of all mammalian life and the evolution of the roots of the human family tree, with a deep division between the ape and human lineages back in Oligocene times (now known to be quite wrong: DNA analysis shows that the split occurred only some 6 million years ago in Africa, during Miocene times). The concept was elaborated a decade later by Osborn's museum colleague Dr William Diller Matthew. Then the famously fraudulent 'discovery' of 'Dawn Man', *Eoanthropus dawsonii*, at Piltdown in southern England in 1912 bolstered the brain-first theory and with it the idea that humans evolved in Asia.

Osborn's Protégé – Roy Chapman Andrews

Being president of the American Museum of Natural History gave Osborn the ideal power base from which to test out his Asian theory. Among the museum's staff was a young man by the name of Roy Chapman Andrews (1884–1960), who had worked his way up through the ranks from lowly bottle-washer to become a zoological collector who specialized in the study of cetaceans. In later life Andrews claimed that he had been inspired by Osborn's Asian theory as early as 1912 but his interests, ambitions and abilities came to the attention of Osborn anyway and so, with the museum president's backing, he was chosen to lead the museum's First Asiatic Expedition.

Andrews proved an excellent choice: he was a first-class organizer and leader and although he was not particularly expert in anything relevant to the expedition he was an enthusiast, if somewhat overenthusiastic at times. A superb shot, he was always well armed and did at times have to use his guns to repel brigands as well as obtain fresh meat for the expedition. Good looking and personable, he is reported to have been very attractive, especially to women. Gossip has it that one admirer told Andrews, 'You can park your shoes next to mine anytime you feel the urge.' In 1914 he married a society beauty, who accompanied him on the First Asiatic Expedition.

Osborn fuelled American press interest in a venture that became labelled the 'Missing Link' expedition, much to Andrews' annoyance but he could not grumble too much because the publicity helped to raise the necessary funds. Europe was deeply embroiled in World War I but the Far East was still accessible through China, especially from America.

Into Asia

The First Asiatic Expedition, led by Andrews, consisted of a number of small teams that travelled through Yunnan in southwest China and through the borderlands of Burma and Tibet in search of any biological, ethnographical and anthropological material of interest to the museum. Osborn, who was very fond of his creature comforts, was not part of the team. In 1907 he had joined the museum's expedition to Fayum in Egypt, but the truth of the matter was that he had travelled with his family and stayed in a separate deluxe camp for a mere three weeks, after which he had gone home, leaving the museum's chief palaeontologist, Walter Granger, to cope with the rest of the dig and the heat, flies and sandstorms that are all part of desert exploration. Granger had wanted to finish in April 1907 but Osborn ordered them to stay on and find more specimens, which they did not. Granger became so ill from infected flea bites that he ended up in a Cairo hospital and was not released to go home until June.

Important zoological material was collected on the First Asiatic Expedition but Andrews realized that he needed a wider range of experts and more time to do anything really worthwhile. Consequently, the Second Asiatic Expedition of 1919 ranged further north into Mongolia with its vast steppes and mountain ranges. Western knowledge of this extraordinary terrain was very limited, with previous exploration being restricted to that of the remarkable American geologist Raphael Pumpelly (1837–1923), who had made a traverse through Central Asia and the Gobi in 1865, and the German geographer Ferdinand Baron von Richthofen (1833–1905, uncle of World War I flying ace, Friedrich von Richthofen) in 1873.

Mongolia was a revelation to these American explorers. As Andrews wrote of the Altai Mountain region, 'there was not a sign of human life, but a dry lake bed ran the entire length of the valley, which swarmed with antelope and wild ass … I have never seen such a concentration of game in a small area. Antelope were running beside the car … herd after herd of wild ass pounded along beside us unable to tear themselves away'. There were hazards too, especially from packs of ferocious feral dogs that scavenged around any settlement. Andrews liked to dramatize and told how one of his narrow escapes from death came when a pack of dogs 'gathered for a feast' on his wife Yvette and himself whilst they slept.

Again the main collections were zoological, especially mammals, but Andrews' reconnaissance showed that there was a real potential for significant palaeontological work. However, he also realized that it would need more specialist expertise and substantial resources to get better results and cover the

huge distances involved when the field season was relatively short because of
the extremes of climate.

Raising Funds for a Return Visit

Andrews had proved himself an effective leader and organizer and so when
he made yet another pitch for yet another Asiatic expedition, this time on a
much grander scale, he still found a receptive backer in the form of Osborn.
As a result, the museum committed US$5,000 and the salaries of any staff
who took part in the expedition. Through Osborn's well-to-do connections
and academic network, Andrews was able to raise a further US$30,000
from the American-Asiatic Association but that was just the beginning.
Andrews estimated that for a successful expedition he needed something
like US$250,000 and that inflated to some US$600,000 by the end of the
eight-year-long project. That he managed to do so shows what an effective
fundraiser he was.

In retrospect Andrews wrote that 'the main problem was to discover the
geologic and paleontologic history of central Asia, to find whether or not it
had been the nursery of the dominant groups of animals, including the human
race; and to reconstruct its past climate, vegetation and general physical
conditions, particularly in relation to the evolution of man'. There was not a
single mile of railtrack in this region, which was nearly half as big as the whole
of Western Europe. Consequently, some means of rapid vehicular transport
was a must. The climate ranged between +40 and -40°C and the terrain was
dominated by the Gobi desert. Food and water were so scarce that hardly
anyone lived there, apart from a few nomadic herdsmen. Andrews realized that
in this terrain motor vehicles could travel up to 100 miles a day and thus cover
a much larger area in the field season, which extended from April to October.
Previous explorers had used the traditional mode of transport – camels,
which could travel just 10 miles a day. So he argued that a properly equipped
expedition could do ten years' work in just one field season.

That was the theory but Andrews was experienced enough to know that
in practice things were not so simple, especially in such a harsh, inhospitable
and uninhabited environment as the Gobi. Motorized transport needed petrol,
oil and spares, people needed tents, food and water and then there was all the
scientific equipment. His compromise was to use fast cars for exploration and

the tried and tested camel caravans for establishing supply lines, stores and encampments and for transporting specimens. A single expedition required half a dozen cars, with 125 camels carrying 100 gallons of oil, 1,000 gallons of petrol, 3 tons of flour, 1½ tons of rice and so on. There were no reliable maps of the region so navigation had to be by compass and sextant, with maps drawn in the field for any fossil sites of importance.

Back to Mongolia
It was in spring 1922 that the first major Central Asiatic Expedition of the American Museum of Natural History drove into Mongolia to search for the Asiatic 'Eden' or birthplace of mankind. This time, the scientific personnel included the palaeontologist Walter Granger (he was also second in command) and the geologists Charles Berkey and Frederick K. Morris. Most importantly they also had a representative of the Mongolian government with them and without his official 'clout' they would not have been able to achieve much. Then there were drivers and field assistants – 26 people in all.

Walter Granger was the key figure to the scientific success of the expedition. Like Andrews he had joined the museum in 1890 as an 18-year-old without any degree-level qualifications and took a lowly position as handyman and assistant taxidermist. In 1896 he switched from ornithology to palaeontology and that opened up more opportunities for the fieldwork that he liked so much. The following year he played a leading role in the museum's excavations of Jurassic dinosaurs at Como Bluff and the Bone Cabin Quarry in Wyoming, which he helped to find. And then in 1921 he had been in China helping with the excavations at Choukoutien, near Peking. All this was invaluable experience for the 1922 Asiatic trip, where he was mainly concerned with searching for ancient fossil mammals to test the Osborn–Matthew theory of an Asian dispersal. All his colleagues later paid tribute to Granger as a person whom they admired and respected and who helped smooth many difficult circumstances in the very trying conditions of the Gobi.

The expedition found their first fossils on the fourth day as they travelled towards the capital Urga (now known as Ulaanbaatar) but they were not human related. Granger and his assistants found 50 pounds weight of teeth belonging to extinct rhino-like animals. Andrews, recalling his initiation into bone-hunting in Mongolia, described how 'in a spot only a few yards from the tents, my eyes marked a peculiar discoloration in the gray upper stratum, and bits of white, which looked like crumbled enamel. Scratching away at the soft clay-like earth, I exposed the grinding surface of three large teeth and felt sure that it was an important specimen'. He continues in this self-congratulatory tone, 'my initial experience as a paleontological collector stimulated me to spend every leisure moment in wandering over the badlands hunting for new treasures. The veriest fragment of exposed bone might lead the way to a skull or skeleton: a single specimen might turn one more page in the prehistory of Central Asia'.

Paraceratherium – *the hornless rhino*
For Granger, Andrews' enthusiasm could be something of a problem and at the museum, damaged specimens became known as 'RCAed ones'. Andrews himself confessed that he was 'inclined to employ a pickax where Granger would have used a camel's hair brush and pointed instruments not much larger than needles'. Altogether they managed to find the remains of large mammals from almost every epoch of Cenozoic times (from 65 million years ago until the present day). Including extinct horses, mastodons and titanotheres ranging in size from early and primitive small ones to much later, advanced and much larger ones.

Some of them reached unprecedented size, including a giant hornless rhino of Oligocene age, now called Paraceratherium. Its skull was 1.7m (5ft) long, it was 24ft long and stood 17ft high at the shoulder. Osborn wrote that 'from the first, the animal seemed incredibly large; it was hard to believe that it was actually a reality'. The mammal equivalent of some of the dinosaurs, it was probably a browser high in tree canopies. Andrews' 1925 expedition found the fossilized remains of four legs belonging to the giant terrestrial mammal. Andrews imagined how 'probably the beast had come to drink from a pool of water covering the treacherous quicksand. The position of the leg bones showed that it had settled slightly back on its haunches, struggling desperately to free itself from the gripping sands. It must have sunk rapidly, struggling to the end, dying only when the choking sediment filled its nose and throat'.

And then, quite unexpectedly, they turned up some Cretaceous dinosaur bones at Iren Dabasu. After some hasty collecting they had to continue to keep to schedule. From Ulaanbaatar they drove south into the Gobi but still

without finding any human related fossils. After many weeks they turned west
to make the long trip back to the Chinese border and on to Peking.

A Parrot-beaked Dinosaur and Eggshells

On Friday 1 September, during a stop on this return journey, the expedition
photographer J B Shackleford, had hung back from the main caravan and
taken a walk towards some low-lying hills. Suddenly he came to the edge of
a plateau and looked down into a large eroded depression in red sandstone
strata. Around the basin the wind sculpted rocks formed a fantastic landscape.
Andrews wrote: 'Almost as though led by an invisible hand, he walked straight
to a small pinnacle of rock on top of which rested a white fossil bone.' It was
the skull of a dinosaur with a strange parrot-like beak.

With one line of cliffs lighting up at sunset into the most extraordinary
red colour, they named them 'Flaming Cliffs', or Shabarakh Us in Mongolian.
Time for collecting was limited because they had to get out of the desert before
the weather deteriorated. Andrews was later to claim this as the site of 'the
most important deposit in Asia, if not the entire world' but they only spent
some three or four hours on this first visit. They collected the skull, some other
bones and bits of fossilized eggshell and they were already making plans to
return the next year.

The 1923 field season saw them back in Mongolia despite the fact that they
had not found any human-related remains. Luckily Osborn and the museum
authorities recognized that what they had found was new and interesting
enough to warrant further investigation and collecting. This time they had
more palaeontologists, including Osborn himself for part of the expedition,
and enough collectors to help to excavate and conserve the fossils for the long
and bumpy ride home to New York. They revisited Iren Dabasu and, according
to Andrews' account, managed to recover 'bones of both flesh-eating and
herbivorous dinosaurs, of several species and many individuals ... piled up one
upon the other in a heterogeneous mass'.

Andrewsarchus – an Unknown Predator

In June 1923 one of Granger's Chinese field assistants, Kan Chuen Pao, made
an extraordinary find, the metre long skull of an extinct kind of mammalian
predator with big canines and and stongly muscled jaws but clearly not any

kind of cat. Unfortunately that was all that remained of the beast. When the skull was safely back in New York, William Diller Matthew was able to identify it as a new mesonychid but it was the 'boss', Henry Fairfield Osborn, who named it *Andrewsarchus*, in honour his protégé. But they did not linger at the site as they were most anxious to get back to the Flaming Cliffs and arrived there on 8 July 1923.

Flaming Cliffs and 'First Horn Face'

They now knew that the site contained the remains of one of the earliest and most primitive horned dinosaurs named *Protoceratops andrewsi* by W K Gregory and C C Mook, both museum palaeontologists. The genus name means 'first horn face' and the species name honoured the expedition leader.

The excavations at Flaming Cliffs were so productive that they would continue in the course of yet another expedition in 1925. Altogether more than 100 skeletons and partial skeletons of the medium-sized-dinosaur were recovered, by far the biggest collection of any single dinosaur made by that time. There were all ages from hatchlings and babies to adults and so for the first time it was possible to understand how a dinosaur grew and developed.

They also wanted to find more fossil eggshells because it was not clear what kind of animal had laid them. Birds and reptiles both produce shelled eggs so it could have been giant birds or perhaps dinosaurs. There were older reports from Europe of eggshells that had been claimed to be those of a dinosaur based on a close association of their remains. George Olsen, one of the museum palaeontologists, soon found a group of three eggs that were almost sausage shaped with a thin wrinkled hard shell, unlike any known bird eggs and more akin to some lizard eggs, so there was the possibility that they had been laid by a dinosaur. The whole group made a detailed search for more egg fossils and soon they were turning up almost everywhere as shell fragments and complete eggs, then clutches of them, and finally they realized that when really well preserved the clutches had clearly been laid within hollow sand mounds.

Dinosaur Eggs and Nest Mounds

The best mound had a circle of five eggs, outside which was a bigger circle of 11 and beyond that another two eggs that might have been part of an even bigger third circle – in other words, at least 18 eggs. It was evident that this was a dinosaur nest mound hollowed out by the mother in the same way that turtles and some crocodiles still do. She then crouched over it to lay her eggs, rotating her body as she did so. Finally, she carefully covered them with sand and left them to be incubated by the sun's heat.

Luckily for palaeontologists but unluckily for the mother, the eggs did not hatch but were preserved for over 80 million years until the American palaeontologists uncovered them. They reckoned that the number of eggs of the same kind probably connected them with the most common dinosaur at the site, namely *Protoceratops*. It seemed that this had been a regular nesting site where these plant eaters gathered in the nesting season in considerable numbers, as some birds do, to lay their eggs, based on the principle of safety in numbers. Eggs of other kinds were found: some were round and larger, others were also elongate but smaller, showing that there were other kinds of dinosaur or other reptiles around.

Oviraptor *and* Velociraptor

One particular nest mound was found to have the skeleton of a strange toothless theropod dinosaur draped over it. When it was described by the museum's president, Osborn, he called it *Oviraptor philoceratops* meaning 'egg robber' with a 'fondness for ceratopsians', because he thought that the position of the skeleton 'immediately put the animal under the suspicion of having been taken over by a sandstorm in the very act of robbing a dinosaur egg nest'. Again, thanks to the unusually good state of preservation of skeletal remains that had not been removed from where the animals died, the expedition was recovering some of the first good information about how some dinosaurs lived and died.

The fossils of a crocodile and pond turtle may not have been the most exciting of the expedition but they did help with the interpretation of the environment in which the animals lived. Although most of the fossils were buried in windblown desert-like sands, it was unlikely that so many creatures could have lived in a barren desert without water or vegetation, especially the plant-eating ceratopians. The discovery of aquatic animals showed that normally there was plenty of water but that, from time to time, the water courses dried out completely or were overblown by shifting sand dunes or dust storms.

Another outstanding find was that of a skull and jaw plus some finger bones, a claw and the hind foot of another unknown small theropod dinosaur. In 1924 it was named *Velociraptor* ('swift robber') by Osborn, who thought that it may have preyed upon the hatchlings of other dinosaurs, but the details of its form and nature were not revealed until further specimens were recovered in subsequent expeditions.

The 'Unidentified Reptile'
Last but not least, one of the smallest and yet most important finds of the expedition was that of a tiny skull in a sandstone nodule, initially catalogued by Granger as an 'unidentified reptile'. Preparation of the specimen back in New York revealed that it belonged to one of the most ancient mammals known at the time. But it did not cause much of a stir as the dinosaur finds stole the limelight when the expedition returned to New York late in the fall of 1923. Nevertheless the museum experts were intrigued and were determined to find more ancient mammal remains on their return the following year.

Although no ancient human-related fossils were found, the team did recover archaeological evidence for the people who had lived in the region a thousand or more years ago.

Mongolia Again – 1925, 1928 and 1930
Andrews was back in Asia for the fifth time in 1925 and yet again they returned to the Flaming Cliffs, where they spent a week looking for more mammals. They found what they were looking for: another seven skulls, some attached to skeletal remains. Andrews, never short of hyperbole, described this period as 'possibly the most valuable seven days of work in the whole history of palaeontology up to date. Those skulls were the most precious of all the remarkable specimens that we obtained in Mongolia'.

Although Andrews managed to return to Mongolia for two further seasons in 1928 and 1929 the expeditions were restricted in their movements by increasingly suspicious Chinese authorities, who found it hard to believe that these Americans should be spending so much time, effort and money looking for a few old bones. Perhaps the hype and publicity that Andrews generated to keep the funds rolling in alerted the Chinese to worry about what was really going on. They suspected that there was some deeper agenda to the expeditions and seized some 100 crates en route back to America, eventually releasing them after examining the contents. Despite the intervention of the US State Department, they were not allowed to return. Andrews was convinced that they 'had barely scratched the surface of the Gobi's secrets'. Meanwhile his wife Yvette must have tired of his love affair with Mongolia: she left him for their accountant.

The Turn of Others
The fossil treasures of Mongolia became internationally famous and inevitably aroused the interest of palaeontologists around the world. But political unrest in China and Russia, followed by the outbreak of World War II in 1939, meant that Mongolia was effectively off-limits. Following the end of hostilities, Soviet dominion was such that they had the field to themselves alone and they took advantage of it. Academic palaeontology had been a thriving subject in Russia since the mid 19th century and there were many very able specialists who were interested in visiting Mongolia.

The Russians had already been in parts of Mongolia from 1925 to 1930, but it was in 1946 that the first major Soviet–Mongolian expedition was mounted. Much of 1947 was spent preparing for extensive work in the eastern Gobi, to which they returned the following year, covering some 14,000km. In an area known as the Nemegt they found the spectacular remains of a huge duck-billed plant-eating hadrosaur (*Saurolophus*) along with a giant carnivorous bipedal (*Tarbosaurus*) and small mammal fossils. They christened the site 'The Dragons' Tomb'.

The Russians were able to work out why so many remains had been gathered together in one area. From their detailed study of the strata, geologists could see that the deposits, 80 million years old, had originally been laid down in the delta of a huge river. Apart from delta channels, there were ponds, lakes and flood plains on which river sediments and anything carried by the river were buried, including the cadavers of animals that had been trapped and drowned in seasonal floods and carried downstream. There were also the remains of the many animals that had lived in the delta itself, feeding on its lush vegetation; and where there is an abundance of plant eaters, there are always the fewer carnivores that prey on them.

Since the Russian expeditions were very well equipped, with heavy-duty military tracked vehicles, all-terrain cars and efficient supply lines, they managed to excavate and recover huge quantities of fossils: some 120 tons were transported back to Moscow. They were about to set out for another expedition in 1950 when they were suddenly recalled by the Soviet authorities and that would be the end of their Mongolian adventures until 1964, when the Mongolian Academy of Science invited the Russians to return to Mongolia to visit a late Cretaceous site that has turned out to be one of the richest dinosaur sites in Mongolia.

The Polish Interregnum

As a young girl in war-torn Poland, Zophia Kielan-Jaworowska read accounts of Roy Chapman Andrews' Mongolian expedition and was entranced. Little did she realize at the time that one day she would be following in Andrews' footsteps, as a member of an incredibly successful series of eight joint Mongolian–Polish expeditions from 1962 to 1971. They were particularly interested in looking for Cretaceous fossil mammals and managed to find some 50 skulls at the Flaming Cliff locality alone and another hundred or so at various other sites, many of which had associated skeletal remains. In addition there were dinosaurs, including three complete skeletons of a new ornithomimosaur (*Gallimumus*), the huge arms of the strange theropod *Deinocheirus*, four new pachycephalosaurs, a new ankylosaur and skeletons of the small fast-running bipedal theropod *Velociraptor* (which possibly hunted in packs) and the relatively small plant-eating *Protoceratops* (which, despite the name it was given, does not have the prominent horns of its descendents but rather a small bony bump on the nose).

The Americans Return

Roy Chapman Andrews, whose intrepid and enthusiastic adventures had revealed the huge scale and diversity of dinosaur remains in Mongolia, died in 1960 but expeditions from his home institute, the American Museum of Natural History, have returned to Mongolia several times since 1990 and are still finding many new fossils of small mammals and dinosaurs. One of the most remarkable is that of the so-called egg-thief, *Oviraptor*, a small, agile ostrich-like bipedal dinosaur, apparently sitting on a nest and incubating the eggs rather than 'stealing' them. The discovery of an oviraptorid embryo within an egg alongside the adult suggests that the parent may have been guarding its nest when smothered by a sandstorm; thus its 'egg-thief' name may be inappropriate.

The fossil treasures of Mongolia are far from being exhausted and no doubt there will be more expeditions and more spectacular finds. Asia may not have been the home of mankind, as Osborn and Andrews had hoped, but its fossil record of life on land during Mesozoic times is outstanding in its richness and quality of preservation.

CHAPTER 5: EMPIRES IN EGYPT

'I crossed the Nile to the west, and proceeding straight to the Memnonium,
I had to pass between two colossal figures in the plain ... They are mutilated
indeed, but their enormous sizze strikes the mind with admiration ... The
groups of columns of that temple ... and the views of the numerous tombs
excavated in the high rock behind it, present a strange appearance to the eye
... As I entered these ruins, my first thought was to examine the colossal bust
I had to take away. I found it near the remains of its body and chair, with its
face upwards, and apparently smiling on me at the thought of being taken to
England.' (Giovanni Belzoni enters the Memnonium of Thebes, 1816)

From its very beginnings, archaeology has been a frequent battleground for the
clash of nations. These days, the arguments are embedded in national identity,
with newly empowered native cultures struggling to win back treasures that
were, depending on one's point of view, either discovered by, given to, or
stolen by overbearing western explorers.

But two centuries ago, Egypt saw a very different type of conflict, as agents
of the great European Empires raced each other, and occasionally came to
physical blows, in pursuit of treasures left unregarded by the nation's rulers.
More than anywhere else, archaeology in Egypt was inextricably bound up in
political power games, and yet it was here that, in the course of a century, it
developed, rapidly from mere tomb-raiding to the science we know today.

Myth, Mummies and Medicine

Egypt was ancient even when the Greeks and Romans ruled here, adding their
own layers of Hellenistic and Latin culture to the deep strata of pharaonic
history. As a result, it was never really 'lost' in quite the same way as some
other ancient civilizations. Indeed, the Romans happily adopted local gods and
customs such as mummification, and proved themselves enthusiastic exporters
of Egyptian antiquities. Egyptian culture therefore traced an unbroken chain
from the pre-Dynastic period, around 3000 BC, to the early centuries of the
Christian era, and it was only the arrival of Coptic Christianity that finally
saw the old ways prohibited and the ancient forms of writing – the ceremonial

hieroglyphs and the everyday hieratic and Demotic scripts – vanish into obscurity. The loss of access to ancient writings, above all, was responsible for transforming ancient Egypt from a well understood historical society into a mysterious, semi-mythical world – from then on, scholars and travellers had to rely on the occasionally biased and frequently unreliable accounts of classical historians such as Herodotus, and fragmentary translations of earlier texts. The spread of Islam across north Africa from the seventh century onwards only increased the problem: the Islamic caliphs and their subjects generally took little interest in the graven images and ruined temples among which they lived. The only exceptions were occasional treasure hunts and a few iconoclastic attempts to destroy the monuments completely. The few European traders to penetrate the Egyptian interior brought back only fanciful travellers' tales.

Renaissance and Enlightenment scholars and collectors took a little more interest, particularly in the surviving hieroglyphic fragments that gradually found their way into museum collections. By the mid 18th century, Egypt (and the pyramids in particular) had become a destination for the more adventurous Grand Tourists, and the establishment of the great European museums saw the beginnings of a trade in Egyptian antiquities. Mummies were the most highly prized objects of all, though for a singularly grotesque reason: misunderstandings of Arabic medicine recipes containing *mumiya*, or raw pitch, had led to a widespread belief in the medicinal properties of powdered mummy. The reality was that the Arabs called the bandaged bodies mummies because many had been coated with *mumiya*, but the western tourists weren't to know this and many a corpse that had survived for millennia beneath the Egyptian sands met its eventual end as expensive medicine for gullible Europeans. This distasteful trade persisted until well into the 19th century.

Perhaps the most influential early report of Egypt, coincidentally dating from 1768, was Scottish traveller James Bruce's account of the 'Tomb of the Harps', the elaborately decorated tomb of the Pharaoh Ramesses III in what is known today as the Valley of the Kings. Bruce's hurried sketch of the ornate wall paintings, and particularly of a harpist, ignited strong British interest in Egyptian antiquities.

Napoleon in Egypt

Despite this growing awareness, it's fair to say that Egypt exploded into the European public consciousness around the turn of the 19th century, in a way that no other ancient civilization has done before or since. One key reason for this was that the ancient dusty land suddenly found itself recast as a stage for the great international conflict of the age, thanks largely to the ambition of one of the most famous men in history: Napoleon Boneparte.

At this time, Bonaparte was an acclaimed young general and technically still a public servant to the Directory that had eventually found its way to power amid the bloody chaos of the French Revolution. The ambition that would soon see him rise to consul and eventually self-appointed Emperor was already becoming apparent and in 1798 he conceived an audacious scheme to steal away the burgeoning British Empire from under the noses of France's old enemy. French troops would 'liberate' Egypt from its Turkish rulers (at the time, it formed part of the huge Ottoman Empire), taking control of the southern Mediterranean. Then, through the building of a proto-Suez canal linking the Mediterranean to the Red Sea, they would be able to strike at British outposts in India and the Far East.

It was an over-reaching and some might say foolhardy plan, but the Directory was only too happy to indulge its wayward, charismatic general if it meant his prolonged absence from the country. Napoleon's invasion fleet set sail on 20 May, and at first all went well; the island of Malta fell without a fight in early June, and following an uneventful landing near Alexandria on 1 July the port city was itself captured. The French force disembarked and moved south to Cairo, where they encountered their first serious opposition: a 60,000-strong force of Mamluk soldiers under the command of the chieftain Murad Bey. Despite the exhausting march south, the French army showed iron discipline under its brilliant leader; the so-called 'Battle of the Pyramids', fought on 21 July 1798, turned into a rout, with just 30 Frenchmen killed as opposed to several thousand Mamluks.

For all this early success, Napoleon's plan was doomed to eventual failure. The British were determined to strangle this nascent French Empire at its birth and ordered the Mediterranean fleet of Rear-Admiral Horatio Nelson to attack the French fleet anchored at Aboukir Bay. The famous Battle of the Nile, joined on 1 August 1798, resulted in a crushing defeat for the French.

From a fleet of 13, only two of Napoleon's ships of the line escaped intact, while several sank to the bottom of the Mediterranean, carrying priceless treasures seized from the Knights of St John on Malta. About 1,700 French sailors were killed (most when the French flagship *L'Orient* exploded) while the British suffered only 218 casualties.

The Battle of the Nile transformed Nelson into a national hero and reduced Napoleon's plans to ruins. Although he continued to throw his weight around Egypt and the neighbouring territories of the Holy Land for several more months, problems with disease and Bedouin attacks on his chains of supply saw his forces steadily diminished. In August 1799, the general left what remained of his forces to administer Egypt, while he left for France to help to secure it against a hostile coalition of neighbours. Judicious use of 'spin' allowed him to paint the Egyptian expedition as at least a qualified success and ultimately assisted his rise to power in the *coup d'état* that established him as leader of a new government, the consulate, in November of that year.

One key element in the spinning of Napoleon's Egyptian adventure was the scientific and cultural expedition that had accompanied the troops. Led by Dominique Vivant, Baron de Denon (1747–1825), a former aristocrat and personal friend of Napoleon through his wife Joséphine, the Commission des Sciences et Arts d'Egypte consisted of some 150 noted academics from a variety of disciplines, accompanied by some 2,000 artists and other support staff. Even as Napoleon's army was clashing with the Mamluks, Denon's party was setting up a well equipped headquarters in the palace of Hassan Kashif on the outskirts of Cairo.

The chief goal of the expedition was to publish a comprehensive survey of Egypt, including accurate illustrations of temples and other monumental buildings, and smaller antiquities of various sorts. While their military comrades found themselves forced into retreat, Denon's men spread out along the course of the Nile, compiling obsessive notes on Egypt's peoples, religions, flora and fauna as well as excavating many hitherto undiscovered monuments.

Denon himself returned to France with Napoleon in 1799, publishing his own memoir of the expedition shortly afterwards. Stranded in Egypt for several more years, the members of his commission, now led by the Comte Claude Louis Berthollet (1748–1822), found themselves with little to do but continue working. Their official report, published in 20 volumes including ten consisting purely of engravings, did not appear until 1809-1826. It was not the first attempt to describe Egypt for western readers, and its lengthy road to publication meant that it was out of date within a few years, but it was certainly the most ambitious such project of its era.

By the time the last volumes appeared, France was a monarchy once again and Napoleon himself five years dead. But through all the turmoil of the Napoleonic Wars and the Restoration, the *Description de l'Egypte* remained an intense source of national pride, and a powerful inspiration for later generations of scholars.

Giovanni Belzoni: the Strongman of Thebes

Fascinating though the pyramids and the Sphinx undoubtedly were, for much of the 19th century they formed a mere sideshow to the main business of Egyptian archaeology: the exploration of tombs and temples in search of portable antiquities that might be shipped back to Europe for display in the great museums, or simply sold to the highest bidder. With Napoleon's Egyptian ambitions thwarted, the Mamluk ruler Muhammad Ali was reinstated as Pasha, overseeing a period of relative peace and good order in which European travellers could go about their business with little danger of attack from bandits – indeed, rival westerners often became the greatest threat. Though later scholars condemned most of these early archaeological collectors and their agents as mere tomb raiders, the more considerate ones certainly paved the way for later generations of more careful workers, and without their efforts even more of Egypt's ancient history would probably have been lost.

When Giovanni Belzoni sailed into Alexandria in June 1815, he had no inkling of becoming a treasure hunter; he was simply an itinerant engineer on the make. Belzoni, perhaps the most colourful character in the entire history of archaeology, was born in Padua in 1778 and spent most of his youth in Rome before fleeing to Holland in the face of Napoleon's advancing army. He arrived in England in 1803 at the age of 25 and became celebrated as a strongman and theatrical performer. Belzoni towered above most of the populace at a height of 201cm (6ft 7in) and went by various stage names, most famously 'The Patagonian Sampson'. His greatest feat was supporting a human pyramid of up to twelve normal-sized men. It was in London that Belzoni met his wife Sarah, who would be his constant companion and play a vital role in his life's work.

Unsatisfied with life on the stage, Belzoni had educated himself in engineering, becoming something of an expert in hydraulics, and it was with this in mind that he set off in 1814 on a tour through newly liberated Europe to Malta, where he hoped to find employment. It was only when fate brought him into contact with an agent of the Pasha, who assured him that Muhammed Ali was very interested in irrigation and water-lifting devices of all kinds, that the 'Great Belzoni' set off for Egypt, taking with him his steadfast and adventurous wife and their Irish servant, James Curtin.

The party was immediately alarmed to discover that the city was stricken with bubonic plague, still a common disease in North Africa at the time. Belzoni calculated that the outbreak would fade as the heat of summer set in, but for the meantime they hid themselves away in quarantine – partly to avoid the disease, but also to conceal the fact that they were themselves ill as they adjusted to the local climate, food and water.

Once recovered, Belzoni sought an audience with the Pasha and delivered a successful pitch for the latest design of hydraulic pump – one that could raise water at four times the rate of a traditional device. Ali agreed to finance a prototype, and Belzoni laboured for more than a year on its construction. The machine was finally ready to be tested in December 1816 and performed well at first, until a practical joke orchestrated by the Pasha himself misfired, leaving the machine wrecked and Curtin with a broken hip. The accident was seen as an ill omen and the Belzonis found themselves stranded in a foreign land with no source of income.

And here fate intervened again. During their stay in Cairo, the Belzonis had made the acquaintance of Johann Ludwig Burckhardt, the renowned Swiss traveller in Africa and the Middle East. On many evenings, Giovanni had listened with rapt attention as Burckhardt wove tales of the wonders to be found on the Upper Nile. In particular, he mentioned the colossal statue of Ramesses II at Thebes. Burckhardt had already obtained it, on paper, as a gift from the Pasha to the Prince Regent, but the diplomatic niceties meant nothing when the behemoth itself, commonly known as the 'Younger Memnon' (from the Greek name for the temple where it lay, the Memnonium) could not be moved. Several attempts had been made but it had proved impossible so far to move it the two miles to the banks of the Nile. What was more, there were rumours that the French hoped to obtain the statue for themselves, through the efforts of their own Italian-born agent, Bernardino Drovetti (1776–1852).

Now Belzoni was fiercely patriotic towards his adopted nation, and equally fierce in his dislike of the French – indeed he had fled Italy rather than be conscripted into the French army. He also had the engineering expertise for the job, was sorely in need of funds, and had a burning desire to see the Upper Nile for himself. Through Burckhardt's good offices, he obtained an interview with the British consul, Henry Salt (1780–1827), and proposed that he would lead an expedition to bring back the Younger Memnon so that it could be shipped abroad for display in the British Museum.

Salt was himself an antiquarian and collector and readily approved the plan. He and Burckhardt offered to finance Belzoni if he could accomplish what had seemed impossible. Later events would prove that the two men left the meeting with very different impressions of their agreement: the high-handed Salt evidently thought (or chose to believe) that Belzoni had agreed to be his employee, while the strong-willed Italian saw himself as an independent agent commissioned for this one particular task. The party set sail to Thebes on 30 June, but had to break their journey at Manfalut for an interview with Ibrahim Pasha, Muhammed Ali's heir and ruler of Upper Egypt. Here, Belzoni came face to face with the French agent Drovetti, who did his best to dissuade him from the plan, and offered him a belittling gift – a granite sarcophagus lid that he had himself been unable to move from its tomb.

When the party arrived at Thebes the enormous temple of the Memnonium (today known as the Ramesseum after its true builder) evidently made a powerful impression on the Italian strongman – his description of it opens this chapter.

Belzoni had brought with him from Cairo the components of a rolling wooden platform, and hired a team of local labourers to help to lift the statue from its resting place and pull it down to the river. Progress was painfully slow, even with several dozen men, and the journey to the river's edge, roughly two miles away, took 16 days. The local ruler, the Cacheff, also had to be bribed into allowing work to continue. There was little to do now but to order a cargo boat from Cairo, and wait until the Nile floods in the autumn brought waters deep enough to float the colossal bust.

In the meantime, Belzoni determined to explore. His first visit to see Drovettii's sarcophagus lid almost ended in disaster when his guides stranded him in a network of narrow passageways, expecting a bribe for his rescue, but he eventually fought his way out and realized there was a much easier route to the tomb's main entrance. However, the local Cacheff insisted the lid was Drovetti's property, so Belzoni was unable to remove it anyway.

To ease their frustration, the Belzonis determined to journey up the Nile. Near Aswan, they visited the temple-strewn island of Philae in the middle of the river (on the return journey they left a group of workmen with instructions to cut away some of the most impressive hieroglyphs for later collection). Continuing up the river and through the Nile's lower cataracts, they were particularly keen to see the great temples of Abu Simbel, where four stone colossi of Ramesses II and his queen Nefertari stared out of the towering sandstone cliff above the Nile's west bank. Burckhardt had been the first to report this monument, its entrance long since covered by shifting sands that had piled up so that only the head and shoulders of the seated figures were visible. When Belzoni first saw it, he immediately recognised that it commemorated the same Pharaoh as the Younger Memnon.

Keen to investigate the temple's interior, Belzoni hired native workers to clear away the huge drifts of sand that had piled up almost to the necks of the enormous figures. Despite his labours, the corruption of local officials meant that he ran out of money with the job half done, and Belzoni made a reluctant return to Thebes to pick up the Younger Memnon and transport it to Cairo.

The statue's arrival in port caused a sensation and visitors flocked to see it as it awaited the arrival of a larger boat to take it on to Alexandria and, ultimately, London. According to Burckhardt in a letter to his sponsors:

'The Committee need not be under any apprehension, that this transaction has caused my name to become of public notoriety in Egypt; which would certainly have been the case, if it had been known that I had a hand in the business, for during the fortnight the head remained at Boulak, the vessel was constantly crowded by swarms of visitors, of all classes. Nobody knows that I have had any thing to do with it. The Kahirines ascribe it entirely to Mr. Salt and Mr. Belzoni, who, they say, send it to England to have it taken to pieces, in order to find the invaluable jewel which it contains.'

With his expenses paid off and £100 commission from Salt for a job well done, Belzoni busied himself preparing for a second journey. He was by now aware that he had serious competition for the antiquities at Thebes and hurried back, only to find that Drovetti's men were already installed among the ruins of the huge Karnak temple. Forced to work on the other side of the river, where he had first searched for Drovetti's sarcophagus lid, he found a rich haul of papyri and other items among the tombs. With another boatload dispatched on its way to London, the Belzoni party joined forces with a pair of holidaying British soldiers and set off back to Abu Simbel.

Passing Philae, they found that the carved reliefs they had hoped to collect had been smashed up with a hammer, and scratched with the French graffiti *operation manquée* ('spoiled job'). The tensions that would eventually put an end to Belzoni's career in Egypt were already rising.

There were mixed fortunes at Abu Simbel too: the party successfully cleared the entrance to the enormous temple and finally got inside but it soon became clear that there were no saleable antiquities to be found. However, Belzoni returned down river well satisfied with his discoveries: he was becoming just as interested in exploration for its own sake as he was in finding valuable objects.

Back at Luxor, on the opposite bank from the French, Belzoni returned to the tombs around the Valley of the Kings, with diplomacy and well placed gifts ensuring that he was given a free rein in the area. Though later archaeologists sometimes cursed him for 'excavation techniques' that amounted to little more than plunder, Belzoni showed himself in a better light when it came to the discovery of hitherto unknown tombs: he was remarkably perceptive when it came to spotting the signs of disturbance that might hide more ancient monuments, to the point where his workmen began to suspect he was some kind of magician. In the course of one miraculous week he discovered five hidden tombs, the highlight of which was the beautifully painted burial complex built for Seti I, father of Ramesses II. Here, Belzoni found a spectacular alabaster sarcophagus and the embalmed remains of a sacred bull.

With their return to Cairo in late 1817 the Belzonis went their separate ways – Sarah set off with James Curtin to visit Jerusalem, while Giovanni remained in Egypt and busied himself defending his reputation from attacks by the French. He was also determined to investigate the pyramids and specifically to look for an entrance to the supposedly solid Pyramid of Chephren. His acute eye soon spotted irregularities on the north side of the pyramid and hard labour eventually revealed the entrance to a sealed-up passageway. Belzoni won the glory of becoming the first European to step inside the second largest pyramid, but found little inside: an enormous sarcophagus set into the floor, and an inscription left by Arab explorers who had preceded him in the early 13th century.

In November 1818, Belzoni set off on what would be his last trip up the Nile. He was determined to record and make castings of the reliefs in the tomb of Seti I and collect a few objects on his own account, but he was also travelling with the collector William Bankes, who had asked him to retrieve a huge obelisk from the island of Philae. With enormous difficulty, Belzoni got the mighty monument on to a boat and guided it down through the rocky Nile cataracts as far as Luxor, where he spent Christmas working in the tomb of Seti I. But his hijacking of the Philae obelisk (which Drovetti considered to be his property) had pushed his opponent to the limit of his patience. When Belzoni crossed the river for a brief investigation close to Drovetti's workers at Karnak, he found himself assaulted by a mob of Arab workers, led by Drovetti and his Italian subordinates. Harsh words were exchanged and a gun was discharged (though without injury) before tempers cooled and Belzoni was able to escape. He returned to Cairo as quickly as possible and made arrangements to leave Egypt for good, before the situation worsened still.

On his return to London in March 1820, the Strongman of Thebes found himself once again at the centre of attention; the general public had been fascinated by press reports of his adventures, and a new wave of Egyptomania had been let loose. He organized a grand exhibition of his finds, staged inside a replica of the tomb of Seti I, and published a best-selling account of his travels. But even with all this success and popular acclaim, the exploration bug would not leave him. Despite the pleas of his wife, he was determined once again to follow in the footsteps of his friend Burckhardt. The Swiss explorer had died at Cairo in Belzoni's absence and never got the chance to join the caravan that would take him south of the Sahara in search of Timbuktu and the source of the Niger River.

Belzoni intended to tackle the same task from the opposite direction, travelling up the river from Benin. Tragically, he was equally doomed to failure: within two months of his landing there in 1823, he, like Burckhardt, was dead of dysentery.

Champollion Cracks the Code

While the agents of British and French collectors squabbled in the race to discover new tombs, temples and artefacts on the ground in Egypt, a parallel intellectual competition was going on in Europe, where some of the finest minds of a generation were struggling to decode the mysteries of Egyptian writing. At any one time the ancient Egyptians had used two distinct writing systems: the decorative hieroglyphs used on monuments and in formal writing, and a handwritten or cursive script (originally hieratic) that later evolved into Demotic around 500 BC.

The secrets of both hieroglyphic and demotic writing had disappeared with the rise of Christianity in Egypt, and the only surviving traces of Egyptian words and names were transliterations found in the Bible, and the works of early historians such as Herodotus and Manetho (a historian whose *Aegyptika*, a summary of Egyptian history written in the 3rd century BC, no longer existed in its original form, except as fragments quoted in other works). Most attempts to decipher hieroglyphs, from the Renaissance onwards, assumed that they were literal picture writing in some form or other, with each image representing a single word – an interpretation enshrined in the *Hieroglyphica*, a work written by the Egyptian-Greek scholar Herapollon in the 4th century AD when the true meaning of hieroglyphs had already been lost. However, with no real clues as to the true meaning of the texts, the early attempts at decipherment were little more than wild stabs in the dark.

Then in 1799, the French had a massive stroke of luck. While digging defences at Fort Julien near the city of Rosetta (modern-day Rashid), Napoleonic soldiers unearthed a slab of smooth grey-black stone about a metre long, covered in closely spaced script in three different languages – hieroglyphs, demotic, and ancient Greek. The Greek inscription revealed that the stone commemorated a number of decrees passed by the Ptolemaic kings (the dynasty that ruled Egypt after its conquest by Alexander the Great in 332 BC). It seemed clear that the other two texts were likely to be renditions of the same text in the lost languages of ancient Egypt, and that this stone could be the key to cracking the hieroglyphic code.

The soldiers who discovered the stone passed it directly to their commanding officer, General Jacques de Menou, who had it sent to the Institut de l'Egypte in Cairo. Word soon spread of what promised to be a breakthrough, but the French soon had other things to worry about: the Battle of the Nile and Napoleon's departure had left them more or less stranded, and in 1801 British troops arrived to finish the job of liberating Egypt. The French academics and soldiers alike retreated from Cairo to Alexandria under the commander of General de Menou, and finally surrendered on 30 August.

Lord Elgin and other leading lights of the British Museum were by now fully aware of the antiquarian booty the French had collected during their time in Egypt, and Elgin's own secretary was one of the advisers sent alongside the expeditionary force to ensure that the French handed over the goods. But while the British were happy to give Egypt itself back to the Ottomans, they wanted the French finds, and particularly the Rosetta Stone, for themselves. After a tense stand-off and much haggling, the French eventually departed with paper copies of the stone, while the British took the stone itself to England, where it retains pride of place in the British Museum.

Now the brightest minds in Europe could finally get to work on the Rosetta inscriptions, but there were still clearly problems. The 55 lines of Greek were easily translated, but with just 14 lines of hieroglyphs and 32 lines of demotic, how could they be matched up? Was the picture writing theory correct? (If so, it threw into question the idea that these were parallel texts, since there seemed to be far too many symbols to convey the meaning of the Greek inscription.) And how did Egyptian grammar work? The first breakthrough came in 1802, when Swedish diplomat and philologist Johan Åkerblad identified certain repeating patterns in the demotic text, allowing him to identify the proper names and a couple of other key words such as 'temple'.

Englishman Thomas Young (perhaps better known today as a physicist) made the next assault: he realized that the names of monarchs were always written in oval frames called cartouches. Using the Rosetta Stone and a bilingual inscription from the obelisk recently recovered by Belzoni and William Bankes at Philae (the island in the Nile), Young identified the names of several rulers and, based on the number of symbols contained in their cartouches, suggested for the first time that, in this special circumstance, each hieroglyph could represent a sound rather than an entire word. He even identified some of their individual sounds and realized that hieroglyphs should normally be read from right to left, though the direction could be reversed depending on which direction certain characters faced. Even more importantly, he built on Åkerblad's work to complete the decoding of demotic.

Young's breakthrough with the cartouches allowed collectors and scholars to identify the names of specific kings mentioned in tombs, papyri and inscriptions, but the mass of hieroglyphic inscriptions remained inscrutable.

The credit for the final breakthrough would be claimed by a young Frenchman, Jean-François Champollion. Born in 1790 in the small town of Figeac, in the Lot region of southwest France, Champollion soon displayed a prodigious gift for languages, and his young imagination was entranced by reports of the French expeditionary force in Egypt. By the age of 11 he had decided that one day he would read and understand the hieroglyphs, and from then on he dedicated himself to attaining mastery of languages that might be useful, ranging from Greek and Latin to Arabic, Persian, Sanskrit and Coptic Egyptian.

Champollion and his older brother Jacques-Joseph (1778–1867) were both ardent republicans and supporters of Napoleon, and their careers in academia were held back on several occasions by the political reverses that wracked France in the early 1800s. In 1809 both were appointed to professorships at the new University of Grenoble (Jean-François on the strength of a geography of Egypt he had written as a student), but in 1816 they were dismissed from these posts after unwisely criticizing the restored monarchy and supporting Napoleon during his brief return from exile. Nevertheless, they resumed their former positions a year later, and by 1821 Jean-François was on the verge of a breakthrough.

Champollion's great advance was the realization that all hieroglyphs – not just the ones in cartouches – could be phonetic. While many of these interpretations matched those already suggested by Young, Champollion extended his interpretations further. He recognised that all three systems of writing had drifted apart and developed specialized grammar over the centuries of separate development. He also realised that the hieroglyphic symbols could have different meanings depending on context: they could represent phonemes (distinct units of sound), but also entire objects.

In 1824, Champollion published his work as *Précis du système hiéroglyphique*.

By unlocking the system of Egyptian monumental inscriptions, he paved the way for a revolution in Egyptology: archaeologists and historians would no longer be scrabbling in the dust for fragments of an incoherent past, but building up an extensive, overall picture of ancient Egyptian history and culture.

The publication of Champollion's book triggered an Anglo-French intellectual dispute of the type that typified much of the 19th century. While Young was fulsome in his praise for the French work, he argued that it was clearly developed from the breakthroughs already made by himself and Åkerblad. He wanted recognition of his part in the translation effort, but Champollion and the French academic establishment insisted that the credit was all French. The dispute rumbled on for some years, although Champollion, promoted by now to curator of the new Egyptian department at the Louvre museum, still allowed Young access to other manuscripts in his charge.

Champollion's attention, meanwhile, was now focused on another Egyptian treasure, known today as the Turin King List. This delicate papyrus had been discovered by Bernardino Drovetti at Thebes in 1822, but poorly treated thereafter, so that it was already fragmented and missing some vital pieces by the time Champollion realized its importance.

Nevertheless, this horizontal parchment, some 1.7m (almost 6ft) long, proved vital in establishing the framework of Egyptian history. The 'good side' of the paper was, of all things, an ancient Egyptian tax return, but some time after it was drawn up a later scribe had, apparently for idle amusement, written out a list of all the rulers of ancient Egypt down to their own time. This list began with a procession of gods and demigods, but then proceeded to human pharaohs that could be matched up with the kings listed by Manetho. As Champollion pieced together the fragmented parchment, he saw that the pharaohs were grouped together in dynasties that seemed to match Manetho's, and accompanied by the precise duration of their reigns – down to years, months, weeks and days. Using this document, then, it was possible to find the precise duration of each dynasty and in theory to calculate the original dates of each reign.

Two major problems remained for later archaeologists. The surviving fragments of the papyrus listed pharaohs as late as the 17th dynasty, but no further. There was no way of knowing precisely when the list was written out, or how much further it continued in its original form. Furthermore, there was no way of putting an absolute date on any of the reigns mentioned in the list – so while Champollion's work had given the Old and Middle Kingdoms an accurate historical framework, they were still drifting in a sea of uncertainty, an unknown distance from the precise dates of later Egyptian history.

In 1828, Champollion finally had the opportunity to see the land of Egypt for himself, as part of a Franco-Tuscan expedition alongside Italian philologist Ippolito Rosselini. Travelling up the Nile into Nubia, the party reached as far south as Abu Simbel, where they found the entrance unearthed by Belzoni had been closed again by drifting sands. Champollion was delighted at the opportunity to live the life of an adventurous archaeologist. Along the way, he collected huge amounts of new material – monumental inscriptions, papyri and so on. Unfortunately, he dented his reputation with later archaeologists by hacking two large wall panels out of the finely decorated tomb of Seti I, discovered by Belzoni back in 1817, and taking them back to the Louvre for study and display.

Champollion remained in Egypt for more than a year, returning to France to take up a position as Professor of Egyptology at the College de France. He now began work on his masterpiece, the monumental *Egyptian Grammar*, but just three years later the ill-health that had plagued him throughout his life finally overcame him. Already ailing with kidney and liver diseases, consumption and diabetes, he died of a stroke on 4 March 1832, aged just 41. Fittingly, Champollion was buried beneath an obelisk-like monument in the Père Lachaise cemetery of Paris.

Pyramid Raiders

The most spectacular and intriguing monuments of all, of course, were the pyramids – specifically the three huge monuments attributed to the Pharaohs traditionally known as Cheops, Chephren and Mycerinus (more accurately, the fourth dynasty rulers Khufu, Khaefre and Menkaure) that lay just outside Cairo. Although they had supposedly been sealed since ancient times, they had long since been stripped of their limestone facings (as with many other monuments, the disregarding locals of the Christian and Islamic eras had seen them as little more than convenient quarries for dressed stone to be used in newer buildings). Greek historian Herodotus, writing in the 5th century

BC, had known that the Great Pyramid of Cheops, largest of them all, was a gargantuan tomb, but the Western merchants and travellers visiting Cairo in medieval and early modern times tended to have a more limited education – and frequently fell in line with the unsupportable theory, first put forward by early Christian historians, that the buildings were enormous granaries constructed by the biblical patriarch Joseph to see Egypt through its famous seven years of famine.

The Great Pyramid had been opened many times since its original construction. Tomb raiders and later generations of pharaohs alike had found their way in, either to steal treasure, or to entomb their own mummies in the hope that a little of the pyramid's magnificence would reflect on them. The first recorded excavation was carried out by el-Mamun, Caliph of Baghdad, around AD 830. He used a battering ram to penetrate the interior of the Great Pyramid, making his way up steep, bat-infested passageways to the Queen's Chamber and eventually the higher King's Chamber.

Some centuries later, around 1565, German traveller Johann Helffrich became the first European to describe the pyramid's interior:

'We climbed with great difficulty a high corridor which lay straight before us, because this corridor was both wide and extremely high. On the sides the wall is set back at about half a man's height, with holes each a good pace distant from the next; to these we had to hold on and climb up as best we could.'

Helffrich's visit to the pyramid was brief, but the effect was stifling and he and his guides were soon 'so full of... unhealthy air that the following night we fell into such weariness and weakness that, for two days, we could stir neither arm nor leg.'

The intrepid Helffrich was not be the most reliable source of archaeological information, but his journals do provide a fascinating record of local beliefs in his own time. He was told, for instance, that the sphinx (then visible only as a head sticking out of the sands) was hollow and accessible through a passage in the sand, and that the Great Pyramid was the tomb intended for the pharaoh mentioned in Exodus, left empty after his army were swept to their death pursuing Moses and the Israelites across the Red Sea.

The first attempt at an exhaustive study of the pyramids, *Pyramidographia*, was published in 1646 by John Greaves, an English professor of astronomy who had travelled to Egypt some years previously and attempted to measure the dimensions of the monuments. His efforts to prove a link between the construction of the pyramids and the ancient British measurement units inadvertently sparked the more speculative and less reputable side of Egyptology that has developed alongside empirical archaeology to this day.

Greaves, like present-day tourists, entered the Great Pyramid through the ragged hole left by el-Mamun's explorations of centuries earlier, and reported the traces of el-Mamun's workers, as well as the vast sarcophagus of Khufu himself, set into the floor. Based on this first-hand experience, he was able to dismiss the fanciful ideas that the pyramids were either granaries or astronomical observatories.

Needless to say, this did not bring an end to speculation about the Pyramids and their builders. It continues unabated to this day, but its heyday was probably in the mid 19th century, when the Astronomer Royal for Scotland, Charles Piazzi Smyth (1819–1900), published his wildly eccentric theories. Piazzi Smyth, building on earlier theories promoted by John Taylor, believed that the Great Pyramid had been built precisely using an ancient system of measurement known as the Pyramid Inch, and was designed under divine inspiration to reflect precisely the dimensions of Earth. He also believed that it was no coincidence the Pyramid Inch and the British Imperial Inch were so close to one another, for he was a follower of the 'British Israelite' movement, which held that the British were descended from the lost tribes of Israel and were therefore God's chosen people. Smyth's heady mix of religion and pseudoscience made his book a bestseller, though he resigned from the Royal Society when it refused to publish his scientific papers on the subject. Ironically, the theory would finally be demolished by an archaeologist (Flinders Petrie, a friend of the Smyth family) who originally intended to prove it true.

Returning to less speculative matters, the early descriptions written by Greaves and others show some intriguing discrepancies from the pyramids as we know them today, which suggests that even in the 17th and 18th centuries, they were still treated as convenient quarries for building stone.

Although plenty of other travellers explored the monuments of the Giza plateau throughout the 18th century, the next major step in the exploration of the pyramids came in 1765, when Nathaniel Davison, British consul at

Algiers and a keen amateur archaeologist, attempted to make his way down the neglected, dust-filled 'descending passage' and also had himself lowered into the near-vertical 'well' that links the ascending and descending passages. He found his descent blocked by rubbish at the bottom of the well, and it would not be until 1819 that Giovanni Caviglia, excavator of the Sphinx and employed by Henry Salt in place of Belzoni, cleared the way between the two. Disappointed by the apparently simple construction of the pyramid and the lack of any hidden treasures within, he unfortunately turned to dynamite, attempting to blast a hole through one of the connecting passageways.

Caviglia was not alone in his willingness to use destructive methods. He shared a love of explosives with a later employer, Colonel Richard Howard Vyse (1784–1853), who conducted an exhaustive 'survey' of the Great Pyramid in 1837. Vyse blasted his way through the passages of the Great Pyramid, but failed to reveal any hidden tombs or treasuries – though he did find the so-called 'relieving chambers' above the tomb, one of which contains the only inscription of Khufu's name in the entire structure.

It has already been seen how Belzoni found his way into the Pyramid of Chephren in 1818, but the entrance to the smaller Pyramid of Mycerinus eluded him. Unfortunately, then, it was left to Vyse to blast his way in, dynamiting a tunnel through the entire structure to reach to central tomb, and only then finding the tunnel back to the north face. Needless to say, the tomb turned out to have had previous and less destructive visitors in later antiquity, but Vyse returned home with the original basalt sarcophagus, and one from a later squatter, to show for his pains. Unfortunately for Egyptology, but with at least some sense of poetic justice, Vyse lost his greatest prize when the ship carrying it back to England foundered. Menkaure's stone sarcophagus now lies somewhere at the bottom of the Mediterranean, doubtless awaiting salvage by some ambitious archaeologist of the future.

Mariette Awakes the Pharoahs

In 1850, a 29-year old Frenchman who would change Egyptian archaeology forever arrived in Cairo. Auguste Mariette (1821–1881) was a talented artist and amateur historian whose imagination was captured by Egypt after he inherited the papers of his cousin, Nestor L'Hôte, who had travelled with Champollion during his one and only Egyptian expedition. A job in his local museum at Boulogne allowed time to devote himself to the study of Egyptian writing and antiquities, leading eventually to a junior post at the famous Louvre. When French government officials decided to finance an expedition to seek out new manuscripts from the early Christian period, they decided that Mariette was the right man for the job.

As it turned out, they were wrong – Mariette spent months in pursuit of various documents, but ended up with embarrassingly little to show for his efforts. Anxious to salvage something from his expedition, and determined to make the most of his time in Egypt, he visited a number of well known tombs and temples and also befriended a Bedouin tribe who said they knew of a previously unexplored site close to the famous Step Pyramid at Saqqara. This proved to be a vast necropolis, the burial ground for the city of Memphis, which had been Egyptian capital between 2600 and 2200 BC. While wandering among the ruins, he came across the head of a stone sphinx sticking out of the sand. A little digging revealed its pair, and gradually an entire avenue flanked by sphinxes emerged from the sand. Mariette began to suspect that he had found one of the most famous lost temples of the ancient world: the Serapeum or Tomb of the Apis Bulls, described in detail by Manetho.

The entrance to the tomb was blocked by fallen stones, but explosives soon blasted these free and Mariette found himself in an enormous complex of underground catacombs. To either side of each long gallery, underground chambers were filled with huge stone sarcophagi containing the mummified remains of the sacred bulls. The bulls had been worshipped since the earliest times as part of a fertility cult associated with the power of the pharaoh, and had been buried in this elaborate complex for more than a thousand years after its establishment in the 13th century BC. Hieroglyphs on the bull burials would ultimately prove extremely useful in establishing the chronology of pharaohs under whose reigns they had lived and died.

Flushed with success, Mariette managed to obtain funds from the Louvre to continue working on the site for another four years. By the time he returned, the French Second Empire had been established under Napoleon III (a nephew of Napoleon I), and a new wave of interest in all things Egyptian had swept the nation. When in 1857 Prince Napoleon, a cousin of the Emperor, announced his intention to visit Egypt in a deliberate echo of the original Egyptian Expedition, Mariette was sent ahead on a bizarre mission. He supervised the opening of new digs across Egypt, noting the finds and then reburying them so that the Prince could 'discover' them for himself.

By this time, there was a new Viceroy on the Egyptian throne – Said Pasha, fourth son of Muhammed Ali – and the adventures of all these Western visitors had not gone unnoticed. Said was a reforming ruler, and was anxious about his country's history being plundered, insisting that his own agents supervise new excavations, including Mariette's. The Frenchman, in turn, was beginning to voice his own doubts about the wisdom of removing finds from their proper historical context.

Luck played its part in what happened next: Mariette met Ferdinand de Lesseps, a retired French diplomat who was then planning the construction of the Suez Canal. De Lesseps was fascinated by Mariette's discoveries and reputation and arranged for an interview with Said Pasha himself. The two discovered that they shared a common concern and within a year Said had created a new Egyptian Antiquities Service, with sweeping power to control the excavation and trade in the country's antiquities. Naturally, the first director was Mariette himself.

Mariette immediately embarked upon the most ambitious programme of excavation seen in Egypt since the time of the Pharaohs themselves. More than 3,000 men were employed at dozens of sites scattered across the country. The huge temple at Karnak (Luxor) was dug for the first time, along with the ancient capital of Tanis on the Nile Delta. Objects from all along the Nile Valley flooded into the newly established Egyptian Museum at Bulaq, near Cairo – most spectacularly, the treasures from the intact tomb of Queen Ah-hotep, mother of Ahmose I (who found the 18th Dynasty around 1550 BC), which were discovered in a necropolis near Thebes.

From now on, all archaeologists in Egypt would have to work under strict licence – and many baulked at what they called 'Mariette's Monopoly'. The British were particularly frustrated at having to take orders from a Frenchman (and indeed the position remained a traditionally French post until the first native Egyptian director was appointed in 1952). But for all his passion and industry, Mariette was a somewhat sloppy archaeologist: when faced with difficult obstacles, he showed an alarming tendency to resort to explosives, and with so many digs going on simultaneously he could not supervise each in person. He was also occasionally careless with his own notes and a great deal of invaluable information about digs as far back as Saqqara was lost when his house suffered flooding in 1878.

Nevertheless, the regulation brought in by Said Pasha and Mariette played a vital role in slowing the plunder of Egyptian monuments at a time when they were being despoiled more rapidly than ever before, fuelled by a boom in western tourism. Antiquities Service officials were soon engaged in cat-and-mouse games with a new generation of tomb robbers.

Bandits and Buried Treasure

Mariette died in 1881 and was buried, appropriately enough, in an ornate stone sarcophagus now preserved in the gardens of the Egyptian Museum at Cairo. His successor was Gaston Maspero (1846–1916), a protégé who had risen to occupy Champollion's old chair at the Collège de France. Maspero was more of a linguist than an archaeologist, but he took his new position seriously; he continued with Mariette's enormous excavations at Saqqara, and soon found himself forced to confront perhaps the most infamous archaeological bandits of the age.

By this time, the trade in illegal antiquities was concentrated around the village of Gourna, on the west bank of the Nile. Here, the el-Rassul clan ran a thriving operation plundering the surrounding New Kingdom cemetery. Most of their finds ultimately ended up in the hands of tourists visiting nearby Thebes; they ranged from papyri and small *shabti* figures to entire mummies (most of the tombs had already been robbed of any intrinsically valuable contents back in antiquity).

By around 1880, the Antiquities Service suspected that most of the papyri now flooding the market had a single source. In April 1881, two of the el-Rassul brothers were arrested and tortured by the regional governor in the hope of extracting a confession. Although they did not talk and were eventually released, the entire family remained under close surveillance and a few weeks later the older brother, Muhammed, confessed the truth – in return for a pardon and a cushy job with the Antiquities Service itself.

Muhammed led a large party of officials, including one of Maspero's deputies, Émile Brugsch, to the Deir el-Bahari cliffs that rise behind the famous temple of Queen Hatsepshut. Here, some ten years previously, his brother Ahmed had discovered the concealed entrance to a New Kingdom tomb, accessible only with a rope down a narrow shaft. This was the source of the el-Rassul family's unexpected wealth, and now it was Brugsch's turn to be lowered down the shaft.

Inside lay an unprecedented treasure – the family tomb of the Pinudjem II, high priest of the god Amun at Thebes from around 990 to 969 BC, packed with a huge cache of mummies that had been stored here at a later time. The sarcophagi had been stripped bare of decoration, and the jewelled decorations of the mummies themselves crudely ripped away, but each coffin was clearly marked with the identity of its occupant. The names were a roll call of New Kingdom history: Thutmosis I, II and III, Ahmose I, Seti I, Ramesses I and II … the pharaohs who had overseen a golden age during which Egypt had spread its influence around the Mediterranean coast.

Evidently this was an organized reburial, probably carried by Pinudjem's successors at Thebes during the Third Intermediate Period. The decline of the New Kingdom saw tomb robbing reach new heights and it seems that the royal mummies were removed from their original tombs and reburied in this plain fashion in order to protect them from further desecration.

The discovery of such a priceless haul evidently unnerved Brugsch, who panicked at the thought that it might be destroyed completely now the secret was out. He immediately hired 300 workmen and set about clearing the tomb. To the lasting ire of later archaeologists, he did not even take the care to record the original arrangement of the mummies before disturbing them. It's possible, though, that this was deliberate – Brugsch was long suspected of trading in antiquities himself and may have hoped to filch some prize artefacts amid the confusion (indeed, when the haul was examined properly back in Cairo, the mummy of Ramesses I turned out to be missing; it surfaced in the 1980s at a museum near Niagara Falls, and its precise route from Egypt to America is still a mystery). What was worse, the mummies were allowed to deteriorate in the harsh desert sunlight before being taken downriver.

The Royal Cache proved to be one of a pair: in 1898 a later director of the Antiquities Service, Victor Loret (1859–1946), uncovered a smaller cache in the newly discovered tomb of Amenhotep. Protecting the mummies of Thutmosis IV, Merneptah, Seti II, and Ramesses IV, V and VI, this cache had been relocated by the high priest Pinudjem himself. It lay beyond the cliffs at Deir el-Bahari, hidden away in the Valley of the Kings.

Flinders Petrie Turns from Pyramidology to Archaeology

The influx of foreign tourists to the Nile valley in the later 19th century undoubtedly encouraged the market for pilfered antiquities, but it had beneficial side-effects too. In England, a group of wealthy Egyptophiles established the Egypt Exploration Fund (EEF) to help to finance future excavations. Their most famous beneficiary was an energetic and enthusiastic young man who had been obsessed with archaeology since his childhood, and who would go on to have a profound influence on the field: William Matthew Flinders Petrie (1853–1942).

'Flinders' Petrie (as he was always known – the name came from a famous ancestor who had mapped the coast of Australia) was brought up within the strict teachings of the Christian sect known as the Plymouth Brethren. Kept from formal schooling by concerns over his asthma, he was largely educated by his eccentric parents. He spent much of his youth alongside his father exploring prehistoric and Roman monuments close to their home town of Charlton on the outskirts of London. This culminated in an expedition to survey Stonehenge with unprecedented precision.

His growing interest in archaeology was diverted to Egypt when he came across one of Piazzi Smyth's works of fanciful pyramidology on a bookstall. By coincidence, the Petries already knew the author's family – Flinders' father William had once been engaged to Smyth's daughter. Intrigued by the theory, they began to investigate it further in lengthy correspondence with Smyth himself. However, they soon realized that Smyth's methods were flawed, his measurements suspect, and his conclusions sadly dubious. By 1879, the Petries had formed a plan to go and measure the pyramids for themselves but, thanks to William's indecision, it was the young Flinders who set off alone for Egypt in the spring of 1880.

Arriving at Giza, Petrie took up residence in an empty tomb and hired a single experienced workman, Ali Gabry, who had once worked for Colonel Vyse. His meticulous survey of the Great Pyramid took two entire seasons, often working at night to avoid interruption. Petrie eventually grew so tired of curious visitors that during the day he stripped to a flesh-pink vest and long johns, reasoning that people were more likely to keep their distance if, from a distance, he looked like a naked madman. Once back in England, he collated and published his work on the Giza pyramids. Its demolition of the

'Pyramid Inch' theory was almost incidental to its real impact – the survey was so accurate that it is still in use today, and its intricate analysis of the building finally allowed archaeologists to accurately discover how it had been built.

Petrie, meanwhile, was already eager to return to Egypt. He had been shocked at the damage that had been done to the pyramids and other monuments by visiting tourists, local thieves and even unscrupulous archaeologists (famously, he likened the rapid destruction of Egypt's monuments to 'a house on fire'), and was determined to do what he could to save the country's antiquities.

As a young, self-trained archaeologist with no formal qualifications and no institutional employer, Petrie was in desperate need of patronage. Fortunately his survey of the Great Pyramid caught the attention of the Egypt Exploration Fund, which was looking for someone to explore the New Kingdom city of Tanis on the Nile Delta. Petrie arrived there in October 1883 and spent the next three years on the site. The EEF funding of £250 per month allowed him to employ a large team of workmen for the first time but, considering this was Petrie's first full-scale dig, he showed a remarkably independent spirit. Although Ali Gabry remained at his side and helped to supervise the work, Petrie did away with the foremen who, he reasoned, bullied the labourers to work quickly and sloppily. Some other archaeologists criticized Petrie as a mere amateur, but his methods proved to be far more precise and exacting than those of his contemporaries.

After three years of successful digging at Tanis and later at the Greek colony site of Naukratis, funding from the EEF dried up due to a number of problems, including the death of its principal benefactor, Erasmus Wilson. Petrie was temporarily forced to take on 'freelance' work while hoping that the situation would improve, and it was not until 1887 that Emilia Edwards introduced him to two new backers who were willing to finance a dig at the Middle Kingdom side of Hawara. Here, Petrie hoped to investigate tombs contemporary with the nearby pyramid of Amenemhat III, so he was at first disappointed to find a Roman-period cemetery. Disappointment turned to wonder, however, as he discovered that many of the mummies buried here were decorated with beautiful wooden plaques, bearing startlingly lifelike portraits of the deceased.

Petrie's next dig would have far-reaching effects for modern archaeology. While investigating the Pyramid of Senwosret II at Illahun, he unearthed a rare domestic site from the 12th century BC. This mud-brick village had housed the workers building the pharaoh's monument, and a lesser archaeologist might have disregarded it completely. But Petrie and his workers carefully picked through the remains, unearthing fascinating evidence of daily life in ancient Egypt. In order to preserve some of the delicate articles they found, Petrie had to develop new techniques for picking up fragile objects – for example, encasing them in wax that was allowed to set before lifting them out of the ground.

Until now, Petrie had maintained a good relationship with the Antiquities Service, but when Maspero stepped down as director in 1886, he clashed almost immediately with his successor. Eugéne Grèbault did little to disguise his dislike of foreign, and particularly British, archaeologists and did his best to turn the Cairo Museum into his own private collection. Thanks to him, Petrie was denied opportunities to work in the Western Valley, and later found himself forced to work around the periphery at Amarna (seat of the heretic king Akhenaten, who had tried to abolish the old Egyptian religion in favour of a monotheistic one) while 'official' archaeologists cleared the royal tomb and then, frustratingly, failed to publish details of the find.

In 1892, Petrie's friend and patron Emilia Edwards, one of the founders of the EEF, died. She left a bequest to University College London for the establishment of a chair in archaeology, and the specification for the post made it clear that there was only one suitable candidate – and so, at the age of 39, Petrie found himself a professor at a distinguished university, finally in control of a small income that would allow him to plan ahead, and with a prestigious post that would help to secure additional backing.

Now Petrie had the freedom to address one of the great unanswered questions of Egyptian history: who were the first pharaohs? The period before the 4th-Dynasty pyramid builders was a near-blank, inhabited only by semi-mythical figures. Digging at the southern site of Tukh near Nagada, he unearthed a huge cemetery of prehistoric graves, in which the bodies had been buried without mummification or sarcophagi, and alongside pottery vessels. Elsewhere, Grèbault's newly appointed successor, Jacques de Morgan, had found similar graves. Petrie and de Morgan respected one another's expertise, but differed in their interpretation of the graves; Petrie believed that they were evidence of an invading tribe, while de Morgan (correctly) thought they were the prehistoric natives of the Nile Valley itself.

Unlike later burials, the Nagada cemetery had no inscriptions or other clues to help in dating it, so in order to figure out the age of the different buildings Petrie developed an invaluable new method: the 'pottery sequence'. With hindsight, the principle (cross-dating) seems simple, but it took Petrie's genius to put it into use. By carefully recording pot fragments from the many different graves, then looking at them as a whole, he was able to identify the way in which the pottery techniques had changed over time. Stratigraphy helped to establish which styles came later, and which earlier. The range of fragments found in a particular grave, therefore, could show the latest possible date at which its occupant was buried. Although the pottery sequences only provided relative dating evidence, they could occasionally be tied to more definitive dates, allowing Petrie to work out the history of the entire site. Before Petrie's breakthrough, archaeology was about papyri, monumental inscriptions and decorative artefacts – glamorous rarities that illuminate brief moments in the vast span of human history. Now, it had found a use for the great mass of ancient material, from prehistoric flints to mediaeval pots – the mundane artefacts that, by simple virtue of their ubiquity, allow us to map great tracts of time to and place individual sites within their context.

Using this method of dating, Petrie soon identified three separate phases of this 'Nagada period' – culminating in 'Dynasty 0', the inhabitants of Egypt in the era directly before it was unified under the first pharaohs.

Petrie now went on to dig at Abydos, the cult centre of Osiris, God of the Underworld. French archaeologist Émile Amélineau, who held the exclusive permission to dig here until Maspero rescinded it, had made a complete hash of excavating the earliest mud-brick tombs, determined to prove his personal theory that Osiris was a historical figure. Picking over the wreckage, Petrie nevertheless made some remarkable discoveries: he identified the tombs of the very first pharaohs – including Narmer, who had first unified Upper and Lower Egypt, and many other previously pseudo-historical figures of the 1st and 2nd dynasties.

Petrie continued digging in Egypt throughout the early 1900s, now in company with a young and spirited wife, Hilda, who was 18 years his junior. By this time, Maspero had been reappointed as Director of the Antiquities Service, and the two co-existed well. Many young archaeologists of the next generation got their start on Petrie's famously spartan digs, and it was only with Maspero's second retirement on the eve of World War I, and his successor Pierre Lacau's determination to effectively nationalize Egypt's treasures, that Petrie eventually abandoned his beloved Egypt in favour of the less famous, but equally intriguing, sites of Palestine.

Carter and the Untouched Tomb

From the 1880s onward, Egypt had been in a state of flux – a protectorate governed jointly by the British and French following the turbulent rule of Ismail the Magnificent. But following World War I, the peace treaties that decided the fate of the former Ottoman Empire explicitly encouraged self-determination, and the crowning of King Fuad in 1922 brought with it a wave of Egyptian nationalism. Pierre Lacau, the new director of the Antiquities Service, saw which way the wind was blowing and lobbied for the nationalization of all Egyptian antiquities, so that finds would no longer leave the country without special exemption. This raised a not insignificant question: with no chance to take even a small haul of treasure out of the country, what incentive was there for rich western collectors to finance digs? And without the work of western archaeologists, would Egypt's ancient sites be left to the tender mercies of the local tomb robbers? Fortunately, the improved administration that came with Egyptian independence saw the introduction of improved security for many ancient sites, and the rise of academic, institutional archaeology helped to ensure that western researchers did not abandon Egypt completely. But on the cusp of this change, the old world of privately funded freelance archaeologists would have its wondrous 'last hurrah' – the discovery of the untouched tomb of the boy king Tutankhamun.

This spectacular find was the fruit of a successful collaboration between two men: Howard Carter (1874–1939) and George Herbert, Lord Caernarvon (1866–1923). The fabulously wealthy earl was a man with two obsessions: fast cars and archaeology. He first visited Egypt in 1901 to convalesce following a car crash, and bought his first digging concession a few years later – an unpromising area where the Antiquities Service felt that an enthusiastic

amateur would do the least harm. Caernarvon soon realized that in order
to find richer pickings he would have to convince people to take him more
seriously. In 1909, therefore, he reluctantly asked Maspero for advice about
securing a professional excavator.

Carter was just the man. In his youth he had trained with Petrie, and
previously worked for Maspero himself, but ultimately resigned from his
position with the Antiquities Service when he found himself sidelined after
standing up for his Egyptian employees in a dispute with a group of boorish
and drunken French tourists. From 1905, he had been earning a precarious
living as a freelance excavator and antiquities trader.

The two were an ideal partnership – Carter had the talent (he had already
excavated the remains of Queen Hatshepsut's tomb at Deir-el-Bahari) and
Caernarvon the almost limitless funds. Despite this, their first seasons were
unpromising; their best finds came from the comparatively late Graeco-Roman
burials at Tell el-Balamun.

However, Carter had ambitious plans. In 1907, Theodore Davis, the only
archaeologist with a licence to dig in the Valley of the Kings, had discovered
a small stone-lined pit containing jars of embalming materials for a hitherto
neglected minor king of the 18th Dynasty. Tutankhamun was probably a son of
the famed heretic king Akhenaten; he became ruler at the tender age of nine,
and ruled for just nine years before his death.

The discovery of the burial pit fuelled speculation that there was at least
one tomb still awaiting discovery nearby. Tutankhamun's mummy had been
a notable absentee from the two great royal mummy caches discovered at
Deir el-Bahari and Luxor. This suggested that the tomb's location had been
forgotten by the end of the New Kingdom period, increasing the chance that
it could also have remained unrobbed.

Carter was convinced that he could find the tomb, but had to endure
several years of frustrating work on less interesting sites, all the time fearing
that Davis might stumble across his prize, before the American finally gave
up his concession and Caernarvon was able to snap it up. The intervention of
World War I delayed things still further, but work began in earnest in 1917.

By the time Carter dug there, the Valley of the Kings had been thoroughly
explored for more than a century and most people thought it had revealed
its last secrets. With no obvious clues to follow, Carter adopted a logical,

exhaustive but time-consuming approach – effectively clearing down to the bedrock across the entire valley. Season followed season with little reward; and then Carter fell seriously ill and digging was suspended completely until his return in 1922.

By the end of the 1922 season, Caernarvon still had little to show for his investment, and the Valley was almost cleared. Only one area remained; a spoil heap on which the builders of the grand tomb of Ramesses VI had long ago built their huts. This had been left until last because its excavation would disrupt tourist traffic through the valley, and now Carter was convinced that it concealed the last resting place of Tutankhamun. Eventually, he persuaded the disillusioned earl to finance one final, short season – if nothing else it would complete the survey of the Valley.

Digging began again on 1 November 1922 and within three days the workmen discovered a set of steps hidden beneath the sand. Caernarvon was still in England, so Carter telegrammed him, re-covered the entrance and set guard over it for three weeks until his sponsor arrived. Soon, the steps were cleared to reveal a monumental stone doorway, with Tutankhamun's name clearly engraved. They had found their tomb.

But what state would it be in? The first signs were promising – once the doors were opened they revealed a passageway sealed with limestone chippings. However, there was still the question of why some of the embalming materials had been given their own separate burial. As work continued, Carter started to fear the worst: beneath the chippings lay a variety of hurriedly discarded objects, and when they reached the end of the passage there were obvious signs of a forced entry. Clearly the tomb had been robbed at some point in its history.

On 26 November, Carter finished making a small hole in the tomb's inner door, inserted a candle and peered through the gap. Lord Caernarvon and his wife, Lady Evelyn, waited with bated breath. Finally, Caernarvon could bear it no longer and demanded to know what Carter could see. Famously, the archaeologist's reply was an awed 'wonderful things'.

The antechamber they had breached was stacked from floor to ceiling with royal treasures: daybeds in the shape of bizarre animals, dismantled chariots, clothing – an entire survival kit, in fact, for the pharaoh's journey into the afterlife. Everywhere, as Carter put it, shone the glint of gold. As the workers began to tear down the doorway it was clear to everyone that they had the find of a lifetime on their hands. The tomb had indeed been breached by robbers (twice, it seems), but on each occasion they had been interrupted and had escaped only with smaller items such as jewellery and cosmetics. Ultimately the tomb was saved for posterity by the construction of Ramesses VI's far grander last resting place nearby. By the time Pinudjem's successor priests launched their operation to recover and re-bury the pharaohs from the Valley of the Kings, they had lost track of Tutankhamun.

Word of the astounding find soon got out and Lacau called on experts from around the world to assist in its preservation and clearance. As the academics converged on the valley, so too did the press and countless tourists and Carter found himself working in a constant spotlight. Europe and the United States, meanwhile, surrendered themselves to Egyptomania in a way not seen since the days of Napoleon and Belzoni.

Clearing the antechamber took some seven weeks – not helped by a stream of VIP visitors (including the polite but persistent Élisabeth, Queen of the Belgians) but on 17 February 1923, Carter was ready to open the doors to the tomb itself. An ugly hole in the bottom of the door showed where the earlier thieves had gained access, and in fact Carter had already used this to make a secret assessment of the state of the inner sanctum. Years before, he had suffered the humiliation of publicly opening a supposedly intact tomb only to find nothing inside, and he was not about to make the same mistake again.

As Carter and his assistant levered away the stone blocks of the wall in front of the assembled dignitaries, they revealed an enormous gilded shrine, the outermost of what proved to be four in total. The extraction of the sarcophagus and mummy of Tutankhamun would take almost a full year, for each shrine had to be carefully dismantled and removed to the antechamber. By that time, Carter's sponsor was dead – the victim of a blood poisoning from an infected mosquito bite obtained in Cairo in late February. Caernarvon's death only added to the media circus surrounding the excavation, triggering talk of a 'Curse of Tutankhamun' that has never entirely disappeared from the popular imagination, no matter how many times it is dismissed by scientists and archaeologists.

Nevertheless, the death of the charismatic Earl did mark the end of an era for Egyptology, and some would say for archaeology in general, for this find was the zenith of a century or more of excavations in the land of the pharaohs, and Caernarvon himself was the last in a grand tradition of private collectors and sponsors of archaeological digs. His untimely demise defused a potentially explosive situation, for it was clear that the Egyptian government would never let the fabulous treasures he had a share in leave the country. Meanwhile, the pressure of working in the public spotlight was beginning to tell and tempers were fraying, leading to a complete suspension of work in the tomb for most of 1924. When it resumed, the new agreement between the Antiquities Service and Lady Caernarvon stated that it would purchase her share of the treasure for a little under £36,000 (one quarter of this going to Howard Carter). The long tradition of Egypt's treasures being for sale to the highest bidder or most daring adventurer was finally at an end.

CHAPTER 6: GREEK MYTH BECOMES REALITY

'I have discovered a new world for archaeology.' (H. Schliemann, 1873)

The West regards Greece as its tap root. For long, received wisdom had it that the first sure fact of Greece's history was the festival of games at Olympia, in 776 BC. Before that, everyone knew, was the 'Heroic Age' age of Homer's epics.

Homer explained that Troy, on what is now the Turkish side of the Aegean Sea, was the scene of bitter war. For the Trojan king's son had stolen lovely Helen, daughter of the supreme god, Zeus, from the Spartan king, her husband. To avenge the insult, the Greeks besieged Troy and eventually conquered and razed it. Homer went on, in *The Odyssey*, to describe the return of Odysseus, the Greek; but it transpired that, while he and his compatriots were at Troy, Agamemnon, king of Mycenae, had been murdered in his palace over another love affair.

Up to the mid 19th century, most readers regarded these stories as impenetrable myths. Repeated intervention by the gods seemed to give that away. Few imagined the possibility of scientific evidence for earlier history. To this day, we distinguish between 'Greek' archaeology and the 'Aegean' evidence of the era up to 1000 BC; but now, indeed, there is archaeological proof for Aegean civilization. The first to provide it was Heinrich Schliemann, in the early 1870s.

Schliemann's own interpretation of the buried ruins of Troy was inaccurate, it turned out, but this hardly dimmed the glory that he quickly gained. For he showed that Troy could be identified precisely and, more generally, that history as early as 1200 BC could be revealed by digging. Schliemann went on to investigate two other major monuments, Mycenae and Tiryns. He wanted to dig Knossos too but, in the end, that was left to Arthur Evans.

Between them, Schliemann and Evans unveiled a whole era of history. Other than that, few men could have had less in common.

Heinrich Schliemann's Odyssey
Heinrich Schliemann was born in northern Germany in 1822. His father was a drunken philanderer but he was also a parson and he evidently taught his

son to love history, including Homer's story of the Trojan War. Young
Schliemann seems to have enjoyed visiting local archaeological sites but at
14 he went to work in a grocery. There, he explained in an account of his
own life, he was thrilled one day when a drunkard burst in, reciting Homer.
But that was not enough to keep him there and he joined a ship to work his
passage to America.

He almost got as far as the Dutch coast when the ship foundered. He took
shelter in an Amsterdam hospital (his health never had been robust) and
soon he landed a job in a business where he showed great talent. Here he
established some of his thoroughness and hard-working routines, not least
acquiring languages; eventually, he boasted competence in 34 (and Dutch
remained habitual for counting). Sent to Russia, he soon set up as a trader in
his own name, travelling all across Europe – staying in the cheapest rooms in
the best hotels. In 1850 Schliemann travelled to California where he cashed
in on the gold rush. Later he described in some detail, how he met the US
President and witnessed the great fire in San Francisco; both claims were lies.
Schliemann increased his fortune during the Crimean War (1853–6) and he
invested very profitably in the Latin American railway boom.

In 1858–9 Schliemann went to the Near East, and visited Petra and Egypt,
before going on briefly to Greece and Smyrna. Five years later, he retired to
live on his fruitful investments and awarded himself a trip around the world
(1864–6), during which he produced an inaccurate book on China and Japan.

In 1868, Schliemann visited Rome and Pompeii before returning to
Greece. Always entranced by Homer, he naively took the poet's description
at face value and assumed that he would easily be able to identify the very
places mentioned in the epics. He conducted his first dig on Ithaca with four
workmen in a search for the ashes of Odysseus – and convinced himself that
he found them, promptly reporting the discovery in a book. One day, with
Homer in hand, he sat down to read about Laertes in the very place that the
Odyssey describes, and found himself surrounded by curious villagers. So he
read the passage out and then translated it for them: 'All eyes were bathed in
tears,' he related, and they bore him off like a hero.

Schliemann went on to visit Mycenae. The going was rough, not least
owing to mosquitoes. Although *cognoscenti* knew the site (a pair of its pillars
were dignifying a garden in Ireland) he was amazed to discover that his local

escort had never even heard of Mycenae. He explored the great chamber of the 'treasury'; and he wondered where lay the tombs of murdered Agamemnon and his companions, reflecting that 'no doubt excavation could recover them'.

Then Schliemann crossed the sea to walk upon the plain of Troy: 'I could hardly control my emotion,' he recorded, in that place he had dreamt of since boyhood. In 1869, having dissolved his first, miserable, marriage, he married Sophia, a Greek of just 16.

Schliemann returned to Turkey in 1871 with his new wife and a permit to dig in search of Troy. On the basis of Homer's description, efforts to locate the place eddied about the respective merits of two different sites. A dig was under way at the site inland but Schliemann aligned himself with the other more recent view that Troy lay nearer the coast, where the Romans said it lay, beneath the mound at Hissarlik. The mound was a 'tell' of the kind common in Mesopotamia, the Near East and in the neighbouring region of Europe across the straits, with layer upon layer of urban occupation. Part of the site was owned by Frank Calvert, an American, who was also convinced that this was Troy. Schliemann put a systematic series of questions to him about his interpretation and about how to dig the mound.

With equipment imported from France and England (notably wheelbarrows) and an increasing workforce, Schliemann cut a great section into the mound. He started sending bulletins to a newspaper in Augsburg and *The Times* in London. The work was terribly dusty, especially on account of the wind pouring through the straits from the north. 'Marsh fever' (probably malaria) struck Schliemann and many of his workmen; and the site was infested with scorpions and poisonous centipedes. He complained that his workers, knowing his interest in decorated pottery, would inscribe plain sherds in the hope of rewards.

The section did reveal walls of the kind that Schliemann had expected to find but they were in the upper parts of the mound and he was convinced that Troy lay at the bottom. Nor did Calvert's part of the site produce much of what they expected, but Schliemann fell out with him over the value of what they did find – notably a sculpture of Apollo – and refused to acknowledge Calvert's own contribution to the project's interpretations. In 1873 he revealed a street and, cutting back along it, two large gateways; and parts of a circuit wall, a

'Great Tower' and a large building were found too. These, he decided, were remains of ancient Troy. Yet the excited reports of his finds in the European press were stirring academic scepticism and criticism. Having excavated what he averred to be 230,000m³ with diminishing returns, he was on the point of calling the search off when he spotted a piece of copper beneath a great wall. Behind the copper was something that glinted like gold.

Schliemann stood still. He glanced at his workmen; they had noticed nothing. He announced a break. Once they had dispersed, he crouched down and started pulling out a hoard of nearly 8,800 pieces of gold, silver, electrum and copper, along with bronze swords. This treasure, he decided, was King Priam's. His wife modelled the jewels and he commissioned a famous photograph of her posing as Queen Helen.

H needed to smuggle the hoard out of Turkey (where he suspected it would simply be melted down). With Calvert's connivance, he stealthily removed it to Athens and showed it only to a selected few; but word leaked out and the Turks persuaded the Greek authorities to find and seize the treasure. There followed some anxious wrangling, especially since Schliemann wanted to dig next at Mycenae and Olympia. Eventually a permit was granted for Mycenae, on the condition that Schliemann should let the Greeks keep everything that he found there but two years were lost in arguing with the Turks about the treasure from Troy. Ordered to pay compensation, he finally sent the Turks five times the fine in order to persuade them to let him resume his dig there. When they did at last issue the permit, it was on an unacceptable condition and he 'exposed' the authorities to *The Times*.

During the negotiations for permission to dig at Mycenae, he had offered to remove the medieval tower by the entry to the Acropolis in Athens. The government took his fund for the job but then used it themselves. For his own part, pretending to be only surveying, Schliemann did start to dig at Mycenae – and his discoveries soon pushed Troy to the back of his mind.

The work at Mycenae was awkward. To prevent Schliemann from concealing another treasure, the government assigned an official to oversee the investiagtion. The official was angry that Schliemann simply cleared Classical masonry and finds away in his zeal to reach the prehistoric levels. Then the work had to stop in order to secure some sculptures against damage by earthquake. In addition, since Schliemann was now so famous, the season was interrupted by visits from eminent figures, including the Emperor of Brazil, who caused a scandal by tipping the local police too meanly.

The Mycenae dig was big. It started with a workforce of 55, which rose to 80 and then leapt to 130. Supervision was difficult and Schliemann was evidently hard pressed to keep abreast of the recording. It is fairly clear that he evaded the protocol for recording some of the more interesting finds.

He began by investigating the domed 'treasury' that he had studied in 1868. Then he found a group of burials richly accompanied by finely crafted jewellery in gold, silver and copper. Soon afterwards came the most dramatic find of his career: five tombs containing skeletons covered with gold masks and breastplates and accompanied by bronze daggers superbly decorated in gold. There were swords, diadems and intricately wrought jewels, Egyptian alabaster, Asian ivory and Baltic amber.

Schliemann felt certain that these were the graves of Homer's Agamemnon and companions as recorded by the Greek antiquary, Pausanius. He considered that the very quality of the finds matched that of Homer's poetry; a gold cup with three handles was the one that Nestor had poured (albeit the bard had erred in describing it as four-handled); and he argued that the find of boars' tusks too corresponded to another detail of Homer's account. Other treasures exposed here had not even been mentioned by the poet; and Schliemann ignored Homer's information about cremation as a rite of burial. The bones crumbled on exposure but Schliemann found one skeleton with 'both eyes perfectly visible'.

The discovery had a mixed reception. In many quarters, of course, there was excitement – the British politician WE Gladstone, contributed a long preface to Schliemann's book, *Mycenae*; but German archaeologists belittled him: one of the gold masks, suggested Ernst Curtius (who had won the permission to dig at Olympia instead of Schliemann), could well be medieval. According to the British consul, observers noticed how 'Schliemann ... recognized Agamemnon's remains the moment he saw them and ... rogered his wife on the spot'.

After a stint back on Ithaca in search of a palace to go with the tombs that he had found before, Schliemann went back to Troy in 1878. The Turks' reluctance to let him return had been overcome not least by international pressure from Bismarck and Gladstone; but the local restrictions were much worse than those imposed by the Greeks. 'I am quite discouraged,' he wrote to Henry Layard (see chapter 7), then British ambassador to Turkey. Schliemann responded with good German discipline, rising to swim before dawn. As for his old habit of secreting the best finds, he seems to have developed new tricks.

His method of digging had improved in the light of experience and thanks also to two new colleagues. Schliemann proved difficult to work with but Rudolf Virchow, a biologist, anthropologist and politician, encouraged him to dig more systematically and showed him how to study the local environment as a source of inference about ancient Troy. Émile Burnouf, funded by the French government, brought the skills of a surveyor to the project and helped Schliemann to take better account of the sequence of layers that the dig exposed. On the strength of this second project, Schliemann published a very large book on Troy replete with contributions from other investigators, including Frank Calvert and the famous Oxford 'orientalist', Max Müller.

Schliemann returned to Troy in 1882. This time, he brought Wilhelm Dörpfeld, an architect and surveyor who had worked under Curtius at Olympia. He was nearly 30 years Schliemann's junior and the two got on well. In the light of what Dörpfeld had learned at Olympia, interpretation of the phases of occupation became an awkward issue but Schliemann eventually accepted Dörpfeld's general conclusion that Homer's Troy lay in the middle of the mound, not at the base.

Schliemann realized, with chagrin, that he had dug straight through it. By his last season there in 1890, he was becoming aware of archaeological complications that would have been inconceivable to him nearly 20 years before, with Homer to guide him. Reviewing his report on the dig, Arthur Evans pointed out in admiration: 'Never before, in any part of the earth's surface, have so many successive stages of human habitation and culture been laid bare by the spade.'

Another golden year was 1884, when Schliemann carried out a brief dig at the site of the Battle of Marathon. Then he turned his attention to planning a campaign at Tiryns, near Mycenae and a monument of the same kind. Having cut a series of test pits there before his season at Mycenae, Schliemann knew about Tiryns.

There was trouble at once, as the Greek archaeologist assigned to monitor him demanded a more organized method of digging that held implications for time. When Dörpfeld arrived, he found that Schliemann had quite misunderstood the architecture. It transpired that it was the remains of a palace to complement the tombs of Mycenae. Schliemann himself was uncharacteristically restrained in his pronouncements; but details of the buildings and their wall paintings were soon to become a point of reference for exciting research across the sea, in Crete.

And it was to Crete that Schliemann turned his attention next, in 1886. Bringing Dörpfeld, he became especially intrigued by Knossos, attributed in folklore to King Minos of the legendary labyrinth built around that giant, half-man, half-bull, the Minotaur. There is a story that, on arrival, Schliemann shocked the villagers by falling to his knees in thanksgiving to Zeus for bringing him. Eight years earlier, a local digger had revealed 'prehistoric' architecture and pottery akin to that of Mycenae and Tiryns. Schliemann set about negotiating to buy the site, but he quarrelled with the owner and the plan flopped. Evidently, Zeus had reserved Knossos for Arthur Evans.

That winter, Schliemann toured the Nile. He was treated like royalty but, invited to visit EA Wallis Budge's dig near Aswan, he stuck his nose back into Homer and replied 'I should like to place my ... science at your disposal by ... explaining to you the tombs, but I have not the time.' Yet he was deeply impressed by the remains at Abu Simbel; and, in the Valley of the Kings he was pleased to find his autograph from 1859, so he added the date of his return.

Schliemann was back in Egypt in 1888 to dig for Cleopatra's palace. That eluded him but there is the mystery about a marble bust that he claimed to have turned up: was it of the queen herself; or, more importantly, had he bought it on his previous tour and planted it? Schliemann then made a third tour, in which he met Flinders Petrie who found him 'the cheeriest of beings; dogmatic, but always ready for facts'.

Schliemann died in 1890. He once boasted that his discoveries had transformed Athens' tourism industry; but the eulogies were warmer farther away. In 1877 his *Times* readers had succumbed to 'Schliemania'; an exhibition was arranged in London and he was received with all honours – though his attempt to buy membership of the exclusive Athenaeum Club failed ignominiously. In Berlin, he was awarded the freedom of the city in 1881 and his Trojan finds were accepted by the museum service. He was invited to work in various parts of the world, even as far off as Yucatan.

In Leonard Cottrell's kindly view, Schliemann possessed 'that exasperating, bewildering yet likeable mixture of shrewdness and naïvety' which can sometimes undermine scholars' false assumptions. He aptly summed up Schliemann's approach as 'a romantic preoccupation with the past' combined with 'inflexible determination and complete literal-mindedness'. Schliemann was intensely energetic; he was driven. He had few qualms over honesty; some even suspect that he planted 'Priam's treasure'. He was headstrong and domineering in his personal life too; none of his many biographers have allowed that the man himself was likeable.

Arthur Evans and the Bull of Minos

The greatest among Arthur Evans's achievements were at Knossos, where he cast bold new light on Schliemann's discoveries at Mycenae and Tiryns. That work was the third phase of a career always lived with energy, confidence and, when he deemed it necessary, assertiveness. Short sighted, he habitually sported a stick called Prodger which he sometimes used for making a point.

Evans was born in England in 1851. His father, Sir John, was one of the leading archaeologists of the day and at 14 Evans accompanied him to the Somme valley, where Boucher de Perthes had found Palaeolithic implements (see chapter 2).

In her biography, his sister Joan explained that 'Evans enjoyed variety of experience against a background of security'; but she also suggested that, his heart a 'secret fortress', one of his 'drives' was a determination to be his own man, not just 'Son of Evans the Great'. He studied at Oxford and during the summer he would travel on the Continent, sporting a romantic cloak until in France, soon after the war with Germany, he was advised to pack it away or risk arrest for spying. Near Trier, he spent a day running a dig of his own in a Roman cemetery. He explored northern Scandinavia, where he and his companions dug into a cave used as a pagan shrine and where he showed the fashionable appreciation of the day for 'folk' arts and crafts. Travelling through the Balkans, he began to develop a passionate commitment on behalf of the region's nationalist movements and here he *was* once taken for a spy.

He settled in Ragusa, in Croatia. 'I love these ... seas that should be valleys, and vales that should be seas ... Blue to-day, tomorrow evanescent lilac, in the sunlight almost white; or robed at dawn and setting in crimson and amethyst.' He loved the life too; the 'customs' intrigued him. He collected archaeological curios, dug into a Bronze Age burial mound and helped a visiting anthropologist to steal some skulls from a tomb. Travelling about, he became familiar with the region's Roman and medieval remains.

From 1877, however, Evans put most of his effort into journalism, sending despatches to the *Guardian* newspaper on the fighting that broke out and its civilian consequences. One assignment took him on a spectacular visit to a Muslim stronghold, carrying a blooming sprig and wearing his cloak with its scarlet lining on the outside. A lot of the wretched events that he reported happened all over again in the 1990s.

In 1882, Evans was arrested by the Austrians, condemned to death and then expelled. That started the second phase of his career. He returned to dank Oxford; he dug a Roman villa but was relieved to leave for Greece, where he met Schliemann and chuckled about how odd he was. In 1884, Evans was appointed to run Oxford University's Ashmolean Museum (the position earlier held by William Buckland). The cliques of patronage were small: three weeks later, his father-in-law was made professor of history.

Evans set about reorganizing the museum. He began to buy from collectors and digs around the Mediterranean, including those of Flinders Petrie (1889). He himself went collecting around the Black Sea and he also returned to Aylesford, in Kent, where his father had dug a cemetery from the last period before the Roman conquest. There he found six urns in good condition and completed a study of them with the art historical approach that became a hallmark of his work; his report is still cited today. His sister ascribed Evans's unusual eye for detail to his short-sightedness.

In 1888, Evans helped to set up a pressure group for preserving the architectural heritage of Oxford and its district. He travelled southwards again and produced a very long article which won the acknowledgements of classicists, resolving an issue about Greek coinage that had interested both his father and his grandfather. He hankered for livelier work but the *Guardian* refused to send him back to the Balkans.

Evans began to notice that many of the objects he was studying and collecting suggested links to Crete. He was especially intrigued by how the variety of finds from Mycenae begged questions about other parts of Greece and beyond – questions missed by Schliemann, in his Homeric preoccupation. Recent German research had suggested that Mycenae owed something to Crete. Then Evans spotted that certain small finds from Mycenae and Tiryns bore marks a bit like Egyptian hieroglyphs. The idea of a link between Crete and Egypt had occurred to him five years before; and discoveries of Petrie's in the Fayyum had recently confirmed such a connection.

In 1894, Evans explored Crete. He noticed that most of the archaeological remains were older than the Classical period. He dated them to the Mycenaean period and before, or what he preferred to call the Minoan period, after King Minos: was Crete an early hearth of civilization? Still collecting, he noticed that the glyphs came in two varieties: hieroglyphs; and a linear pattern of signs like an alphabet. He worked out that Knossos was the key to these puzzles; and he set about buying the site. Unlike Schliemann's concern with Homer as historian, the defining phase of Evans's career began with a question about strictly archaeological evidence.

This new chapter of his life began slowly. Stimulated by Greek military pressure on the Turks all around the Aegean Sea, Crete was enduring negotiations, uprisings and communal massacres. Evans bided his time with explorations on Sardinia and in Libya. In Libya, he showed that ruins locally understood as prehistoric monuments were Roman olive presses.

He returned to Knossos at last in 1900, bringing a couple of seasoned British archaeologists with him, and they set to digging with 30 workers. In less than a fortnight, they began to reveal two successive phases of building. The upper one had been abandoned at about the time of Mycenae and Tiryns after an occupation of about five centuries; and the remains beneath it dated from about 2000 BC. The upper was a large palace; and here they found a lot of clay tablets inscribed like Babylonian ones but in the linear alphabet-like script that he recognized from the gems that he had been collecting. In the lower complex, they found imports from Egypt and Babylonia and brilliant frescoes on the walls. 'A great day!' wrote Evans in his diary, 'large pieces of ... fresco ... The figure ... life size ... the face ... noble ... The arms are beautifully modelled. The waist is of the smallest ... far and away the most remarkable human figure of the Mycenaean Age that has yet come to light.' Some of the pottery was painted most beautifully. Remarkable too were correspondences between these figures and Egyptian pictures of foreigners called Keftiu; and, sure enough, archaeologists in Egypt confirmed that they had found pottery of the kind that Evans now termed Minoan – the Keftiu were Cretans.

It was hard work; and security proved a problem. Heat and malaria curtailed the digging season. Back in Athens, Evans found evidence that seals from Knossos had been sold; but he already knew the inscriptions so well that he could work out which of his own workmen to blame.

Then he discovered that sieving the earth yielded fragments of clay impressions from the sort of signet rings that he had been collecting. A throne room was discovered with masses of inscribed tablets – just what the archaeologist looking for ancient administration should expect. An Egyptian statue was found, more frescoes, and then the plaster relief of a charging bull – soon recognized as key evidence for the Minoans' most distinctive cult, the Bull of Minos. The second season revealed much more of the complicated architecture: halls, stairs, and galleries with wooden colonnades; corridors of power, a veritable 'labyrinth', indeed. (The writing, known as Linear B, was deciphered by Michael Ventris in 1952.)

At times, Evans felt overwhelmed: 230 men were at work; 'everything is so deep .. we have mostly two storeys to deal with, which requires a lot of propping up'. Yet the finds were inspiring: a royal gaming table inlaid with crystal, ivory, gold and silver; the remains of ivory statuettes 'beyond anything that could be imagined'; and captivating frescoes of flowers and the sea and of elegant young women enjoying 'tittle-tattle and society scandals'; 'even our uneducated workers', he remarked, were enchanted. The idea grew that Crete should be distinguished from Mycenae: if Greece was the root of European tradition, then Crete was the root of Greek civilization, symbolized in the myth of King Minos.

Back in England, Evans was honoured like Schliemann. Like Schliemann, he had been providing *The Times* with bulletins. In 1911, he was knighted.

The dig was expensive, not even counting the reconstructions of architecture. 'You are a rich man's son,' he was warned. 'At the other pole to you stands Petrie' – parsimonious Petrie. In 1908, however, the problem was solved when Evans inherited first his father's estate and then that of Dickinson, the paper-makers (John Dickenson was his maternal uncle).

He resigned from his job in Oxford to devote all his time to making sense of Knossos. At first, he was interrupted with the flattering request to put himself forward as a candidate for Parliament; but Evans was no great speaker and the campaign was a fiasco that he soon regretted. He continued his digging seasons and spent the rest of his time in study. One of his principal academic results was a correlation between the archaeological evidence for Minoan history and the Egyptologists' chronology of Kingdoms, Old, Middle and New.

Evans also worked hard on reconstructing the palace for the visiting public. Early on, he began to replace parts of the wooden fittings that had perished and then to reconstruct whole rooms. Now entire buildings were erected. There was also the need to publish his results, both for scholars and in his old medium, journalism. However, newspaper editors had some trouble with his handwriting, so readers were treated to 'The Royal Lamb' for 'The Royal Tomb', or, for 'naked female figures', 'naked French figures'. His last dig at Knossos was in 1931 but publications about the Knossos digs kept him occupied util the mid 1930s at his home near Oxford. He died in 1941.

The immense standing that Evans enjoyed was not necessarily all to the good. If Schliemann's experience with archaeological evidence finally began to correct his dependence on Homer, Evans's conviction about Crete's historical primacy eventually clouded his sensitivity to the archaeological evidence. While he lived, the characteristic assertiveness with which he expressed that conviction prevented an appreciation of the relative importance of Crete, the Cycladic Islands and the Greek mainland in the later part of the 'Aegean' era.

What inspires the archaeologist? For Schliemann, it was Homer and, eventually, the landscape; for Evans, it was landscapes and, perhaps finally, Homer too. In 1922, Evans's crew uncovered a house demolished by what must have been an earthquake. Nearby they found the heads of two enormous oxen set into corners of a cellar – a sacrificial offering? That afternoon, there was a big earth tremor and Evans remembered Homer: 'In bulls doth the Earth-shaker delight'. Four years later, he was wondering of an evening about whether the abrupt end of one phase at Knossos had been caused by an earthquake when another 'quake struck: 'A dull sound rose from the ground

... crashing of roofs ... shrieks and ... cries ... dust ... rose ... so as almost ... to eclipse the full moon'. 'It is something,' he thought, 'to have heard with one's own ears the bellowing of the bull beneath the earth who ... tosses it with his horns.'

CHAPTER 7: CITIES FROM THE DUST

And they said one to another, Come, let us make brick, and burn them thoroughly. And they had brick for stone, and slime had they for mortar. And they said, Come, let us build us a city and a tower, whose top may reach unto heaven; and let us make us a name, lest we be scattered abroad upon the face of the whole earth. And the Lord came down to see the city and the tower, which the children builded. And the Lord said, 'If as one people speaking the same language they have begun to do this, then nothing they plan to do will be impossible for them.' Come, let us go down, and there confound their language, that they may not understand one another's speech. So the Lord scattered them abroad from thence upon the face of all the earth: and they left off to build the city. (The Biblical story of the Tower of Babel, recounted in *Genesis* Ch. 11, v 1–9)

Ask any educated person of either the Renaissance or the Enlightenment period to identify the source of the first civilizations, and they would immediately point to the same area on the map – Mesopotamia, the 'land between two rivers' covered today by the modern states of Iran and Iraq. The rivers in question are the Tigris and Euphrates, which wind their way from up in the Taurus Mountains down to the Persian Gulf. This was the land situated to the east of Israel and was home to semi-legendary empires such as those of the Persians, Assyrians, Hittites and, oldest of all (it was thought), the Babylonians.

This opinion was largely based on the biblical Old Testament – still considered, at the time, an unimpeachable historical source. Most of the tales of these exotic Eastern empires were found there, or among classical texts. Few had seen the evidence for themselves, though a number of widely circulated books claimed to contain accounts of these distant lands. These ranged from the fantastical *Travels of Sir John Mandeville* to the more reputable accounts of Venetian trader Marco Polo (whose authenticity has also been questioned in recent times). As late as 1582, Leonhard Rauwolf, an educated physician and botanist from Augsburg, travelling in search of medicinal herbs, could credibly report that the ruins of ancient civilizations were guarded by poisonous, three-headed vermin.

Although the names of ancient cities such as Nimrud, Babylon and Nineveh were familiar from the ancient sources, their precise locations remained unknown. The most prominent relics of the past were the great stepped ziggurats that still towered above the predominantly flat landscape – most travellers understandably associated them with the biblical Tower of Babel.

The most influential report of the time came from a wealthy Italian traveller, Pietro Della Valle (1586–1652). Frustrated in love, Della Valle left Naples and travelled in the East for a dozen years, at first on a pilgrimage to the Holy Land. From there, the lovelorn Italian was drawn further East by the alluring portrait of a Nestorian Christian girl from Baghdad. He successfully courted and married her, but she died in childbirth after five years, so he had her mummified and continued to travel with her, ultimately reaching India, before returning to lay her to rest on Italian soil. Whilst travelling in Mesopotamia, Della Valle's guides showed him the ziggurat at Hillah and assured him that these were the remains of the Tower of Babel. His description of the ruins inspired the German Jesuit scholar and polymath Athanasius Kircher, some 60 years later, to write an entire book on the subject.

Della Valle was also the first to describe Persepolis, the ancient City of the Persians, founded by Darius I around 500 BC and laid waste by the forces of Alexander the Great 170 years later. In stark contrast to more ancient ruins, many of the columns and walls of Persepolis were still standing, and the Italian's description soon turned them into a fashionable destination for travellers on the trek east. Huge gate pillars and wall reliefs were decorated with the exotic creatures of Persian mythology, themselves artistic descendents from the strange beasts of Assyrian and earlier times.

Despite this promising start, European travellers east of Jerusalem remained a rarity throughout the 17th century. Jean Chardin, an enterprising French jeweller, took a draftsman with him and made the first eyewitness sketches of Persepolis during his work as court jeweller to the Sultan of Baghdad in the midle of the century on his return to the west, his work saw him awarded a knighthood by King Charles II of England and he was elected to a Fellowship of the Royal Society. A generation later, German physician Engelbert Kampfer followed in Chardin's footsteps, returning with detailed descriptions and a sketchbook that was soon acquired by Sir Hans Sloane.

The Mystery of Cuneiform

The first attempt at a comprehensive scientific survey of Mesopotamia ended amid disaster, but the expedition brought back the first accurate examples of the region's ancient cuneiform writing. King Frederick V of Denmark was the inspiration behind this expedition, which set out from Copenhagen in early 1761 aboard a Danish man-of-war. They reached Alexandria without much difficulty, but the intention was to base themselves in Yemen, on the east coast of the Persian Gulf, and they did not arrive here until December 1762. Illness and disease soon took their toll on the sensitive Europeans:

'Mr von Haven [the expedition's philologist] *died very soon, on the 25th of May, at Mokha, and Mr Forskål* [the naturalist] *on July 11 at Yeri, another town in Yemen. After the sudden loss of these two companions, the rest of us decided to go to Bombay aboard the last of the ships that were sailing this year from Mokha to India. On this voyage Mr Baurenfeind* [the official artist] *died at sea, near the island of Socotra, on August 29th, and Mr Cramer* [the surgeon] *on February 10th 1764, at Bombay.'*

This brief account of the party's misfortunes was written by its sole survivor, Carsten Niebuhr (1733–1815), a self-educated geographer and surveyor who had set out on the expedition at the age of 27 and must at times have pondered the wisdom of his decision. For all the misery that the travellers experienced, he nevertheless ended his account on an almost deadpan note: 'Although death has almost entirely wiped out our company, I do not think that this should deter others from making journeys to Arabia.'

The hellish outbound journey would surely have been enough to send most people scurrying for home, but Niebuhr was determined to return with something to show for it all. He remained in Bombay for more than a year, before setting off home overland, and it was this route that took him to the ruins of Persepolis, past Della Valle's 'Tower of Babel' at Hillah, and on to Baghdad and Aleppo. During his travels he gathered convincing evidence for the locations of the lost ancient cities of Babylon and Nineveh.

After a stopover in Cyprus and a second tour of the Holy Land, the intrepid Dane finally returned to his homeland late in 1767. Over the following decade, he published three exhaustive volumes of notes on his travels, including precisely copied illustrations of monuments and inscriptions.

It was the latter that proved to be Niebuhr's lasting legacy. Cuneiform had been noted by Della Valle and Kampfer, but their copies of the inscriptions provided little evidence for the academics eager to begin work on its translation. The biggest challenge was the fact that cuneiform had vanished from use well before classical times, so there were no contemporary accounts of its use, and apparently no convenient 'parallel texts' similar to the Rosetta Stone that would unlock the hieroglyphs. Nevertheless, applied study allowed Niebuhr to make a start on understanding the language. He concluded, for instance, that cuneiform was an alphabet similar to the Roman one: its 42 basic symbols (reduced to 39 by modern scholars) were too few to represent individual words or even complete syllables, but too many for a language that only wrote down its consonants (such as ancient Egyptian). What was more, Niebuhr detected the traces of three different writing systems and found that parallel texts did in fact exist – even if they consisted of inscriptions in three unknown languages.

Grotefend Cracks Cuneiform

A generation later, this was enough for a young German schoolteacher to take up the challenge of cracking cuneiform based on little more than brilliant intuition. At 27 years old, Georg Friedrich Grotefend (1775–1853) began his seemingly impossible quest with barely a passing understanding of eastern languages, but reached his conclusions in less than a year – even if they had to be read out to the Göttingen Academy of Sciences by a more respected academic colleague.

The key to Grotefend's breakthrough was the daring assumption that one of the cuneiform scripts (today called Old Persian I) bore strong similarities to later Persian languages, to the point where certain formal inscriptions might even start with the same form of words. In particular, he looked at the genealogical pedigrees that opened Royal decrees. These typically repeated the word 'king' many times, and also indicated whether a certain ruler was himself the son of a king or a common man. Soon Grotefend had identified groups of symbols that probably meant 'king', and 'son', and had a number of other groups that were likely the names of ancient Persian rulers. By looking at how his cuneiform pedigrees compared with those recorded by classical historians, the assiduous teacher was able to begin matching names – for example, the names of Xerxes and his father Darius sprang out because Darius had seized power after a period of instability and bloodshed, and so his own father, Hystaspes, was merely a prince.

Despite Grotefend's ingenious work, he never received the recognition he deserved. His lowly position in the hierarchy of German academia meant he missed the opportunity to publish a full account of his decryption (it eventually appeared as an appendix to someone else's book) and his discovery faded into obscurity to such an extent that later translators pretty much started from scratch.

The East Indiamen

Throughout the 18th and well into the 19th century, many of Britain's 'imperial' interests abroad were in fact privately run commercial ventures conceived with an eye to turning a profit on valuable commodities imported from the Far East. The corporate behemoth of its day was the Honourable East India Company, a British merchant trading company that had been granted monopolistic trading rights across the East as early as 1600. By giving the company such a wide-ranging licence, Queen Elizabeth I was hoping to create a rival to the thriving Dutch merchants, who were already establishing trading outposts and military garrisons across Southeast Asia.

Good Queen Bess's plan worked out eventually – even if it took a couple of centuries, several wars, and plenty of behaviour that could hardly be described as 'honourable', before Britannia could truly be said to rule the waves. By the turn of the 1800s, the Company's agents had effective control across most of the Indian subcontinent and a fair portion of the East Indies. The Company maintained its grip through a mixture of commercial power, bribery and threat, enforced where necessary by its own private army. Company agents performed a diplomatic role in every major city with trading links to the subcontinent, and a job in the Company's service was a tempting career for young men on the make, be they the younger sons of noble houses, or self-educated clerks.

The East India Company's influence spread far and wide, and it's little wonder that several of the most significant figures in the exploration of the Near East were in fact Company men taking advantage of their official travels to indulge a private passion for antiquities.

Claudius Rich in Babylon

Born at Dijon, France, in 1787, Claudius James Rich definitely fell into the latter category – a young man making his way in the world. Moving with his English parents to Bristol as an infant, he soon showed a prodigious talent for languages and mastered Turkish, Persian, Arabic, Hebrew, Syrian and even a smattering of Chinese. Word of the young boy's talent spread widely enough to attract the attention of a director of the East India Company.

Fostered by the Company, Rich travelled first to Constantinople, then on to Alexandria where he briefly assisted the British Consul-General and perfected his Arabic. Posted to Bombay in 1807, he determined to explore along the way. Disguising himself as a Mamluk, he was able to visit Damascus and even enter the city's Great Mosque undetected. His lengthy land journey next took him through Mesopotamia, where his interest in the region's ancient civilizations was first piqued.

In Bombay, Rich met and won the hand of Mary Mackintosh, daughter of the Chief Magistrate, but they did not remain in India for long – Rich soon found himself posted to Baghdad as the Company's resident, an all-purpose diplomatic 'fixer'.

It was not until 1811 that Rich found the time to investigate the ruins of Babylon, whose location had been reported by Niebuhr some decades earlier. Setting out from Baghdad that December with a party of ten workmen, he remained on the site for little more than a week, but in that time compiled an astonishingly comprehensive survey of the ruins and even conducted an exploratory dig that yielded a variety of stone inscriptions, clay cuneiform tablets and document seals. The following year, Rich published his *Memoir on the Ruins of Babylon*, which – alongside a handful of finds sent back to the British Museum – inspired a wave of interest in ancient Mesopotamia.

Rich returned to Babylon in 1818, this time taking with him a larger retinue. He was also joined by Sir Robert Ker Porter (1777–1842), a noted Scottish artist. Porter, like Rich, had been a child prodigy, elected to London's Royal Academy at the age of 14. His early work had specialized in heroic depictions of the British Empire – most famously a vast panoramic rendering of the *Siege of Seringapatam*, 130ft long. On the strength of this, he had found a position as court painter to Tsar Alexander I in 1804, where he fell in love with a beautiful Russian princess – though it took seven years and a brief exile to Sweden before her father would consent to the match. He received a knighthood from King George IV in 1813, but soon returned to Russia, and it was here that he became interested in Mesopotamia for the first time. Poring over the various illustrations of a single monument from Persepolis, he noted that they varied hugely depending on which particular features had caught the attention of the different artists.

In 1818, the Porters headed south, across the Caucasus on a route that took them through Teheran, Isfahan and Persepolis to Baghdad, where they first encountered Rich and his wife. Porter soon gained a reputation for the accuracy of his draftsmanship, and he spent the next two years travelling widely around Mesopotamia. He risked his life scaling the sheer rockface at the entrance to the tomb of Darius the Great at Naqhi Rustam near Persepolis, and accompanied Rich on both his return to Babylon and his journey to Birs Nimrud, the huge eroded ziggurat that stood above the River Tigris near Mosul. In 1821 he returned to Britain and published a journal of his travels that only increased public interest in the region. That same year, Rich died at the age of just 34, paying the price for his refusal to abandon the sick and dying in the cholera-stricken city of Shiraz. Porter would lose his own wife to typhus a few years later and spent his remaining years as British consul in Venezuela.

Rawlinson and the Key to Cuneiform

One of the most intriguing stops on Porter's itinerary had been the impressive inscription at Behistun (present-day Bisutun in western Iran). Here, carved above a ledge some 100m up the side of a sheer cliff face, he could vaguely make out the figures of various chieftains clearly paying tribute to a great king, surrounded by a huge mass of illegible cuneiform writing. Unable to reach the ledge or translate the writing, Porter interpreted it as a commemoration of 'The Ten Tribes before Shalmaneser'. On this occasion, however, Porter was mistaken. And it was to be almost three decades before the scene was properly identified. That breakthrough would fall to another Company man, Henry Creswicke Rawlinson (1810–1895).

The son of Oxfordshire landowners, Rawlinson signed up with the military service of the East India Company at just 17. On his way out to India, he spent four months aboard ship with the newly appointed Governor of Bombay, the distinguished soldier Sir John Malcolm. Malcolm had risen to prominence partly through bravery on the battlefield, but also through his diplomatic abilities and mastery of various eastern languages. He had already written the first popular histories of the Indian subcontinent, based largely on his own translations of various Indian epics, and his stories fired the young Rawlinson with interest in the linguistic and historical mysteries of the East. During his years in India, he busied himself with the study of Persian and other languages and as a result was well suited to his next posting – helping to train troops for the Shah of Persia's army. Arriving in 1835, he soon heard tell of the Behistun inscription, and in 1837 he took leave from his duties to go and see the mighty outcrop for himself. Frustrated with the view from below, he was lowered over the jagged precipice at the top and, while hanging a hundred metres above the valley floor, painstakingly recorded the closely packed cuneiform symbols arranged in blocks along the monument's 20m length.

Here Rawlinson knew he had the work of a lifetime, for the inscription was, he suspected, the same text rendered in the three different forms of cuneiform writing. By this time, Grotefend's breakthrough in the translation of 'Old Persian' was largely forgotten, so Rawlinson had to begin from scratch. Through the following years, and despite constant interruptions from his military duties, the young soldier had the drawings constantly at his side as he rose through the ranks and he returned to the site frequently. After distinguishing himself in the First Afghan War, he was knighted in 1844 and granted an appointment as consul-general at Baghdad that finally allowed him some spare time for his studies.

Rawlinson's decryption of the Old Persian inscription at Behistun now became almost as rapid as Grotefend's earlier breakthrough. He published a full translation in 1846 and was widely acclaimed during his subsequent return to Britain. Working on the premise that the inscriptions were indeed parallel, Rawlinson and other leading philologists attempted to unravel the structure of the other languages, known today as Elamitic and Babylonian. By the early 1850s, however, a note of despair had set in: the Old Persian provided a key to the meaning of the other two inscriptions at Behistun, but when this key was used in attempts to unlock other texts, it stubbornly refused to turn – the result was gibberish.

The breakthrough, when it came, was sudden. Irish linguist Edward Hincks suggested that Babylonian, unlike Old Persian, used symbols to represent syllables rather than individual letters, thus each symbol would incorporate a vowel sound, plus its preceding or succeeding consonant. Then Rawlinson himself suggested an additional level of complexity known as polyphony – put simply, this meant that each symbol in the more ancient languages could have several different pronunciations depending on their position and context in a word or sentence.

The matter was finally settled in 1857, when William Henry Fox Talbot (better known to history as the inventor of the photographic negative) wrote to the Royal Asiatic Society. He had applied the methods suggested by Rawlinson and Hincks to one of the inscriptions lately arrived from Nineveh (see below), and proposed that these two scholars should attempt their own translations (a third competitor, the Franco-German Jules Oppert, was later invited to join in). When a commission reviewed all the translations, they proved to be remarkably similar – confirming that the mysteries of cuneiform had at last been mastered.

Layard and the City of Nineveh

Although the early 19th century linguists played a key role in bringing the world of the ancient Near East back to life, their explorations 'on the spot' brought back little in the way of archaeological treasure. Most of the material that made its way to the west was in the form of small inscribed tablets and seals.

In 1839, a young man set sail from Dover with dreams of changing all that. Austen Henry Layard had recently qualified to practise law, and ostensibly his plan was to travel to Ceylon and establish himself in business there. However, for this ambitious 22-year-old, the journey was of more interest than the final destination.

Layard (1817–1894) had lived a peripatetic childhood, dragged this way and that across Europe in a constant tug of war between his asthmatic father's quest for a lenient climate, and his overbearing lawyer uncle's ideas about how a young Englishman should be bought up. A brief but happy period in Florence fired his interest in antiquities, particularly when the old palace where they rented the lower floors from cash-strapped nobility proved to have a mysterious locked door. The young Henry purloined the key and slipped inside, and was horrified but fascinated to find the door concealed a private chapel where the embalmed remains of a medieval lady were preserved in a glass coffin. The sight gave him nightmares for months afterwards, but ensured a lifelong fascination with the gothic and uncanny. He eagerly devoured much of his father's library and was especially fascinated by the *Arabian Nights' Entertainment*, the popular anthology of Eastern tales introduced to Europe by Antoine Galland in the early 18th century.

Henry's sojourn in Florence was brought to an end by a stern edict from his uncle Benjamin Austen, who 'advised' that the Layard boys should be sent to English boarding schools to complete their education. Their parents remained in Florence for the sake of their father's health, so Henry saw little of them in the years that followed. Although he did reasonably well at school, his less travelled classmates viewed him with suspicion and he made few friends. Henry consoled himself in reading tales of the exotic East and, when staying at his uncle's London house during the holidays, visiting the British Museum. Benjamin Austen considered such interests as pointless distractions and had already formed his own plan that the boy should study law as an unpaid clerk, so Henry was unceremoniously pulled out of school at the age of 16 and found himself living alone in a lodging house whilst working from morning to night at his uncle's nearby offices.

The one recompense for all this agony was Benjamin Austen's Sunday lunches, to which Henry was invited. The attraction was not in the food but in the guests, for his well connected aunt frequently invited notable figures, including the painter JMW Turner, the poet William Wordsworth and an up-and-coming politician called Benjamin Disraeli. Most inspiring of all, though, was Sir Charles Fellows, a distinguished traveller who had recently returned from Asia Minor.

With Henry seemingly in his thrall, Benjamin Austen now issued a another edict to his parents, suggesting they should return to England, but the autumn of 1834 saw Henry's father take a turn for the worse that ended in his premature death. Once Henry was over the shock, he began to rebel against his uncle, holidaying each summer in different parts of Europe and losing himself in their art and antiquities. He made little attempt to conceal his contempt for the law from Austen, and his uncle in turn made it clear that he would not consider making Henry a partner unless he changed his ways.

Salvation arrived in the shape of another uncle, Charles Layard. Charles worked as a government agent in Ceylon, where Henry's father had also been an official before his illness. He suggested that if Henry completed his apprenticeship, he would easily find work in the colonies.

Although this did not make the prospect of a career in law any more attractive to Henry, it did at least offer a prospect of escape and foreign travel. The young Layard knuckled down to pass his exams, and at the same time began to plan an ambitious overland journey to Ceylon. His uncle had introduced him to a potential travelling companion, Edward Mitford, who was travelling to Ceylon as a coffee planter and was anxious to avoid the long sea route on account of seasickness. Sir Charles Fellows enthusiastically endorsed the scheme, advising Henry on his route, and securing various letters of introduction and a commission from the Royal Geographical Society.

Layard and Mitford's travels took them across central Europe to Montenegro, then on into the Ottoman Empire. They crossed the Bosphorus at Constantinople (now Istanbul) and, travelling light but well armed, began their explorations of Asia Minor. The native Turks were largely welcoming, and they were able to map a new route through the ancient Christian settlements at Lystra, across the Taurus Mountains and down to Tarsus on the shores of the Mediterranean. Along the way, Layard made detailed notes and drawings of the various monuments and inscriptions they found.

From here, they continued to Jerusalem, where they decided to go their separate ways temporarily. Layard was keen to see for himself the city of Petra, discovered by Johann Ludwig Burckhardt some 30 years before, while Mitford was discouraged by reports of ferocious natives and bandits along the way (and was possibly tiring by now of Layard's endless archaeological diversions). The pair agreed to rendezvous at Aleppo; Layard recruited a local Christian Arab lad as his servant before setting out in company with a party of armed Bedouin.

Despite a hostile reception at Petra, Layard was able to enter the city through a mixture of diplomacy and veiled threats about what might happen if his party was harmed. From here, he travelled on through present-day Jordan, heading for Damascus. Twice along this route, he and his servant Antonio were ambushed. The first time, Layard escaped unmolested after holding the bandit chief at gunpoint. The second time, a party of deserters from the

Egyptian army got the better of them, stealing their money and clothes. Eventually they tracked down a local guide who got them to Damascus, where Layard threw himself on the mercy of the local British Consul.

Reunited at Aleppo, Mitford and Layard set out on the next step of their journey, to Baghdad, scene of Henry's boyhood fantasies. As they travelled along the banks of the Tigris, they caught their first glimpse of the mounds of Kuyunjik, thought to conceal the ruins of the great city of Nineveh. Further downriver, Layard took a diversion to see the great hill of Nimrud (said to be the ruins of a city associated with the biblical hunter Nimrod). Local legends about the treasures that lay hidden in these lost cities were intriguing, but there was little time for more than a cursory investigation. Layard resolved that he would return when time allowed, and dig out the mysteries of Nineveh for himself.

The journey from Baghdad into Persia finally brought an end to Layard's travelling partnership with Mitford. Forbidden from taking their intended course thanks to a territorial dispute and local hostility to the British, Mitford opted to take the open route along the coast of the Persian Gulf, while Layard was eager to negotiate a passage through less well-known territory.

In order to secure a permit to travel, Layard now had to track down Taki Khan, the local chief in a rugged region of the Bakhtiyari tribe. Arriving at the Khan's stronghold of Kala Tul in the Zagros Mountains, he found that the leader was absent on tribal business and his court was in a state of consternation. The Khan's son was dangerously ill with a fever, and the local physicians had exhausted their knowledge with little result. Layard was carrying with him a selection of medicines and willingly volunteered doses of quinine to help ease the fever, but on two occasions these went unused after the Khan's wife consulted the local mullah, who advised against the western medicine. The boy was close to death when his father returned, learned of the situation and begged Layard again for help. This time the quinine reached the sick child, and the following morning his fever broke.

Layard was swift to extract promises of safe conduct and assistance from the grateful Khan. These allowed him to explore various ruins in the region, first noted by Rawlinson a few years earlier, but upon his return to Kala Tul he found that the Khan had been arrested by the Persian Shah for non-payment of taxes. Layard found himself caught up in a daring but doomed rescue attempt that ultimately left him lost in the harsh mountains of the region. His misfortunes did not end there: when he reached civilization at the town of Shustar, he was put under house arrest by the local governor and had to make his escape once again. Joining up with a messenger on East India Company business, Layard headed for Baghdad, but the pair were ambushed twice by bandits along the way and arrived at the city gates with nothing but the dirty rags the robbers had left for them.

Despite all his misadventures, Layard had now decided to abandon his journey to Ceylon. With his funds running short, he readily accepted a commission from the British political agent in Baghdad to personally courier a message to Sir Stratford Canning, the Ambassador at Constantinople. Along the way, a happy accident delayed Layard at Mosul for some three days, during which time he made the acquaintance of the French Consul, Paul Emile Botta. When Botta discovered that his visitor shared his passion for archaeology, he took him across the river in order to show him the trenches he had been digging among the mounds at Kuyunjik. To Botta, they were a disappointment; he had hoped to find the fantastic ruins of the Assyrian capital Nineveh, but had turned up little of value, and was now switching his efforts to another site at Khorsabad, some 15 miles away. To Layard, however, they were an inspiration.

At Constantinople, the British Ambassador offered Layard another diplomatic courier mission, which detained him in central Europe for almost three years. On his return, he received details from Botta of the fabulous discoveries he had begun to find at Khorsabad. Layard showed the letters to Canning and argued passionately that the government should fund a British expedition. Henry Rawlinson, now British Consul in Baghdad, added to the pressure. Eventually Canning gave in and agreed to fund Layard's explorations personally, with a promise that, if they proved a success, he would try to secure government funding for more ambitious excavations.

For his first archaeological dig, Layard chose to target the unexplored mounds at Nimrud, some way down the Tigris from Mosul. The Pasha or governor of Mosul had an untrustworthy reputation, so at first Layard claimed he was off on a hunting expedition. He set off down river accompanied by a local British merchant, two servants, and a mason he had hired at the last moment before setting off on 8 November 1845.

They came ashore at the village of Naifa, where the villagers made them welcome (relieved at first that they were not bandits). Layard engaged a local foreman and hired six men to help him dig. They struck lucky immediately – even the surface of the great mound was scattered with fragments of pottery and ancient tablets, and digging down they immediately hit one wall of what proved to be an oblong chamber made of huge alabaster slabs, each bearing a cuneiform inscription.

When his foreman Awad beckoned him aside to show him the fragments of gold leaf he had collected (most likely flaked off the gilded ivory objects found on the floor of the chamber), Layard assured him that they were his to keep; he had no interest in gold for its own sake. However, the incident highlighted a common problem faced by early European archaeologists employing native workers: the labourers rarely saw the merit in the stone and pottery that interested the archaeologists and often assumed that they were really looking for precious stones and metals. This could lead to finds being hidden, stolen, and even destroyed. What was more, Layard knew that the Pasha at Mosul would share this suspicion.

The dig was growing and could not remain secret for long, so Layard took pre-emptive action, returning to Mosul and making his intentions clear to the Pasha. After giving assurances that the Pasha could have any gold that he found and was welcome to send his own agent to keep an eye on operations, he was allowed to continue.

At the end of November, Layard's spirits received a boost when he discovered a wall decorated with bas reliefs showing a battle scene. Enormous sculptures of lions soon followed and Layard resolved to continue working through the winter, returning briefly to Baghdad in order to spend Christmas in the company of Henry Rawlinson, and discuss how the finds might be removed from the site and transported back to Britain.

Layard's most exciting find came on 20 February 1846, when he arrived back from a visit to a local village to find the site in a state of uproar. The workmen had discovered an enormous human head, which they claimed was the mighty hunter Nimrod himself, and one man had already run off in a state of terror towards Mosul. Layard immediately suspected that it was the top of a giant winged bull figure similar to those found by Botta at Khorsabad, and so was likely to be one of a pair acting as gatekeepers to an important room in the palace. A small trench proved his instinct right by nightfall, but Layard's delight soon turned into dismay when a messenger from the Pasha arrived. The markets of Mosul were filled with superstitious gossip about the dig and the governor wanted to halt work on excavating the heads. Eventually Layard had to travel back to Mosul himself to obtain permission to continue working while leaving the figures untouched.

Spring arrived in the valley and work on the site continued, unearthing yet more ornate rooms in the palace. Meanwhile, Layard wrote to Canning in Constantinople, requesting more funds from the British government and official permission from the Ottoman Sultan to continue his work and remove his finds. Armed with this, he would be able to stand up to the whims of the Pasha. When the letter arrived, signed by the Sultan's Grand Vizier, Layard felt confident enough to launch a second front within sight of Mosul itself, opening exploratory trenches on the mounds at Kuyunjik, the suspected site of Nineveh. At first the site proved just as frustrating for Layard as it had for Botta, turning up just a few fragments of sculpture and brickwork. Nimrud, meanwhile, continued to produce ever more spectacular finds – the remains of palaces built throughout the city's period of dominance in the eighth and ninth centuries BC, when it was famous and recorded in the Bible under the name of Kalakh.

By now, Layard had accumulated an enormous hoard ready for transfer to the British Museum, but moving the huge statues and other objects created problems of its own. Rawlinson sent a steamer up river, but the rapids proved too strong for its engines, and it was forced to turn back. Instead, Layard had to build rafts of wood an skin and float them down to Baghdad. There, the cargoes would be loaded on to small boats that would carry them down to the port city of Basra. In order to transfer the huge stone slabs (some up to 2.4 m (8ft) high), Layard ordered that the backs be cut away from them. This destroyed the cuneiform inscriptions often found on their reverses (which Layard insisted were repeated patterns anyway) and stained his reputation with later generations of archaeologists.

By autumn 1846, news reached Layard that the British Museum was offering a grant of £2,000 to continue his work – not a great deal, even by the standards of the time. Nevertheless, this was enough to finance a considerable expansion of the dig. Layard hired more workers and their first task was construction of a semi-permanent village of mud-brick huts for accommodation during the coming winter, partly so the digging could continue uninterrupted and partly in order to deter the thieves who were taking an increasing interest in the excavations. Layard's encampment was a strange echo of the long-lost houses that once clustered around the stone-built palaces of the Nimrud kings, and which would have formed the bulk of any Mesopotamian settlement.

As the dig continued, more discoveries came to light: a second palace, with more sculpted reliefs, more lion and bull statues, and – a particular highlight – a black marble obelisk or stela engraved on all sides with images of a king (later established as Shalmaneser III, c. 840 BC) receiving tribute from his subjects.

Layard's plans for a second shipment to Britain were disrupted by the theft of felts, ropes and other packing materials during the construction of the rafts. Layard suspected that the thieves came from one particular village, and resolved the situation with imperialist vigour. kidnapping the sheikh at gunpoint and threatening to take him and his evidence to the Pasha unless the stolen material was returned. The felts soon reappeared on the back of some anonymous donkeys, along with a peace offering of a lamb and a kid.

Although this headstrong action put an end to trouble with local thieves, a regional famine saw the wandering Bedouin growing bolder. Fearing a raid on the excavations, Layard decided the time had come to attempt his biggest shipment yet – an entire ceremonial lion and bull.

The whole operation was fraught from start to finish. The bull toppled to the ground as it was being lowered onto a cart for transport down to the river (mercifully it was undamaged). One wheel of the cart then became stuck in a disused grain pit and it had to be left in its place overnight; Layard left an armed guard to watch over it, but a skirmish with Bedouin thieves in the night left the bull with a permanent bullet wound. Finally, both sculptures became stuck in the sand close to the river bank, but eventually before they were freed and hauled aboard large rafts for transportation direct to Basra. The operation was conducted in a circus-like atmosphere, with some 300 men hauling the carts, led by an impromptu band, circled by horsemen and followed by a crowd of curious onlookers.

With his funds almost exhausted, his greatest finds safely away and Bedouin raids in the district increasing in frequency and violence, Layard reluctantly decided to close down the dig at Nimrud, carefully reburying what he had not removed. Returning with his retinue of workers to the relative safety of Mosul, he had just enough reserves left to conduct an exploratory dig of his own at Kuyunjik. For several days, his workers found nothing of value or particular interest – the same fragments of smashed pots and tablets, and signs of a fiery destruction, that had deterred Botta a few years previously. Layard had almost given up, and was making preparations for a return to England when the remains of a new palace appeared. He was soon able to collect evidence that this had belonged to Sennacherib, one of the most famous Assyrian kings.

Despite this success, Layard's health and lack of further funding now made his return to England a priority. He was granted a heroic send-off by his loyal Arab workers, and arriving in London some six months later, found himself the centre of attention there, too.

The first sculptures from Nimrud had arrived in London at around the time he was leaving Mesopotamia – June 1847 – and their display in the British Museum had caused a sensation. Now Layard was feted in society and welcomed as a 'star turn' in his own right at his uncle's Sunday lunches. But his requests for new funds to finance further digs at ancient Nineveh itself met with official disinterest, and Layard's disappointment was compounded the following year when the second consignment of material from Nimrud arrived at the British Museum in a shocking state. An inquiry revealed that the boxes had been unpacked, inspected and even plundered by curious British residents at Bombay before being carelessly re-crated and sent on their way. The result was a public outcry, which Layard capitalized on with the publication of his first book on Nineveh in February 1849. This two-volume work provoked a sensation not seen since the *Description de l'Egypte*, causing *The Times* itself to thunder at the government's lack of support for Henry Layard's work.

Reluctantly, the Treasury paid up: he was offered an official post at the Constantinople Embassy and £3,000 to finance further digs. He felt this sum was still a mean one, but was reluctant to cause too much of a fuss. By October 1849, he was back in Mosul, accompanied this time by an artist, a doctor and a Turkish expert, Hormuzd Rassam. He soon found himself reunited with many of his old team of foremen and labourers, and even his trusty horse, Meijan.

Although Layard continued to supervise digging at Nimrud during his second expedition, he now focused his main efforts on Kuyunjik. Nevertheless, Nimrud provided the first spectacular find – the great hall of the palace of King Sennacherib. Bas-reliefs decorating one side of the hall recorded the precise methods used for transporting the enormous bull statues, while the other side showed scenes of warfare and tribute. When the cuneiform inscriptions that accompanied these scenes were translated, they told tales of how Sennacherib had subdued 'the kings from the upper sea of the setting Sun to the lower sea of the rising Sun' (in other words, across an Empire that stretched from the Mediterranean to the Persian Gulf). One passage was particularly interesting, for it told of how Sennacherib had captured 46 cities and fortresses belonging to Hezekiah, King of Judah. This was the first independent evidence to support the Bible's tale of Sennacherib's conquest of Jerusalem, immortalized in Byron's famous lines as the Assyrian coming down 'like a wolf on the fold'. This discovery was soon followed by the unearthing of Sennacherib's treasury, filled with delicate objects given in tribute to the mighty ruler.

Meanwhile at Nineveh, Layard's foreman 'Fat Toma' Shishman had made an intriguing find amid the ruins of Sennacherib's other palace – a library of several thousand cuneiform tablets. As digging continued and moved across the mound to the palace of the great conqueror's successor Ashurbanipal, Hormuzd Rassam found an even more impressive library numbering about 26,000 tablets. With so much material to excavate, Layard did not think to catalogue each item on site; he simply ensured that they were packed and shipped separately to the British Museum. Therefore it was hardly his fault when the tablets were irretrievably mixed together thanks to careless handling in London. Known today simply as the Library of Ashurbanipal, this vast collection of tablets contained about 10,000 individual documents, and its translation hugely increased our knowledge of the region in ancient times.

By 1850, Layard was nearing the end of his resources and aware that he had pushed his health to the limit. The time was coming when he would conclude his digging, but for now he was ready to ship an enormous consignment of 500 cases back to Britain, and he wanted to take the opportunity to accompany them downriver and explore southern Mesopotamia. Visiting Baghdad was the conclusion of his childhood fantasies, but the city was no longer the one depicted in the Arabian Nights and the country around it was teeming with potentially hostile Bedouin. Nevertheless, he ventured far enough to explore Della Valle's 'Tower of Babel' – the ruined ziggurat at Hillah – and follow in Rich's footsteps around the ruins of Babylon. Along the route from Mosul to Baghdad, he left a team of diggers to confirm there was something interesting among the mounds at Kalat Sherghat (German archaeologists would later confirm that these were the ruins of Assur, the capital of Assyria before Nimrud/Kalakh), while in the marshes to the southeast of Baghdad he identified the remains that later proved to be the Babylonian city of Nippur.

On 28 April 1851, having once again supervised the reburial of the ruins at Nimrud and Nineveh, Layard departed Mesopotamia for good. In order to return to London, he had resigned his post at Constantinople; by July he was back in England and already anxious about securing an income. Fortunately, the mania for all things Mesopotamian had only grown in the meantime and he was able to write several more books before eventually beginning a successful second career in politics, culminating in his appointment as British Ambassador to Constantinople in 1880. By the time of his death in 1894, he had seen a new generation of scholars and archaeologists pick up the baton of his work and confirm many of his own speculative theories.

George Smith and the Search for Gilgamesh
The hoard of clay tablets found by Layard amid the ruins of Ashurbanipal's library at Nineveh contained enough work to keep scholars busy for generations, but the translation of their most famous content fell to one man. George Smith (1840–1876) was an ordinary young working-class man with an extraordinary gift for languages. He worked as an engraver of banknotes, but he spent all his spare hours at the British Museum poring over the mysteries of the cuneiform tablets. This eventually brought him to the attention of Henry Rawlinson, now returned to England, knighted, and a director of the East India Company (amongst other influential positions). Rawlinson soon persuaded the Museum trustees to offer Smith a post as his assistant on the four-volume collection of Assyrian inscriptions he was compiling.

Smith's first great discovery may seem dry and scientific, but it proved invaluable to the construction of a coherent history of the Mesopotamian civilizations. He found a record of an eclipse of the Sun, which astronomers calculated must have occurred in 763 BC. Such records are gold dust to archaeologists, for they help to establish fixed points in the midst of the ever-shifting, always-debatable ancient calendars that are usually based on 'regnal' years (measured since a particular monarch's ascent to the throne).

The general public, however, were much more impressed with Smith's next find: the oldest written work of literature, recorded across several cuneiform tablets. First published in 1872, the work is known today as the Epic of Gilgamesh. It tells the tale of a godlike king and his quest for eternal life, culminating in his encounter with Utnapishtim, an immortal ruler who survived a great flood by building an ark.

Six days and seven nights came the wind and flood,
the storm flattening the land.
When the seventh day arrived …
The sea calmed, the whirlwind and flood ceased.

I looked around all day long – all was quiet,
and all the people turned to clay.
The horizon was as flat as a roof.

The habitually religious Victorians were fascinated by this apparent confirmation, in a text dating back more than a thousand years before Christ, of the Biblical flood myth, but there were some crucial fragments missing. Taking advantage of the wave of public curiosity, Smith appealed for funds that would allow him to travel to Nineveh in person and look for the missing tablets. The *Daily Telegraph* newspaper soon came forward with the money and by early 1873 Smith was picking over the remains of Layard's earlier digs. Amazingly, he found what he was looking for almost immediately, along with an extremely valuable genealogy of Mesopotamian rulers that further helped to cement the chronology of these early civilizations. Later that same year, Smith returned on a larger expedition financed by the British Museum. This led eventually to the publication of the Mesopotamian creation myths as *The Chaldean Account of Genesis* (1880), but Smith did not live to see the fruits of his labours – he died at the age of 36, struck down by dysentery on his way to a third expedition in Mesopotamia.

John Peters' American Misadventure

The wave of interest in archaeological evidence for biblical events triggered by Smith's discoveries would have far-reaching effects. One immediate consequence was that religiously inclined American archaeologists became interested in Mesopotamia for the first time. In 1884, the University of Pennsylvania announced its sponsorship of an expedition to be led by the orientalist and protestant minister John Punnett Peters (1852–1921).

Rather than reinvestigate sites that had already been explored, the American expedition eventually settled on a dig at Nippur, a large complex of mounds to the southeast of Babylon. Peters proved an unfortunate choice to lead the expedition: convinced of his superiority to the locals, he followed stern religious principles and was reluctant to make concessions to the traditional way of doing things. It took him two years to negotiate a permit for digging with the Ottoman government, and having done this and arrived in the area with a Turkish armed guard, he saw little need for the small gifts and polite visits that would smooth things over with the local sheikhs. Digging finally began in early 1889 (though Peters took the bizarre step of locating his camp on top of the very mound he was supposed to be excavating) and things went from bad to worse when he ordered his guards to shoot any suspected thieves on sight.

On 15 April, 1889, the inevitable happened when a Turkish soldier shot an Arab man whom he suspected of trying to steal a horse. Soon the local villagers were in uproar, demanding that the soldier be handed over to them. Unwilling to hand one of his men over to certain death, Peters decided to abandon the dig, but before they could break camp the Arabs attacked in force, burning the expedition's huts and stealing whatever they could lay their hands on. Rather than defend the camp, the Turkish guards fled with their own loot.

To his credit, Peters learned the lessons of his humiliation. The following year he returned, taking much greater care in his relations with the local sheikhs and their villagers, and was able to continue digging the site for a further five years. The result was a hoard of cuneiform tablets in a far more ancient system of writing than any known to that time. Dating back as far as 3000 BC, they contained early versions of the Epic of Gilgamesh, including the conclusion of the story in which the king finally dies, only to become Lord of the Underworld. American excavations on the site have continued, off and on, for more than a century, and established that Nippur was a holy city of temples rather than a civil capital; its sacred status ensured that it survived intact while the various city-states of Mesopotamia – Ur, Babylon, Assur and Nineveh – rose and fell from power. According to some archaeologists, Nippur may be one of the very first cities, dating back to at least 5000 BC.

Koldewey Digs Up Babylon

The great city of Babylon had coexisted with Nineveh in the first millennium BC, but its roots stretched much further back in history. When Claudius Rich had dug among the ruins in the early 19th century, he had found baked clay tablets, seals and inscribed stones, but little in the way of architecture. Rather like the lower-class buildings of Nineveh, the bricks of the city seemed to have become one with its soil.

In 1899, however, an ambitious German archaeologist arrived at Babylon with the intention of changing all that. Robert Koldewey (1855–1925) had trained in architecture before becoming fascinated by the buildings of the distant past; his first archaeological experience was assisting on a dig at Assus in Asia Minor. Gifted with great charisma and a passion for his subject, he engaged the interest of the Berlin museums, the German Oriental Society, and even the Kaiser himself in his scheme to explore the ruins of Babylon.

The key to Koldewey's astounding success in the following decades were the great care he took with his excavations, and his sharp understanding of the newly established principles of stratigraphy. Careful excavation allowed Koldewey's workers to distinguish for the first time between unbaked but still-intact mud brick and the surrounding 'matrix' of clay, revealing a host of buildings that would have been lost to the clumsier techniques of earlier times. Stratigraphy allowed Koldeway to work out the precise sequence of construction across the site with unprecedented accuracy.

With a history stretching back for several millennia, Babylon was rebuilt many times, each time adding another layer to the strata of crumbled mud brick below. Koldewey would be prevented from reaching the very earliest remains of the city (dating back to Babylon's original heyday around 2400 BC) by the sheer depth of deposits and the relatively shallow water table. Instead, much of what he found was from the Neo-Babylonian city, rebuilt after the place was sacked by the Assyrian king Sennacherib around 689 BC. During its brief flowering of less than 90 years, the city finally threw off centuries of Assyrian rule, assisted in the sacking of Nineveh in 612 BC, and forged an empire of its own under Nabopalassar and the famous Nebuchadnezzar II. During this period, Babylon was filled with stunning architecture, including the enormous Ishtar Gate (reconstructed by Koldewey at the Pergamon Museum in Berlin) and the famed Hanging Gardens.

Babylon went into gradual decline after its absorption into the Persian Empire in 539 BC, but it survived long enough for its wonders to be described by classical writers and so Koldewey had some idea of what to look for beneath the soil. The Hanging Gardens were supposed to be an artificial ornamental hill built by Nebuchadnezzar to comfort his homesick queen, a Mede princess from the mountainous regions of northern Iran. When Koldewey came across a stone basement with vaulted ceilings, he believed he had found the foundations, but archaeologists today believe that the gardens themselves were elsewhere in the city and the stone cellars were probably a storeroom.

Babylon's other great archaeological mystery, of course, was the semi-mythical Tower of Babel. In the Bible, the tower was supposedly built by the vain people of the city in an attempt to reach the heavens, and so that they might never be forgotten. In order to halt its construction and teach his overreaching progeny a lesson, God scattered the people and cursed them to speak different languages, so that humanity might never again be unified in such a common cause. Although travellers from the time of Della Valle onwards found their local guides happy to identify almost any convenient ruin as the remains of the famous tower, the historical sources were all fairly well agreed that the true tower had stood at Babylon, where it had been described by the Greek historian Herodotus as the Temple of Zeus Belus.

Koldewey soon found evidence of the enormous structure Herodotus had seen – originally a stepped temple 91m on each side, with seven tiers rising to a total height of 91m (300ft). However, this was clearly contemporary with the 'Neo-Babylonian' buildings of Nebuchadnezzar, and could not have been the tower as described in the Bible and other early writings. So Koldewey continued digging until he unearthed the corner steps of a much older temple below. This was the original ancient tower, probably built around 2000 BC and destroyed during Sennacherib's attack of 689 BC.

After 18 years on the site of Babylon, the assiduous Koldewey would probably have continued digging into his dotage, had it not been for the pressing intrusions of a modern world which, by 1917, was engulfed in war. As Iraq became a battleground, and the British Indian Army pounded the exit route to Baghdad with heavy artillery, Koldewey reluctantly returned the monuments of Babylon to the sands from whence they came.

Leonard Woolley and the Deathpits of Ur

While Koldewey was under fire at Babylon, the archaeologist who would assume his mantle as master of Mesopotamia was languishing as a Turkish prisoner of war. C Leonard Woolley (1880–1960) was the son of a London clergyman. Educated in classics at Oxford, he was assistant keeper at the Ashmolean Museum when in 1905 Arthur Evans recommended him for a role overseeing a dig at the Roman fort in Corbridge, Northumberland. Although the young historian had no formal education in archaeological methods, he threw himself into the work with a mixture of enthusiasm and precision and was soon a rising star in archaeological circles.

His first foreign excavation was a dig at the Hittite city of Carchemish, in Syria, between 1911 and 1914. Here he supervised a young and impetuous student – TE Lawrence, who later found fame for leading the Arab revolt against the Ottomans during World War I. In early 1914, Woolley and Lawrence spent several months in the Negev Desert on a combined archaeological survey and military reconnaissance, but with the outbreak of war in November, the two went their separate ways. Woolley volunteered for service and was put in charge of a coastal patrol in the eastern Mediterranean coast. Unfortunately in August 1916 his yacht, the *Zaida*, hit a mine and sank – Woolley spent the rest of the war as a captive of the Ottomans. On his release he spent another season at Carchemish, before returning to England.

Koldewey's discoveries at Babylon, and the ongoing work translating the Nineveh library and other cuneiform tablets, had raised many intriguing questions about the origins of Mesopotamian civilization. Now that Iraq was being run by the British under a League of Nations mandate, the time was clearly right for a return and the British Museum and the University of Pennsylvania agreed to sponsor an expedition that would excavate the mounds associated with the ancient cities of Ur and Eridu near the mouth of the Euphrates. Earlier explorers had dabbled at both of these sites, and they were thought to date back to the very first Mesopotamian civilization – the mysterious Sumerians. In 1919 a short season of digging by military archaeologist R Campbell Thompson suggested that a full-scale excavation would prove extremely fruitful, and Leonard Woolley was soon selected as the man for the job.

Woolley's expedition arrived at Basra in late 1922 and set about obtaining the relevant permissions to dig and recruiting local workers. When he arrived at Ur itself, he found Hamoudi, his foreman from the Carchemish dig, already waiting for him. In early 1923, Woolley struck two exploratory trenches close to the ruined ziggurat and almost immediately found archaeological and literal gold. The very first trench came down on what was clearly a high-status burial ground, with skeletons accompanied by jewellery made of precious metals and stones. With admirable restraint, Woolley realized that his untrained workmen did not yet have the skills to excavate such a delicate and potentially important site, so he ordered it closed and switched his attentions to the second trench, which had found a less fragile relic – a section of an enormous mud-brick wall. By early spring, when soaring temperatures made digging impossible, Woolley had established that this was part of an enormous temple complex.

The dig at Ur would continue until 1934 and there was so much material to excavate that before long the workmen had plenty of experience. Statues, houses, even small and delicate everyday items were recovered, but most important were the numerous cuneiform tablets that helped to reveal the history of the early city. Unlike the later tablets found at Nineveh, these had never been properly baked, so Woolley found himself completing the process several thousand years later – firing the clay in a makeshift kiln so that later accumulations of mud and sand could be removed.

Woolley maintained good relations with his labourers, and avoided pilfering by paying *baksheesh* – a bribe or reward (depending on one's point of view) for each find, equivalent to the price the seller might get from a black-market dealer. Relationships among the camp's European contingent were sometimes a little more strained, particularly where Woolley's forthright wife Katharine was concerned. The explorer Gertrude Bell was a frequent visitor, as was the novelist Agatha Christie, who took it into her head to visit the dig in 1925 (and later married one of Woolley's field assistants, Max Mallowan, after Katharine introduced them). Her time at Ur undoubtedly influenced the writing of *Murder in Mesopotamia* (1936) and her murder victim in that novel, the outspoken Louise Leidner, is often compared to Katharine Woolley.

Woolley waited until late 1926 before returning to what he had dubbed the 'gold trench'. Here, it soon became clear that they had struck the side of an enormous burial ground. It eventually proved to contain more than 1,800 individual graves, often adorned with jewellery and other relics of everyday life around 2600 BC. But most extraordinary of all were the Royal Tombs – multi-roomed sepulchres with mud-brick walls, containing high-status burials and elaborate grave goods. From these tombs Woolley's team carefully excavated treasures such as jewellery, gold cups, musical instruments and the beautiful box-like 'Royal Standard'.

Then during the 1928–9 season came a macabre find that would fascinate the entire world. In one corner of the cemetery, Woolley's workers discovered a single tomb containing the skeletons of 74 people, 69 of which were women, laid out in ranks. Each skeleton wore the decayed remnants of fine clothing and jewellery, and most had a cup lying beside them. There was only one conclusion: that this was a mass human sacrifice and, even more chillingly, one conducted by willing victims who had administered poison to themselves. Although the tomb's principal burial here was missing, presumably destroyed in the intervening millennia, there were several signs that the occupant must have been a king – fabulous objects such as harps and the beautiful 'ram in the thicket' (in reality a statue of a goat on its hind legs, made of gold and lapis lazuli).

The discovery of this mass burial prompted Woolley to reassess the other tombs in the same light. He concluded that the burials of each of these high-ranking nobles was accompanied by a human sacrifice ranging from a few servants to the 74 found in the so-called 'Great Death-pit'. Writing in 1954, Woolley conjured up a ghostly image of such a burial:

'Down into the open pit … comes a procession of people … in all their finery of brightly coloured garments and head dresses of carnelian and lapis lazuli, silver and gold … and all take up their allotted places at the bottom of the shaft … Each man and woman brought a little cup of clay or stone or metal,

the only equipment needed for the rite that was to follow ... The musicians played up to the last; then each of them drank from their cups a potion ... and then lay down and composed themselves for death.'

Even this was not to be the last great find from Ur, for in early 1929 Woolley trumped the Death Pit with a discovery that was to prove a subject of debate and controversy for decades to follow. As he dug down into the city's earliest levels, below the cemetery, he found a thick layer of silty deposits overlying the early settlement. Clearly, the city had once suffered from a sudden and cataclysmic flood, and Woolley was quick to associate this evidence with the ancient tales of the deluge found in Mesopotamian literature.

Others had their doubts of course; similar evidence for a later deluge some way to the north at Kish was found at around the same time. So now the believers had two floods to choose from – and later in his career Max Mallowan added a third, intermediate in date, at Fara. The difficulties of pinning down such an ancient event have led most archaeologists, philologists and historians to assume that, rather than referring to a specific event, the Mesopotamian flood tales are a conflation of several related stories, each warning of the dangers of floods that must have been fairly frequent on the flat plain surrounding the mighty ancient rivers of Mesopotamia.

CHAPTER 8: BIBLE QUESTS

Now Jericho was straitly shut up because of the children of Israel:
none went out, and none came in.
And the Lord said unto Joshua, See, I have given into thine hand Jericho, and
the king thereof, and the mighty men of valour.
And ye shall compass the city, all ye men of war, and go round about the city
once. Thus shalt thou do six days.
And seven priests shall bear before the ark seven trumpets of rams' horns:
and the seventh day ye shall compass the city seven times, and the priests shall
blow with the trumpets.
And it shall come to pass, that when they make a long blast with the ram's
horn, and when ye hear the sound of the trumpet, all the people shall shout
with a great shout; and the wall of the city shall fall down flat, and the people
shall ascend up every man straight before him. (The Ark of the Covenant
at Jericho – *Joshua* Ch 6 v. 1–6)

The Bible presented an enormous challenge to 19th century archaeologists.
For centuries it had been seen as an unimpeachable historical source – if
not the actual transcribed word of God. Recognition that it was the work of
multiple authors who sometimes contradicted themselves and often wrote
centuries after the events they chronicled led to the first wave of 'biblical
criticism' in the 18th century. But as the expeditions of Carsten Niebuhr and
others began to open the way for western travellers in and around the 'Holy
Land', they offered an intriguing possibility for physical confirmation of the
Bible in the form of contemporary evidence.

Of course, the Church had once overflowed with alleged 'evidence'
– famous relics ranging from the fingers of saints to thorns from the crown
worn by the crucified Christ. But many of these had been lost during the
iconoclasm of the Reformation, and those that survived in Catholic countries
typically had dubious and unprovable provenances. Most famous of all were
the widely distributed fragments of the 'True Cross', discovered around 320 by
the Empress Helena (the Christian mother of Constantine, who had legalized
the religion across the Roman Empire). According to the Roman chronicler
Socrates Scholasticus, at some time in the 310s Helena travelled to Jerusalem

on a pilgrimage, ordering that a temple to Venus built on the site of the Holy Sepulchre should be pulled down. Beneath it, she was said to have discovered the crosses of Jesus and the two thieves executed alongside him, as well as the famous titulus reading 'Jesus of Nazareth, King of the Jews', and the nails that had held Jesus to the cross. The tale of the discovery makes Helena another candidate for the title of the 'first archaeologist'.

Soon these relics were dispersed across the Empire. The nails were allegedly incorporated into Constantine's armour and horse fittings, and the titulus was periodically displayed for veneration as early as the late 4th century, though it later vanished and the object displayed today in the Church of Santa Croce on the outskirts of Rome seems to be a medieval fake or copy. The Cross itself was split into countless fragments (though there is no truth to the old saw that the fragments if put together again would have amounted to an entire forest of crosses). Meanwhile, a grand church was built around the Holy Sepulchre itself, destroying any evidence for the true nature of the site in first-century times.

Other famous relics found by the church had accumulated a similar patina of mythology and awkward gaps in their histories. There are, for instance, at least four claimants to the title of the Holy Lance used to pierce Christ's side on the cross. The most famous of all extant relics, the Turin Shroud, only appeared in its present form around the 14th century (though somewhat similar images of Christ flitted in and out of various chronicles for centuries before – most significantly the Mandylion or Image of Edessa, said to have been venerated in Constantinople between the 10th century and the crusader pillaging of the city in 1204). And similarly the Veronica or *vera* (true) *icon*, another cloth miraculously imprinted with the image of Jesus, had a history allegedly tracing all the way back to Christ's journey to the Cross, when the cloth was used to mop his face – but it did not appear in Rome before about 1200, and disappeared again when the city was sacked in 1527.

Since the history of the known relics was contradictory and completely indistinguishable from folklore and hearsay, surely the answer was to find new objects that could be incontrovertibly linked to the stories of the Bible?

In Search of the Biblical Truth: from Robinson to Kenyon
The godfather of this new school of so-called 'biblical archaeology' was

American traveller Edward Robinson (1794–1863), who travelled through Ottoman-ruled Palestine during 1838. Noting the similarities between modern Arab placenames and many of those in the Bible, he published his *Biblical Researches in Palestine and Adjacent Countries* in 1841. His most significant achievement lay in the discovery and clearance of 'Hezekiah's tunnel', a water conduit whose course corresponded exactly to that described in the Old Testament books *Kings* and *Chronicles*. Conveniently, an inscription found within the aqueduct shaft described the date, purpose and even method of its construction.

Robinson's timing was fortuitous, for it coincided with the work of Paul Botta, Austen Henry Layard and others in Mesopotamia. While the American was wandering through the Holy Land and speculating on the links between modern towns such as El-Jib and biblical names such as Gibeon, his French and British contemporaries were digging up the actual palaces of Sennacherib, Nebuchadnezzar and other incidental players in the Old Testament's grand story of the Israelites.

Perhaps inspired by these successes, French archaeologist Louis Felicien de Saulcy obtained permission from the Ottoman governor to carry out various excavations in Jerusalem from 1863. His most important site was the so-called 'Tomb of the Kings' – an extensive first-century tomb complex. Unfortunately for de Saulcy's later reputation, he fell into the trap that has so often ensnared archaeologists digging for evidence of the Bible, convincing himself on little evidence that he had found the last resting place of the ancient kings of Judah. In fairness, he was only following a tradition that had thrived among medieval European travellers, but most of the locals had different traditions and it now seems that this is the tomb of a wealthy Jewish family described by the historian Josephus in his *Antiquities of the Jews* around AD 93.

Layard's successes had helped to inspire the formation of the Palestinian Exploration Fund (PEF) in Britain, with the aim of encouraging similar digs in Palestine that might unearth clear evidence of the biblical Hebrews themselves. Their first expedition was conducted by a party of soldiers from the Royal Engineers, led by Charles Warren (1840–1927), a young lieutenant who had recently worked on the survey of Gibraltar. Warren's new survey had several aims, the most significant being to investigate the Holy Sepulchre and dig beneath the Temple Mount for remains of King Solomon's famed

Temple, destroyed by the Romans after the Jewish Revolt of AD 66–73. The most interesting finds were of more ancient water supply conduits – notably 'Warren's shaft', a near-vertical passage modified from a natural fault in the bedrock, which was discovered by crawling along Hezekiah's tunnel and then upwards.

With the conclusion of Warren's excavation, the PEF switched priorities to another scheme: the ambitious Survey of Western Palestine. This invaluable project again employed British soldiers as its workforce (including a young lieutenant, Herbert Horatio Kitchener, who would find later fame in the Boer and First World Wars). Between 1871 and 1878, it successfully mapped all of the Levant west of the River Jordan, recording not only topography, but also geology, botany and archaeology, and producing a monumental eight-volume catalogue of its results.

Following a hiatus in the 1880s, the fund was pleased to secure the services of the renowned Flinders Petrie for its next project. The mound of Tell el-Hesi on the coastal plain was to be the target, and here Petrie found evidence that this mound and many others like it found across the near East were in fact the remains of ancient cities, whose levels had slowly risen as each successive generation of mud-brick houses was flattened to make way for the next. Petrie's work here helped him to recognize the importance of changing pottery styles as useful dating indicators, leading ultimately to the development of his pottery sequencing techniques at Egypt's Nagada cemetery a few years later (see chapter five). It was during his single short season on the Tell, too, that he realized the significance of stratigraphy in piecing together the site's long history. Today, this principle seems like common sense – that material is laid down on a site over a long period of time, so that younger objects lying on top of it and older objects 'sealed' beneath can be used to pin down the dates. There is more to it than this, of course – and it would be Mortimer Wheeler in the mid-20th century who transformed stratigraphy from one among a number of analytical techniques at the archaeologist's disposal into the overriding principle guiding all archaeological excavations. However, Petrie's recognition of the importance of 'superposition' – the deposition of more recent objects on top of older ones – was a major step forward.

Petrie now returned to Egypt for another two decades or more, but his dig had opened the way for many others that followed, and many ancient sites, famous from the Bible, were excavated in the period up to the First World War. Petrie himself, and Frederick Jones Bliss, who continued his work at Tell el-Hesi, believed mistakenly that their site was the remnant of biblical Lachish, once the second city of the kingdom of Judah.

The fall of the Ottoman Empire with World War I, and the British mandate in Palestine (which lasted until the foundation of Israel in 1948), saw the establishment of a new Antiquities Service, modelled on the Egyptian example. The increased regulation of archaeology in the Holy Land was parallelled by a growing consensus over the early history of the region. Although the idea that the first five books of the Bible (the Pentateuch) were an accurate chronicle of Jewish history 'as it happened' had now been swept aside in favour of the 'documentary hypothesis' that they were put together from the works of several different authors, none writing before the 10th century BC, there was still a belief that the books might reflect earlier, oral histories, and as the archaeologists dug around they increasingly found evidence to back up this idea. The biblical archaeology movement extended its reach well beyond the confines of Palestine, looking at evidence among the records of other countries that had dealings with the early Israelites. So Thutmosis III was identified with the pharaoh of Joseph's time, and Shoshenk I was seen as the biblical Shishak, leader of the Egyptian assault on Jerusalem in the time of Jeraboam.

The field was led by William F Albright (1891–1971), an American professor whose parents had been Baptist missionaries. Typically, many of the other authorities working in the field had also come to it because of their religious beliefs and so, intentionally or otherwise, they tended to interpret their discoveries with a biblical gloss. The rough timeline of early Palestine offered by the Pentateuch served too often as evidence in its own right for establishing the dates of various sites and pivotal events, which meant that, unsurprisingly, the biblical archaeologists reached the conclusion that the Bible's record was substantially correct.

It was not until the 1950s that a serious flaw emerged, when Kathleen Kenyon (1906–1978), digging the famous walls of Jericho, came up with a date for their destruction by fire of around 1550 BC. This disagreed by a whole three centuries with the estimate of her predecessor John Garstang. More importantly, it suggested that Jericho's walls had fallen at a time when, according to the widely accepted chronology, the Hebrews were still residing in Egypt, long before Moses led them back into Palestine and Joshua helped them to overthrow the Canaanites.

Kenyon's dating of Jericho stirred up a hornets' nest of controversy, though recent carbon dating of burnt remains suggests she was substantially correct, and when a new generation of archaeologists began to look more critically at the supposed evidence for biblical history they found more and more discrepancies. Today, the consensus has shifted and most experts see very little evidence for the Hebrews in the right place at the right time. For instance, according to the standard dates, there is almost no evidence for the existence of a flourishing Israelite civilization at the supposed time of Solomon. Clearly something is wrong, and reactions to the evidence have ranged from those who want to discard the Pentateuch entirely as a meaningful historical record, to those who propose radical revisions of the accepted timeline of Palestine and its neighbours (with knock-on effects to other civilizations) in order to bring archaeology and the Bible back into line with each other.

Burckhardt and the Lost Cities of the Levant

While excavations in the Holy Land have always been laden with political and religious significance, archaeologists working in the area have rarely felt at risk of their lives. The same cannot be said for the variety of travellers who went in search of some of the Bible's great enduring mysteries. Their tales are the true stuff of *Boy's Own* stories and adventure movies – quests for ancient and mysterious relics, fabulous treasures and hidden cities, that ended with disappointment as often as success.

The most famous lost city of all has exerted a lasting influence on the Western imagination since its rediscovery in 1812. Immortalized by poet John William Burgon as the 'rose-red city half as old as time', Petra was the capital of the ancient Semitic peoples known as Edomites and Nabateans – traders who commanded caravan routes between Mesopotamia and Egypt, the Red Sea and the Mediterranean. Surrounded on three sides by impenetrable desert, the only access to this fantastical city (recorded in ancient manuscripts as Rekem) was through a steep-sided canyon known as the *Siq* (the shaft). By the early 19th century, the ruins of the city were inhabited by Bedouin tribesmen who guarded its secrets closely, and Petra had retreated to semi-

30. A small section of the Ishtar gate, revealed by Robert Koldewey during his excavations at Babylon. Built around 575BC on the orders of Nebuchadnezzar II, the gate was originally painted in bright blue, and decorated with creatures both real and fantastical.

31. The Tower of Babel: Pieter Brueghel the Elder's painting of the fabulous Biblical tower captures the essence of a vast but ultimately futile engineering scheme. Since it was painted several decades before Della Valle's first reports of Mesopotamian ziggurats, it bears more relation to the classical architecture of ancient Rome.

32. *Austen Henry Layard supervises the lowering of one of the spectacular winged bulls from Nimrud on to a platform for transport back to England. Layard's work in Mesopotamia sparked a wave of interest in ancient Iraq that rivalled the earlier Egyptomania.*

33. *Leonard Woolley displays a bull-headed harp, one of several delicate musical instruments found alongside the bodies of musicians in the Great Death Pit of Ur during the 1928–9 digging season.*

34. Layard's colourful reconstruction of an Assyrian palace was based on sketches he made on the spot and the fragments of original paint he found on the walls and statues. The 1849 publication of The Monuments of Nineveh was an instant bestseller, and helped secure backing for a return to Mesopotamia.

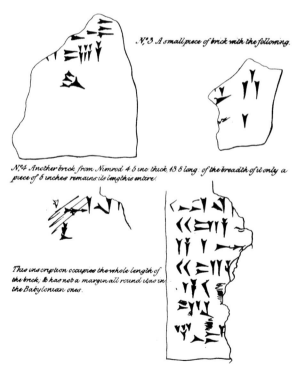

35. Claudius James Rich's careful notes on the cuneiform fragments he collected from around Babylon and Nimrud reveal the inquisitive spirit of an early proto-archaeologist.

36. An imaginative 18th century rendition shows the walls of Jericho falling before the power of that most mysterious of biblical artefacts, the Ark of the Covenant. According to scripture the Ark was always transported beneath a veil of skins from an unidentified animal known as a tachash.

37. Two intrepid explorers approach an entrance to the network of caves in which the Dead Sea Scrolls were discovered. A mixture of incompetence and academic politics fostered countless conspiracy theories about the scrolls' content before their eventual publication in the 1990s.

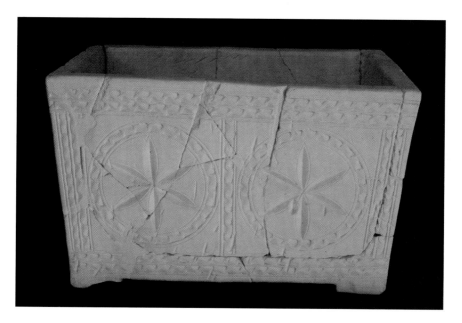

38. One of the cache of first-century stone ossuaries found by archaeologists from a tomb at Talpiot, Jerusalem, in 1980. 'Rediscovered' and publicised by Hollywood director James Cameron and documentary maker Simcha Jacobovici, these ossuaries were used as evidence for a theory that this was the tomb of Jesus' own family.

39. An early postcard shows the white stony ruins of the city of Great Zimbabwe at a time when most Western visitors were convinced it was the home of the Queen of Sheba or other colonists from beyond southern Africa itself.

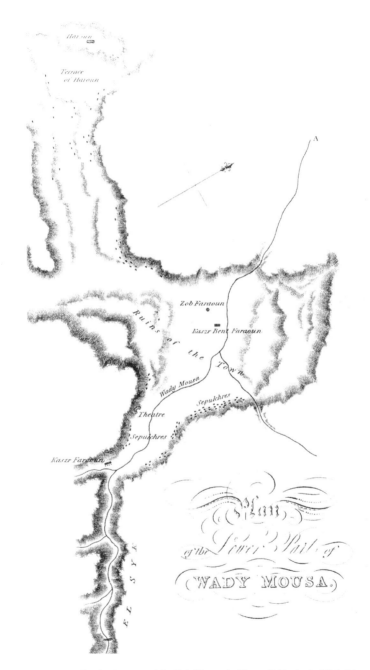

Haroun

Terrace
of Haroun

A

Zob Farnoun

Kaszr Bent Faraoun

Ruins of the Town

Wady Mousa

Theatre

Sepulchres

Sepulchres

Kaszr Faraoun

EL SYK

Plan
of the Lower Part of
WADY MOUSA.

40. *Johann Ludwig Burckhardt's first map of the 'forbidden city' of Petra, hidden in the Wady Mousa valley of southwestern Jordan. Burckhardt's tales of exploration in the Holy Land inspired many of those who would follow with the intention of digging up the Bible.*

41. The 'treasury' at Petra. The ancient city had been forgotten for a thousand years when Burkhardt came across it in 1812 while travelling in search of Timbuktu. The building is so called because the locals believed a giant urn on top of its portico was filled with treasure.

42. *Aurel Stein at the beginning of his career: he was always good company but found later that he was happiest in the wilderness with his assistants, or at his alpine summer camp in Kashmir.*

43. *Some 1,500 years ago the cliff and caves at Dunhuang were sculpted with Buddhist devotional reliefs and carved out to form shrines and monastic cells. Aurel Stein knew about the caves, but he had expected the archive to be sealed up in one of the cells by Wang Yuan-Lu. How he persuaded the little hermit to let him make a large haul of the ancient manuscripts and silks was long regarded as a scandal by the Chinese authorities.*

44. *Alfred Maudslay at Chichén Itzá in 1889, taken by Henry Sweet. Like Waldeck, and Stephens and Catherwood, Maudslay would clean out and convert ancient chambers of monuments for his accommodation. This one is in the 'old' part of the site; note the typical 'Maya arch' above Maudslay.*

45. *The Temple of the Inscriptions at Palenque was studied by Stephens and Catherwood, who were intrigued by its hieroglyphic tablets. In 1952 it was shown that the pyramid marks a famous king's tomb. The steps on the left side of the picture lead to the Palace where Stephens and Catherwood, and then Maudslay, stayed.*

46. *Tikal, amidst the forests of northern Guatemala, had not been recognized as a monument when Stephens and Catherwood were travelling, although the rumour of 'turrets white and glittering' may have been a first report. AP Maudslay was the first archaeologist to carry out extensive research on the site and it is now well known to archaeologists and tourists alike.*

47. John Stephens at the time of the expeditions to Central America and Yucatán. A man of flair and energy, he had a streak of desperation – and a pleasant appreciation of good-looking women.

48. A painting by Frederick Catherwood showing the survey of a Maya ruin. It is probably intended as a picture of the artist himself at work.

49. *Platforms at Iximche (in the mountains of Guatemala), which were visited by Stephens and Catherwood. Iximche belonged to the Kakchiquel Maya at the time of the Spanish Conquest and the platforms supported shrines.*

50. *EG Squier's expedition measuring a monument at Tiwanaku. The inspiration for this picture may be Frederick Catherwood's composition of his own survey. Clearly inspired by Stephens and Catherwood, no doubt Squier wanted to give a similar impression of intent study.*

51. *Ephraim Squier as he would have looked at the time of his research and political activity in Ohio. Squier was an intense personality of whom most quickly grew wary.*

52. *'MH' Mitchell-Hedges and 'Mabs' Richmond Brown size up a ruin in Central America before joining the dig at Lubaantun. Much later, MH claimed that his daughter found 'The Crystal Skull' at Lubaantun.*

53. *Hiram Bingham: an inveterate explorer and a strong man with a sense of vision and the determination to make a mark for himself.*

54. *Machu Picchu among the mighty Andes. It was identified by Hiram Bingham as one of the Incas' last strongholds but it is now thought to date to the reign of the great emperor, Pachacuti, about a century earlier. Bingham showed that the site is linked to others in the same district but today access is tightly supervised for the sake of preserving the whole area from erosion and pollution.*

55. *Sir Mortimer Wheeler: energetic visionary, charismatic archaeologist, flamboyant soldier, leader of men –
and of many women. A well known early television 'personality', he was for a long time considered, in Britain,
the epitome of 'the archaeologist'.*

56. *The exposed remains of Mohenjo-daro, in Pakistan: misunderstood by Alexander Cunningham and confidently, if inaccurately, interpreted by Mortimer Wheeler. Mohenjo-daro is a key to understanding the enigmatic ancient world of the Indus civilization.*

57. *The ruins of the great medieval Hindu temple at Konark (in eastern India) are famous for their sculptures. They include the god of the Sun, the mighty wheels of his chariot, the stallions that draw it and, famously, dancers and other attendants, many of whom are shown happily engaged in various imaginative sexual antics. When Mortimer Wheeler inspected the monument, he ('of all people', puzzled his biographer) was disgusted at the levels of 'smut'.*

mythical status.

The man who rediscovered the reality of the city set a template for many who came after. Johann Ludwig Burckhardt (1784–1817) was a Swiss-born explorer and a naturalized Briton (his name is frequently rendered as Jean-Louis or John Lewis). Like Giovanni Belzoni, the Italian treasure hunter he later befriended in Cairo near the end of his life, he had been a refugee, driven eventually to British shores by the maelstrom of the Napoleonic Wars. Here, he became a trusted associate of several significant figures of the time, including Henry Salt and Sir Joseph Banks, president of the Royal Society. In 1808, he learned that the African Association was seeking young and vigorous men to explore the mysterious interior of West Africa, where the course of the mighty Niger River remained largely uncharted, and the fabled city of Timbuktu was supposedly hidden. Burckhardt volunteered his services and was soon accepted. His plan was to travel overland from Cairo, crossing the Sahara to reach Timbuktu in a trading caravan.

Burckhardt might be called the first 'method' explorer: while other European travellers abroad typically sweltered in unsuitable clothing in the name of propriety, and suffered from the heat and the diet, Burckhardt's preparations for his journey east included long-distance, bare-headed walks in the English countryside during a heatwave, sleeping in the open air on rough ground, and subsistence on a diet of water and vegetables (as well as lessons in Arabic at Cambridge University). Once abroad, he was to adopt the clothing and persona of an Arab trader, which not only helped in the heat, but also served to disguise his European origin. The example he set would soon be followed by other explorers.

The first stop on the journey was Aleppo, a bustling Syrian city at the junction of several trade routes, where he could lose himself in his disguise and also perfect his Arabic. From this relative safety he struck out on short expeditions to explore the area, including one visit to the spectacular ruins of Palmyra, the city supposedly built by Solomon, and later occupied by Greeks, Romans and Persians. After several months, on 14 February 1812, he joined a caravan heading south to Damascus, where he spent a further three months before continuing towards Cairo through the lawless, rugged country of Syria and Jordan. Several times he found himself stripped and robbed and on some occasions blackmailed by apparently friendly guides, but conversely he found the local people in general offered him the greatest hospitality.

In mid-August, as he passed through what is now southwestern Jordan, Burckhardt heard tell of wonderful ruins in the Wady Mousa (Valley of Moses), close by Jabal Haroun, the mountain where the grave of Moses' brother Aaron was said to lie. Burckhardt was determined to see the ruins for himself, even though he was warned that the present inhabitants were hostile and suspicious of strangers. Undaunted, he obtained the services of a local guide and set off for the valley, ostensibly in order to sacrifice a goat at the shrine of Haroun.

As Burckhardt followed his guide into the valley on 22 August, he found himself confronted with architectural treasures that had been forgotten for more than a thousand years. The houses, shops, markets and public buildings of Petra were now mere piles of rubble, but the spectacular tombs the inhabitants had cut out of the living rock had survived almost untouched. Grandest of all those the intrepid Swiss saw on his journey through the valley was the building known locally as the Khasneh, or Treasury – so called because the residents believed a giant urn on top of its portico was filled with treasure.

There was little time to explore, for the guide soon became suspicious of Burckhardt's continued diversions into the various tombs along their way. The locals were obsessed with the idea that outsiders would come to steal the supposed treasure, and only repeated threats as to the fate that might befall his guide if he incurred the wrath of Haroun kept this visitor safe. By nightfall, a goat had been sacrificed and eaten in a hurried meal and Burckhardt was on his way out of the valley, filling his notebook with descriptions of the buildings he could remember.

Within two weeks, Burckhardt was safely established in Cairo and sending back reports of his discoveries that would fascinate and inspire later travellers (who usually had the sense to arrive with armed escorts). The city of tombs was soon identified with the ancient Petra recorded in the writings of the 1st-century geographer Strabo, and the 3rd-century bishop Eusebius.

Burckhardt never made it to Timbuktu; he remained at Cairo for five years, waiting in vain for a caravan across the desert. He was far from idle, though: his explorations of the upper Nile valley led him into Nubia and from here he crossed the desert to the Red Sea. His studies had fostered a fascination with Islam that now led him on to Mecca and Medina, before he finally returned to Cairo. Here he encountered and inspired the recently arrived Belzoni, who undertook to see the upper Nile for himself and set out on one final journey to the monastery at Mount Sinai. By April 1817 his health was failing, and just as the caravan he had waited so long for was preparing to leave, he was struck down with dysentery. He died a few months later.

'Liar' Bruce and the Lost Ark

While Burckhardt's record of his travels made him a celebrated figure in his own lifetime, another roughly contemporary traveller had to put up with mockery and accusations of outright lying. Scotsman James Bruce (1730–1794) was only at the start of his journey when he discovered the famous Tomb of the Harps in Egypt's Valley of the Kings, and inadvertently helped to set off the craze for all things Egyptian. Aged 38, and already experienced as British consul in Algiers, he had decided to set out in search of the source of the Nile, along the way, his wanderings would lead him to Abyssinia (present-day Ethiopia), and the possible last resting place of the most fantastic biblical treasure of them all.

Abyssinia exercised a powerful fascination for many Europeans on account of its very ancient Christian community. Centred on the great city of Axum, the early Abyssinian kingdom converted to Christianity around AD 300, when it was the dominant maritime power off the Horn of Africa. Thereafter it went into decline and became isolated from the rest of Christianity, allowing the Axumite religion to develop its own peculiarities. Occasional third-hand accounts fuelled rumours in Europe that here was the kingdom of the famous Prester John, a mythical Christian Emperor had been variously located in Asia and Africa since the Middle Ages. A potential saviour of Christian Europe, he had been conjured into existence as a response to the implacable threat of Kublai Khan's Mongols, but lived on as an insubstantial ally against later Ottoman threats.

Only a single embassy had ever reached Axum – a party of Portuguese Jesuits. Their mission ended in disaster when their attempts to impose Catholic dogma on the local Christians triggered a virtual civil war. The missionaries were executed for their troubles, and for a long time Abyssinia became effectively a closed kingdom so far as Westerners were concerned – indeed, there was a standing order that any Portuguese attempting to enter the country should be beheaded.

Bruce's plan must have seemed foolhardy when he set out in 1768. Striking out along the Red Sea coast to Massawa, he then travelled to Axum and finally Gondar, where he remained for a year and sought an interview with the king. The tales he told of his services to the king, which included commanding a troop of cavalry and helping to cure the queen of smallpox, did little to increase the believability of his tale. He did eventually reach Lake Tana, source of the Blue Nile, but during his three-year return journey he stumbled upon the river's union with the greater White Nile at Khartoum, and ruefully admitted that he had found just one of the Nile's sources.

Bruce stayed at Axum for a mere two days, but he saw many wonderful sites, including the towering 4th-century stela, 24m (79ft) tall, that was torn down and carried away by Mussolini's troops in 1937 following the Italian invasion (and only returned home in 2005). The details of Bruce's travels were so amazing that, on his return to Edinburgh in 1774, he was widely accused of making it all up. The affair caused a scandal in Georgian society and no educated man was without an opinion on the matter (Doctor Johnson was particularly vicious in his slandering of Bruce). Eventually, things got so bad that the unfortunate traveller was nicknamed 'Liar Bruce', and found that a new edition of the *Adventures of Baron Munchausen* had been dedicated to him. It was almost a century before his true achievements were properly recognized.

One of Bruce's most infamous claims was that the Axum church of Saint Mary of Zion was, according to the locals, the last resting place of the fabled Ark of the Covenant – the casket in which Moses had placed the stone tablets of the Ten Commandments. According to the Bible, the Ark had supernatural powers, most famously the ability to lay waste opposing armies. When Solomon built his Temple at Jerusalem, it was enclosed in its own shrine, the Mishkan. At some point during the following millennium, in one of the many invasions and sackings suffered by Jerusalem The Ark vanished. It was still mentioned as residing in the temple during the reign of King Hezekiah (around 725 BC), and is generally assumed to have disappeared during Nebuchadnezzar's sack of Jerusalem in 598 BC.

Even so, rumours of its survival persisted: some said that it lay in a secret vault beneath the Temple Mount in Jerusalem, others that it had been carried off to Mesopotamia, or even taken to Egypt by an invading pharaoh. The Axumite story was even more fantastic: they claimed that the Queen of Sheba, the most famous visitor to the court of Solomon, had hailed from Abyssinia, and that when she returned home she was carrying Solomon's child. When the boy, Menelik, grew up he was sent to his father's court, where he either stole or was entrusted with the Ark. There were several variants on this basic story, but all ended with the same astounding claim: that the Ark was still lying in the church at Axum, watched over constantly by a guardian monk – a near-hermit and the only man ever allowed to see it.

The Axumite claim to the Ark of the Covenant has been reintroduced to Western readers on several occasions since, but proof has always remained tantalizingly out of reach. Although the tale of Solomon's son flies in the face of the other fragmentary evidence (since the Ark was still supposedly in Jerusalem during Hezekiah's reign), the ties between Axum and Israel do go back well before Christian times, and the Christian community here evolved among a more ancient ethnic group of Falasha Jews. The name Falasha itself means 'exile', but recent DNA analysis suggests that the Ethiopian Jews have none of the distinctive genetic traits of true Semites and may simply be a group of native converts (which itself raises intriguing questions).

The other well known claim to the fate of the Hebrew relic was made famous in the 1980s by Steven Spielberg's film *Raiders of the Lost Ark*. According to this version, the Ark was carried away by the Pharaoh Shoshenk I, who with his army besieged Jerusalem around 1270 BC. In the movie, the Ark is concealed in a shaft called the 'Well of Souls' beneath the lost Egyptian city of Tanis (in reality, the Well of Souls is a cave below the Temple Mount in Jerusalem – another favoured site where the Ark might have been concealed – and Tanis was never 'lost' in the dramatic circumstances described in the movie). Some have argued that, while Shoshenk besieged Jerusalem and demanded tribute, he never sacked the city and so the Hebrews were unlikely to have handed over the Ark.

Other, more outlandish theories include the idea that the Ark was found by the Knights Templar during their occupancy of the Temple Mount (following the First Crusade, around 1120), and concealed in either Britain, France or, in the most far-fetched variation on this theme, at the bottom of the so-called Oak Island 'Money Pit' off the coast of Nova Scotia. Between 1899 and

1902, the eccentric British Israelites searched for the Ark at the Hill of Tara, Ireland's ancient capital: they were convinced that the Ark had been carried to Tara, which they considered the spiritual centre of the British Empire, by an Israelite princess. This was particularly ironic since Irish nationalists also viewed Tara as the spiritual centre of their land; the damage done by the amateurish Britons did a great deal to unite Irish archaeologists, politicians and landowners in finally doing something about protecting their hitherto ignored ancient monuments.

Karl Mauch in Search of King Solomon's Mines

The Queen of Sheba remains a fascinating mystery to many, and the tales of her visit to Solomon, and of Solomon's famous mines in the unknown territory of Ophir, inspired one explorer to adventures far to the south of Abyssinia. Born in Württemberg, Germany, Karl Mauch (1837–1875) trained in geology and was obsessed from his youth with the idea of locating the site of Ophir. As a young man he found employment as a tutor, but in 1865 he set off for Africa, working his passage on board ship. He arrived in southern Africa at a time when it was still a jumbled mosaic of small territories – some independent under native tribal leaders, others settled by British and Dutch colonists. For the first year, he wandered across the Transvaal and neighbouring areas, mapping the geology, testing the soil, and ultimately discovering a rich goldfield in Bechuanaland. Although this offered him the chance of unexpected wealth, Mauch chose to leave others to exploit his discovery rather than let himself be derailed from his initial plan.

Native tribes wherever he went told tales of a great stone city, built by a lost white tribe, somewhere in the interior. Reports of the mysterious ruins had been filtering back to the West from Portuguese navigators as early as the 16th century, and others had already made the association with Ophir, but Mauch apparently first heard the stories from native sources in Africa. By 1868 he had a reasonably accurate description of their location and planned to set off with a German missionary, Alexander Merensky. When the minister had to pull out, Mauch determined to push on with only a troop of porters and an unreliable interpreter for company.

The German ruefully admitted that he cut a peculiar figure forging his way through the bush in a handmade leather suit, carrying an umbrella to protect himself from sun or rain. He took constant scientific measurements of soil composition, weather conditions and local flora as he travelled, and measured the stars to keep track of his position. By mid-August, he had penetrated into uncharted regions of modern Mozambique and was heading for the kraal (homestead) of the local chieftain, Mapansule, when a dispute with his porters escalated and he found himself abandoned in the midst of hostile territory. When 'rescue' finally arrived in the form of a scouting party of Mapansule's Banyai tribe, Mauch soon discovered that the chief in fact planned to keep him as a sort of trophy.

There was just one hope. Mauch had heard tales of a German hunter called Adam Render who had abandoned the European lifestyle to settle in the region with a pair of native wives. It turned out that Render lived nearby, and a letter from a beleaguered fellow countryman soon brought him to Mapansule's kraal, where his intervention secured Mauch's release and saw him safely installed in the neighbouring territory of the friendly Chief Pika.

Prior to meeting him in the flesh Mauch had written with scorn of Render's adopted lifestyle, but the two soon became firm friends and Render was instrumental in helping Mauch to reach his goal. Talks with Pika and his sons soon revealed that he was temptingly close to the great stone settlement, and an expedition to the top of a mysterious nearby mountain (said to be inhabited by a ferocious walking pot) unearthed hints of advanced metalworking and brought the white-walled city within view for the first time.

The ruins lay just eight miles away but were inside the territory of a rival chieftain, Mangapi, so diplomacy was required. Mauch came up with a hunting expedition as pretext for crossing on to Mangapi's land, then sent a messenger to the chief when they were just a short distance from the city. The plan backfired somewhat when Mangapi himself arrived and insisted that Mauch's party come to his village. However, Mauch had managed to get his first look at the ruins from reasonable proximity and could see that they were unlike anything else in sub-Saharan Africa: conical towers and long walls made from neatly cut, mortarless bricks.

After more visits to Mangapi, Mauch was finally able to see the ruins close up. He soon discovered that the site consisted of two distinct parts: the hilltop ruins containing numerous curving interior walls; and a second round enclosure at the foot of the hill containing overturned ruins and a conical beehive-shaped building. The stonework was decorated in various patterns and there were some traces of wood used in the construction.

While the ruins were now abandoned, they had been used for rituals within living memory and the natives were eager to volunteer local folktales of hidden treasures and other ruins, sending the somewhat credulous Mauch on wild goose chases. Chief Mangapi's growing suspicion limited his access to the site and he only managed to make one more clandestine visit. Nevertheless, the German managed to draw up surprisingly accurate maps of both enclosures, which were verified by later visitors to the area.

But Mauch's other ideas did not stand the test of time. Considering he set out to find the mythical city of Ophir, it's little surprise that he unconsciously bent the facts and fitted the native stories he heard around his preconceived theory. The fact that the lower enclosure was known locally as the 'House of the Great Woman' was, to Mauch, clear evidence of the Queen of Sheba's palace. The features of the natives showed that they were partly descended from Semitic people. And the ferocious walking pot was transformed into a folk memory of the Ark of the Covenant itself.

What Mauch did not realize was that the natives were little wiser than he was. They had moved into the area just a few decades before, and had developed their own mythology to explain the ruins that seemed to be beyond their abilities, which they were now repeating to their German visitor.

The truth, of course, was that no Queen of Sheba, no Hebrew miner, ever came here. This great city, once home to 10,000 people, was the ancient capital of an entirely indigenous regional empire, whose history is lost forever. But in the case of the ruins now known as Great Zimbabwe (the name means 'house of stone'), the truth was particularly inconvenient.

When Mauch brought back news of his discoveries, the West embraced them enthusiastically. H Rider Haggard fictionalized them into that apologia for Empire, *King Solomon's Mines*, and for generations afterwards, the idea of white settlers bringing civilization to the barbarous Africans was instilled into every schoolboy. The first travellers who enthusiastically followed in Mauch's footsteps did little to rectify the situation, adding layers of interpretation that showed how Great Zimbabwe was in fact a replica of a solar temple, a Phoenician settlement, or the work of a prehistoric super-race – anything, in fact, but a native African structure.

The motivations for this denial in an age of white colonization are all too clear to modern sensibilities, but even after British archaeologist David Randall McIver visited the site in 1902, and comprehensively demolished the 'evidence' of Mauch and his followers, the myth refused to die. Only the end of white minority rule in what was then Rhodesia finally saw an end to the story and the adoption of the ruins as a symbol of national identity – even to the extent of renaming the country in their honour.

Looking for Jesus
Direct evidence of New Testament times and characters has always been the most teasing challenge for archaeologists working in the Holy Land. This field of investigation has perhaps attracted more charlatans, rogues and credulous victims than any other in the history of archaeology, and here the controversies continue to this day.

Historical evidence contemporary with Jesus remained frustratingly elusive until the middle of the 20th century. The most obvious written accounts, the gospels, were only known from manuscripts composed at least several decades after the events they chronicled; and although historians such as Josephus mentioned Jesus by name and told stories roughly in line with those of the New Testament, these were generally seen as later interpolations into the original history. In addition, some crucial archaeological evidence apparently contradicted the Bible; for instance, there was apparently no evidence for the existence of Nazareth before 2nd century AD.

Then in 1947 a unique find came to light: the famous Dead Sea Scrolls. The story goes that a Bedouin goatherd searching for a lost animal in the hills around the Wadi Qumran threw a stone into one of the many caves in the area, hoping to scare his quarry out, only to hear the sound of breaking pottery. Inside the cave, he discovered ancient jars containing carefully protected scrolls.

This 'lost animal' story could of course be a convenient cover for a spot of archaeological prospecting (it certainly played that role many times for Egypt's native tomb-robbers), but whatever the truth, the documents ended up in the hands of a Bethlehem antiquities dealer. Fortunately, they were offered for sale to Hebrew and Christian scholars who recognized their potential value, and thus the whole cache was recovered. Trained archaeologists rapidly moved into the area and found several more caves, but one of the largest collections of fragments was, embarrassingly, missed by the professionals: the Bedouin who stumbled across it spirited away most of the documents in Cave 4 before their academic visitors realized what was going on. Eventually the fragments had to be bought back from their discoverers at a handsome price.

Despite the publicity surrounding their recovery, the scrolls now disappeared from view for several decades in a maze of academic bureaucracy that fuelled rumours and conspiracy theories about their content. By the late 1980s, just a handful of scroll translations had been published and the treatment of the manuscripts had become an international scandal. The situation only changed when some scholars and institutions decided to ignore academic protocol and publish unauthorized copies of the scrolls, which led eventually to their formal release.

Translated *en masse*, the papyri provided a fascinating insight into the political situation in the time of Jesus, though they disappointed some of the wilder conspiracists. The Dead Sea Scrolls proved to be a hidden library, most likely hidden by members of the Essene sect of messianic Jews at the nearby settlement of Khirbet Qumran. They dated to between 250 BC and the late 1st century AD, and included the earliest fragments of many books of the Old Testament, as well as 'apocryphal' texts such as the Book of Enoch (now no longer included in the accepted Bible). Some scholars have even argued that they contain an early fragment from the Gospel of Matthew. Other works, such as the Temple Scroll more than 8m (27ft) long, are apparently interpretations of Judaic law as it applied to the Essene sect, while the War Scroll appears to be a military manual for the apocalypse that the Essenes believedto be imminent.

Perhaps the most bizarre find of all is the famous Copper Scroll, which has lately been the subject of much academic speculation, several popular paperbacks and a couple of thrillers. As the name suggests, this scroll is made from a roll of flattened metal, etched with a form of Hebrew language found nowhere else among the scrolls. It purports to be a list of treasure caches and their hiding places, and most popular theories suggest it recounts the hiding place of treasure from one of the Temples in Jerusalem – either the First Temple, sacked by Nebuchadnezzar, or the Second Temple, overthrown by the Romans in AD 70. The fact that the Qumran scrolls seem to have been hidden at some time around the Jewish Revolt is certainly suggestive, but some academics see the entire scroll as a work of fiction or imagination – and so far no one has been able to use it as a treasure map.

The Dead Sea Scrolls neatly bracket the era in which Jesus supposedly lived, but (disbarring a few radical interpretations of the Essene texts) they make no mention of Christ himself. Until very recently, some of the best evidence for the early 1st century came from the port city and capital of Caesarea Maritima, built by Herod the Great around 20 BC. Archaeological digs at the Roman theatre in the 1960s unearthed a dedication to the emperor Tiberius from Pontius Pilate, prefect of Judea, confirming for the first time that Pilate was a real historical figure. Another inscription elsewhere in the city offered crucial evidence that Nazareth did indeed exist before the 2nd century AD.

The Lost Tomb

The most intriguing discoveries of all regarding the historical Christ have only come to light in the last few years. In 2002, US television's Discovery Channel and the Biblical Archaeology Society called a press conference to announce a stunning discovery: a collector had come forward who claimed to have recently obtained a small casket made of chalkstone – an ossuary or burial urn for bones – dating from the mid 1st century. What made it special was the inscription on one side, which read *Yaakov bar Yoseph Achui de Yeshua* – 'James son of Joseph, brother of Jesus'. Could this really be the ossuary of Christ's brother, and the long-sought proof of his historical reality? Experts in the history of the period, the dating of stone artefacts and Hebrew writing styles had already studied the box and said they believed it was not a fake, but of course the announcement brought sceptics out of the woodwork, and a fierce debate was raging even as the casket itself was shipped off to Canada for a special exhibition.

Then things got stranger. In January 2003, the same antiquities collector, an Israeli called Oded Golan, revealed another find that was as potentially important for Jewish historians as the 'James Ossuary' promised to be for Christian ones. It described repairs carried out to the Temple of Solomon by Jehoash, son of King Azahiah, and was a good match for a similar account given in the Second Book of Kings. If genuine it would be important evidence for the historical reliability of the Old Testament.

With two such significant artefacts on its hands, the Israeli Antiquities Authority (IAA) determined to set up a scientific commission to investigate the inscriptions. Even before it had reported, the police had reached their own conclusions: Golan was arrested and questioned in March 2003, and a raid on rented warehouse space revealed a huge range of 'historical' artefacts in various stages of production. In December 2004 the collector was charged, along with four others, with running a forgery ring over 20 years or more. The controversy shook Israel's antiquity collectors and museums, and cast doubt on many important pieces of biblical 'evidence'.

It was in this climate of suspicion that the IAA report was published, pointing out various errors that counted against the Jehoash inscription being genuine, and suggesting that the patina over the letters on the James Ossuary had recently been painted on to the older stone. Despite this apparently damning evidence, the IAA has so far refused to let others conduct a critical review of its scientific results, fuelling the doubts of some who suspect a whitewash.

Golan's trial is still ongoing at the time of writing, but in early 2007 another even more astounding claim was being aired in the media. James Cameron, better known as director of blockbuster movies such as *Aliens* and *Titanic*, announced that he had produced a documentary entitled *The Lost Tomb of Jesus*, focusing on a burial complex in the Talpiot district of Jerusalem, discovered during building work in 1980. Cameron and director Simcha Jacobovici highlighted the fact that several of the ten ossuaries found in the tomb bore names with biblical associations – ranging from Mary and Joseph to 'Judah son of Jesus', 'Mariamne' (identified with Mary Magdalene), and even 'Jesus son of Joseph'. The names on the inscriptions had actually been published in academic journals back in 1996, but the documentary producers went further, producing a statistical analysis that claimed the chances of finding this particular combination of names in a single tomb was more than 600 to 1. The documentary even claimed that the James Ossuary came from this site. (One of the original ten ossuaries did go missing, but the original excavators denied that it had an inscription, and evidence presented at the trial of Oded Golan also suggests that he had had the James Ossuary in his possession since at least 1976.)

The documentary aired on the US Discovery Channel on 4 March 2007 to enormous media interest, and a predictable backlash from professional archaeologists and biblical scholars. Of course, the fact that this was a television documentary rather than a peer-reviewed scientific paper denied them the necessary information to make reasoned criticisms, so the controversy rumbles on.

If nothing else, the publicity around the James Ossuary and the 'Lost Tomb' shows that the public still retain an enormous appetite for biblical archaeology, yet all the statistical reports in the world cannot ultimately decide what are essentially matters of faith.

CHAPTER 9: RAIDS ON BUDDHISM

India ... the source of incalculable plunder ... the base of Asiatic expansion ... the most complete demonstration of ... modern imperialism.
(Indian Revolutionary Socialists, 1942)

Archaeology in India began under the British administration, during the Victorian period. The first key figure was Alexander Cunningham (1814–93) who had arrived as a soldier and gone on to distinguish himself in military service; but he took up archaeology and in 1861 he was appointed as the government of India's archaeological officer. He spent more than 15 years travelling across northern India, describing monuments with passionate conviction.

Cunningham carried out a good part of his army duties in the mountainous northwestern part of Britain's 'sphere of interest', where the 'Great Game' of rivalry was building up as Russia consolidated its interests in Central Asia. It was during the height of this tension, in 1900, that Aurel Stein (1862–1943) crossed to Inner Asia from India – the prelude to 'the most daring and adventuresome raid upon the ancient world that any archaeologist has attempted', reckoned Leonard Woolley, the excavator of Ur in Iraq. Stein's biggest discovery was at Dunhuang, but the Chinese long regarded his scoop of manuscripts from the caves there as looting. Cunningham too is sometimes accused these days of 'mining' India's archaeology.

Alexander Cunningham Uncovers India's Past
Cunningham was born in London. His father, Allan, was a poet, esteemed by some as second only (among Scots) to Robbie Burns. Thomas Carlyle said of him that 'he has a heart and mind simple as a child's but with touches of a genius singularly wild and original'. Walter Scott, the novelist, admired him too and helped to obtain posts for both Alexander and his elder brother Joseph in the British army of India.

Alexander Cunningham was trained as an engineer and arrived in India in 1833. By the end of that decade he was entrusted with a mission to Ladakh and Kashmir, through territory unseen by Europeans since Alexander the Great's invasion. At Gwalior, he led an assault in which rebels' guns were turned on their own side. He then distinguished himself as an engineer in both of the Anglo-Sikh Wars. He was sent to establish British power in the foothills of northern India and to settle political boundaries between Kashmir and Tibet and in Rajasthan. In 1856, he went to Burma as chief engineer and, two years later, to the North-West Provinces, where he rose to Major-General.

All this while, Cunningham was cultivating an interest in archaeology. Within months of his arrival he was studying Roman coins from the Buddhist shrine or stupa at Manikyala (in what is now Pakistan) – interpreted, in those days, as the ancient city of Taxila. His report was published as part of a study by James Prinsep, the leading expert on the coins and inscriptions of India. Prinsep acknowledged young Cunningham most handsomely; the admiration was mutual. In 1835 Cunningham dug the Buddhist shrine at Sarnath, again in cooperation with Prinsep.

On his first mission to Kashmir, Cunningham built on another of Prinsep's projects by collecting more than 1,000 coins covering no fewer than 15 centuries. His technical description of the country included remarks on monuments and finds along with an attempt to identify the route of Alexander the Great's invasion. In his second mission to Kashmir, Cunningham reported on the ancient Hindu and Buddhist shrines in which he discerned Greek influence from the Bactrian kingdom established to the north after Alexander's campaign. He also described key features of the way of life, with useful tips for travellers, such as how to cross a river on the inflated hide of a buffalo. He was sent a third time on a political mission, but the Indian, Tibetan and Chinese negotiators failed to arrive and instead he turned his attention to the landscape and claimed to identify the site of one of Alexander's hardest fights. Inspired at one point by the mighty scenery, his father's influence broke out in verse:

Eternal silence reigneth there
Upon his snow-girt throne;
And the unsyllabled dull air
Sleeps echoless and lone.

In the same period, Cunningham took part in a project to work out the history of Delhi with reference to its monuments. More important was his response to the publication in France, of two Chinese pilgrims' accounts of travelling through India in the 5th and 6th centuries. He proposed to find the places that they mentioned on the ground. The archaeology, he urged, would be a better source for historians than 'all the rubbish' in the later Hindu religious texts: it would cast lively light on India's political and religious history, dispelling the notion of her 'timeless' past and implying the possibility of changing Indian culture in future (bear in mind that the proposal was addressed to the funding authorities). He added forcefully that the government should also pay for the preservation of such archaeological remains.

In 1849, Joseph Cunningham commissioned an archaeological report on the ruins of the great Buddhist complex at Sanchi; and two years later Alexander Cunningham joined in with the work. The project dug several of the stupas or shrines in the neighbourhood and found relics of a pair of the Buddha's disciples in two of them. They also found ancient architectural fragments carved so finely that Cunningham attributed them to a Greek sculptor; and he wondered whether some of the evidence here cast light on the origins of the Druids. The carvings and inscriptions, urged Cunningham in his report on the project, 'are almost equal ... to the ... discoveries made by ... Layard in the mounds of the Euphrates'. The shrines of Sanchi (Bilsa, as he called it), stood, he continued, 'still as cities under magic's wand / Till curious Saxons ... / Unlock'd the treasures of two thousand years.' Sixty years later, however, he was forcefully blamed for digging these 'treasures' out too hastily.

In 1861, Cunningham persuaded the first Viceroy, Lord Canning, to appoint him to record monuments. During the next four years he documented almost 170 more or less single-handedly. He was guided by the routes of the two Chinese pilgrims but he also discovered several sites not known from the ancient sources.

His first tour, from Gaya to Benares, included the Buddhist shrine at Bodh Gaya, the great Buddhist monastery of Nalanda and the ruined capital of Rajgir, and he tested the sites by digging. His second tour covered Delhi, the sculptures of Mathura, the Allahabad district, Ayodhya and some of his old stamping ground in the North-West Provinces where he became yet clearer about the influence on the region's Gandharan sculpture of the Greek (Hellenistic) art introduced by Alexander the Great.

The third tour was through the Punjab. In this trip, he identified Taxila correctly as the site that we now know, undertaking a general survey and some test digs; and he returned to Manikyala (previously mistaken for Taxila) and surveyed here too. His fourth tour took him across the central part of northern India: he went back to Gwalior and described the forts, palaces, temples and inscriptions; and he surveyed Khajuraho, attempting to date the temples by their inscriptions – and condemning the most famous sculpture there as 'highly indecent', 'disgustingly obscene'. Cunningham also condemned 'the plundering natives' who had disturbed so many of the Punjab's sites but he overlooked the treasure hunting of Raja Ranjit Singh's two French generals in the 1830s – after all, the terms of his own contract granted him a share of his finds.

Cunningham's budget was cancelled in 1865. He returned to England and devoted himself to desk-based research. He formulated a chronological framework for making sense of India's archaeology. In 1868, the imperial government called on regional administrations to report on archaeology but Cunningham was not brought back to India until 1870, when the government decided to create an archaeology service. He was consulted about the scheme and, in large part, it was his specifications for an Archaeological Survey of India that were adopted. He was invited to run the Survey but only accepted the post after securing twice the salary offered. The rest of his plan was pared down, however, so that in the end the staff comprised Cunningham and two equally energetic trainees, Joseph Beglar, an Armenian engineer, and Archibald Carlleyle (another Scot) who was working as a museum curator in Agra.

The three crossed the subcontinent to and fro on foot and by horse, elephant and camel or carried by litter and, latterly, by rail. In line with his first observations of Kashmir, Cunningham's instructions covered not only the technicalities of archaeology but also how to record features of local life. He was also keen to promote the new technique of photography. It all looked very strange in some of the remoter parts. At Jaugada, in Orissa, Beglar suffered villagers' curiosity about his foreign ways and his camel (a novelty there); and he complained of 'passive resistance' as he tried to record an inscription by the emperor, Asoka the Great – apparently they were possessive about it on the suspicion that it held the clue to a lost treasure. As for Carlleyle, he seemed to succumb to 'bush madness', straying into an area outside direct British authority and more than once losing his camels and his temper.

Cunningham himself revisited several of the important monuments that he had studied before. but most of his visits were to new sites. In 1872 he studied Harappa and cut some test pits there. He 'found very little worth preserving'; but he did comment on a seal, found there earlier, showing a bull and some unidentifiable letters. He guessed that Harappa dated from about 400 BC. Not until 1924 would the true date and significance of Harappa and its connections with Mesopotamia be recognized. Thanks to his assumption that written evidence was the most basic source for history, it never even dawned on Cunningham that archaeology could reveal an era long before 400 BC.

Nor would Cunningham's other judgements be accepted today. Consulted about preservation at the Agra Fort, he recommended that the most cost-effective way to preserve the private audience hall, the Diwan-i-Khas, would be to replace the roof and ceiling in corrugated tin; but even the bureaucrats baulked at that idea. He also endorsed the proposal to peel off the glorious Buddhist paintings from the cave walls of Ajanta in order to preserve them.

On retiring, Cunningham sent his gold and silver coins back to England. The rest of his collection, Buddhist sculptures from the North-West, copper coins and his archive, was sent a little later but lost off Sri Lanka. He returned to England in 1885 and was knighted two years later. The Archaeological Survey of India is still going and today has responsibility for the country's many superb Protected Monuments.

Aurel Stein's Desert Treks

Born in Bucharest in 1862, Aurel Stein had graduated in Germany with a doctorate in the ancient languages of South Asia and Iran. His next research took him to England. He had always been fascinated by the eastern travels of Alexander the Great and Marco Polo; and, during his year of military service in Hungary, he had learned surveying, probably to follow up the childhood interest in historical landscapes encouraged by his father. He developed an intuition for the study of places.

His researches took him to England and his learning and sense of purpose impressed Henry Rawlinson, among others in London. Rawlinson helped to place Stein in his first job, an administrative position at the Punjab University in Lahore, where he arrived in 1888. Yet this posting and the travels that he then began in Kashmir were the only unusual features of Stein's career as an 'orientalist' at this stage. Most of his colleagues stayed put in their European universities, surrounded by texts; more broadly, Stein was guided by conventional academic goals; and, like Cunningham, he sought a reliable income and ultimately security in retirement.

In Lahore, Stein soon became friendly with Lockwood Kipling, curator of the Central Museum (described as the Wonder House by Kipling's son, Rudyard, in *Kim*) and its collection of Gandharan sculpture. Encouraged by Kipling, Stein found himself following Cunningham's footsteps northwards into Kashmir as part of research on a medieval chronicle. He began to survey Kashmir, using Xuan Zang as one of his sources, and in 1898 he attached himself to General Blood's police action in order to reach one especially remote and dangerous district.

As Stein was finishing his research on Kashmir, there came news from Kolkata (Calcutta) of an interseting new historical link between India and the north, this time beyond Kashmir and even the Karakoram Mountains. Scraps of writing in an ancient Indian script but of an unknown language had been found at Khotan, on the southern edge of the terrible Taklamakan Desert, along the ancient Silk Road trade route from China to the Mediterranean Sea. Would this new evidence confirm ancient Chinese reports of a distinct civilization in the middle of Inner Asia?

Stein promptly set out a proposal for seeking archaeological evidence to confirm how Indian – specifically Buddhist – ideas had taken root in that region of Inner Asia. He pointed out to the authorities that the Russians were planning an expedition to the same region and suggested that the indomitable Swedish explorer, Sven Hedin, was preparing to go too. His proposal was accepted and in the spring of 1900 Stein set off with a surveyor, two other assistants, his faithful terrier, Dash, and 16 ponies. This was the beginning of the most distinctive phase of his career.

The first stage of the journey was past the headwaters of the Indus and over the Karakoram Mountains from Kashmir to Sinkiang. In the first stage the trail clung to the mountainsides vertiginously; the weather was bad and the snow already so soft that the ponies slid hazardously. Reaching Gilgit, Stein was impressed by the orderly facilities provided for British India's northernmost outpost. The mountain scenery was staggering (and Stein's photography most effective). Beyond the frontier the hazards were ice, dust and scree; and here the expedition transferred to yaks.

They reached Tashkurgan, which Henry Rawlinson had identified with a site mentioned b, the ancient geographer, Ptolemy. Since it was overlooked by a Chinese garrison, Stein carried out his archaeological survey while the soldiers dozed after lunch in case they should mistake his work as spying. Matters had suddenly become delicate with news of the Boxer Rebellion in Peking; indeed, Stein's luggage included a set of revolvers and ammunition for George Macartney, the region's veteran British representative. Yet, confident that the disturbance would hardly reach this far, Stein took the time to try to emulate Sven Hedin's climb up a mountain of nearly 8000m – leaving all but two of his party behind, suffering from the altitude.

Once into the edge of the Taklamakan, passing the skeletons and carcasses of previous travellers' pack animals, Stein began to learn about how to travel across and through a terrain of uncertain surfaces and unreliable wells. Winter was closing in already but he had chosen this wretched season in order to avoid the ordeals of the summer. His water was carried as ice by camel. He learned not to rely solely on his assistants to attend to details such as his animals' condition.

Stein had a list of sites that had been mentioned as the find spots of ancient documents and he set about locating and checking them. Pausing at Khotan, he was shown a document similar to those reported from Kolkata but he immediately detected it as a forgery – and he recognized the name of one of its purveyors from the research at Kolkata. It did not take him long to show that the research at Kolkata had been based on fakes.

Further enquiries for ancient documents led him out into the desert, where Stein soon learned to recognize the remains of ancient settlements from a less arid era. The preservation of the posts and lintels of little buildings, and of scraps of textile and paper, is utterly astonishing to any archaeologist accustomed to a more humid environment. Stein found coins that helped to date the first of these sites to the Tang period of Chinese history (AD 618–907). One of his leads corresponded to Hedin's report describing wooden walls decorated in plaster with figures of the Buddha and Buddhist gods: no archaeologist himself, Hedin had been satisfied simply to point to 'a new field of archaeology' there in the desert at Dandan-uilik.

At the last oasis Stein recruited 30 workers with the lure of good wages. From there, the journey took six slow days across soft sand. At night Stein had to sleep with his fur over his head, breathing along the sleeve, since 'It was uncomfortable to wake up with one's moustache hard frozen'. Once they reached Dandan-uilik, the problem was solved in part by hacking up the ancient remains of the village's orchard for firewood.

Dandan-uilik had been looted for years but already, in the first day of exploration, Stein found the remains of frescoes and plasterwork showing Buddhist images; and within a couple of days more his men – in response to the offer of a reward – found parts of written documents, mostly in the ancient Sanskrit language from India. Then he found a script that must have served as the prototype for the forgeries studied at Kolkata (eventually it transpired that the script's language had not been known before). In less than three weeks, 14 buildings had been dug and the whole site surveyed, including its avenues and orchards.

A couple of weeks later Stein had followed further leads to a place known as Niya. Here the documents that he found were on wood, which helped him to assign the site to the period before the introduction of paper from China. Here too other artefacts of wood were preserved, including houses and 'two parallel rush fences that still form a little country lane just as they did nearly 17 centuries ago'. He also found bits of wooden furniture, part of a guitar, a mousetrap and a piece of tapestry. Two miles to the north, he found more buildings and among them a scatter of wooden slips bearing Chinese writing. Digging here he found that they marked an ancient rubbish tip, with written wooden tablets mixed up in potsherds, rags, straw, leather 'and other less savoury refuse ... still pungent'. Some of the wooden tablets and their clay seals showed portrait heads drawn in Classical style and the images of Greek gods. Later, Stein referred to Niya as 'my own little Pompeii'.

Moving on, he discovered the ramparts of another settlement and inside, he investigated a Buddhist temple ornamented with plaster figures where he found the oldest known writing in Tibetan, both on paper and in grafitti. There was also a Chinese inscription dated to 719, which puzzled him since Xuan Zang mentioned no place in the region. It was clear that, after Xuan's journey, the Chinese had occupied an older site but were driven out by the Tibetans, who scrawled their grafitti on the walls.

The last part of his trek took Stein through sandstorms to another of Hedin's sites, but this one yielded very little. A runner arrived with the news that Queen Victoria was dead: 'my two Indian followers,' he recorded, 'understood, and in their own way shared the deep emotion which filled me.'

Finally, word of 'an old house' at Rawak led the party to a big Buddhist shrine collapsing among dunes, where they found 91 large, damaged plaster statues. They were made in a manner akin to the Gandharan style that Stein had learned from Kipling. When he returned to Rawak on his next expedition, he found that the site had been wrecked by treasure hunters. His own visit may well have prompted them; even as he travelled out of the desert he heard rumours that his camels were laden with gold rather than scraps of paper.

In 1906 Stein set off on his second and most momentous expedition, which eventually led him to Dunhuang. The idea that he was a treasure-seeker had spread so widely by then that he had to carry handguns through the Afghan panhandle into Sinkiang.

The intervening years had been partly devoted to writing up *Sand-Buried Ruins*, a 'personal narrative', and then an academic tome. The main target of Stein's second expedition was Lou-lan, another site of Sven Hedin's, between the Taklamakan and Gobi Deserts, where the explorer had found the ruins of wooden houses, bits of paper with Chinese writing and an Indian inscription on wood. Stein knew that a French expedition under Paul Pelliot was also making for Lou-lan.

Stein spent time investigating other sites on the way, including Rawak and Niya. His confidence was justified when Hedin's map proved remarkably accurate in leading him to Lou-lan. Hedin had worked out that the site had been a garrison during the Han period, more than 1,700 years ago. Excavation over 11 freezing days showed that it had held out as a lonely outpost for years beyond the collapse of the government that it had been ordered to serve. Unsuspected too was the discovery of tablets with a script from northwesternmost India. Stein also found a tape measure of Hedin's which he was later able to return to the heroic Swede at a London dinner. Stein was surprised too by the arrival of forwarded mail – the runner had almost perished of thirst but his first request, on arrival, was that Stein should check the seals on the mail to ensure it was still intact.

Stein pressed on and came to a new site, known as Miran. Excavating here for nearly three weeks yielded masses of Tibetan texts and scraps of leather armour. There were also the remains of a Buddhist monastery decorated with fine plaster heads and lively wall paintings, some in a Classical style that had surely been brought along the Silk Road – one document even bore a name in Roman style, 'Tita'. The dig was done in freezing wind which scattered a choking dust from cloth, snapped wooden tools, straw and human excrement (of 'age-persisting smelliness', as Stein put it). Owing to limited basic supplies, the expedition had to leave before he could bring down and pack as many of the paintings as he wanted. Tough work was made harder by a bout of the malaria that he had picked up in India.

The travel onwards was difficult too, with six donkeys dying of dehydration and exhaustion, but in this part of the trek Stein made another discovery. Seven years before a French explorer had reported finding towers and when Stein spotted one of them he recognized it as a brick watch-tower. He found another the next day and beside it he noticed bundles of reeds sticking out of the ground in a line that stretched three miles to a third tower. Digging in, he discovered that the reeds crowned a wall of clay; and during the following days he traced it toward Dunhuang (Sha-chov). Here in the Gobi desert in March 1907 he had found an extension of the Great Wall of China.

Meanwhile, Stein's curiosity was keenly piqued about a rumour of manuscripts and their archivist, Wang Yuan-lu. After waiting for the archivist for more than six weeks, he was discouraged to find that the man 'looked ... extremely shy and nervous, with an occasional expression of cunning'. He soon found out that 'To rely on the temptation of money alone as a means of overcoming his scruples was manifestly useless'. For the hermit Wang lived at the Caves of the Thousand Buddhas, at the foot of a giant figure of the Buddha.

Stein had known about the Caves of the Thousand Buddhas all along, since a Hungarian colleague had described a visit to them in 1879. The surprise was the archive.

Stein decided to broach the matter less directly. For this and the whole amazing sequence of events that followed, Stein depended on his 'indefatigable, zealous' Chinese assistant. Through him, Stein flattered Wang by asking about the shrine that the archivist was restoring. Some of the new sculpture was hideous but Wang's sincerity was compelling. Then Stein carefully mentioned the popular travellers' saint, Xuan Zang (Hsüan-tsang), his own 'Buddhist Pausanius' (Schliemann's antiquarian authority), whose ancient route he had followed earlier from India; and, sure enough, 'a gleam of lively interest' lit the little hermit's face and he led Stein out to admire his paintings of the saint's adventures.

That evening, Wang sent Stein some specimens from the archive. They were translations by Xuan Zang himself of texts that he had brought from India, though Wang had not known that. With this revelation, it was then easy to persuade him that destiny – perhaps Xuan Zang himself – had chosen Stein to fetch the manuscripts back to India. Wang took him into the archive: 'Heaped up ... without any order, there appeared in the dim light of the priest's little lamp a solid mass of ... bundles rising to ... nearly ten feet.'

Stein completed his trawl, he thought that Wang 'was almost ready to recognise that it was a pious act ... to rescue for Western scholarship all those relics ... which were otherwise bound to get lost ... through local indifference'.

Stein's name would become black in China for what ensued. After arranging surreptitiously to study samples of the archive, Stein quickly found with the help of his Chinese assistant that the collection comprised manuscripts relating to the introduction of Buddhism across the Himalayas and the Karakoram to Inner Asia, along with paintings, votive silks and brocades and enormous banners perhaps intended for hanging from the cliffs above. There was also the world's oldest known printed book. Only too aware of rival expeditions converging on him from Europe and Japan, Stein recognized at once that this literary treasure was a key to the whole field of research in which they were all engaged. He offered Wang a donation for the shrine in return for letting him take some of the archive to a 'temple of learning in Ta-Ying-Kuo', England (the British Museum). Wang was persuaded

For the next six weeks he devoted time to finding out more about this northwestern end of the Wall. He raised eight labourers, 'torpid and enfeebled by opium' and he managed to find documents written on wood and coins as well as utensils, rugs and other things of daily life on the outer limit of the Han Empire 2000 years ago. 'With the experience daily repeated of perishable things wonderfully preserved one risks gradually losing the true sense of time,' he wrote. As the sun sank low in the evening, the line of the wall showed up as a shadow; he remembered his father's tale of looking for Roman defences in the Hungarian plain.

Having packed up his takings in readiness for shipment to England, Stein started a final trek eastward. He found another Buddhist shrine and completed his survey of the Great Wall's western section, where he found a later wall at right angles, marking a change of policy for China's western frontier.

At last, he turned back westwards, making first for Turfan, lying more than 130m below sea level and watered by a system of underground ducts. A German expedition had beaten him to it and Stein was disparaging about how their 'burrowing' had disturbed all the ancient monasteries except for one group of temples a little out in the desert. Further on, he found that expeditions from Russia, Japan and France, as well as pilgrims, had disturbed the sites.

He then made a daring crossing of the Taklamakan, at the other side of which he identified a site mentioned by Marco Polo. He now wanted to tackle just one more challenge: crossing the Kunlun mountains, 'overwhelmingly grand', between the Taklamakan and Kashmir. It nearly proved his last, as he got frostbite in the feet. His manual recommended helpfully that 'the aid of an experienced surgeon should be sought at once'. Whether or not on account of the altitude, his porters refused to carry him by litter and so he had to endure agonizing rides by yak and camel. He made it to safety but some of his right toes had to be amputated.

Three years of research followed in England, Stein was publicly honoured there and as well as in Hungary. In 1912 (the year after Arthur Evans), he was knighted.

That year saw him back in the North-West Frontier Province with the title of Superintendant of Archaeology. He felt a strong pull to Afghanistan, across that Frontier: he was fascinated by the idea of finding Alexander the Great's town of Balkh (Bactra) in Bactria; but the Afghans hesitated to let him in. So he mulled over other options and settled on returning to Sinkiang and the Silk Route by tracing an ancient pilgrimage and military route from Kashmir, first through territory recently opened by diplomacy and then the mighty

Pamir mountains before swinging back west to Central Asia and Iran. This expedition was to take 32 months.

Once back in Sinkiang, he visited old haunts, including Niya, where he dug again. On reaching Miran he found that the main scene of the wall paintings that he had left behind in 1907 had been hacked out by a Japanese who had read Stein's report. The gracefully decorated dado beneath it was left, however, and Stein took that. He made next for desolate Lou-lan where, despite his labourers' misgivings, he investigated a cemetery and found 'a wealth of beautiful designs & colours' among the goods accompanying the well preserved bodies. An assistant of his had found further military ruins in the district and Stein was able to amplify the picture of China's former western salient. Returning to some of the outposts that he had seen before, he found his own footprints and Dash's preserved in the stillness.

Next came a trek across rough salt desert back to the main frontier defences near Dunhuang. It would have been risky except that the route was marked by a trail of coins, arrowheads and other finds dropped by ancient travellers. On meeting Wang Yuan-lu again, Stein heard that Paul Pelliot had taken more of the archive and the Chinese authorities had tried to garner the rest; but Wang had kept a sample of his own and Stein bargained for four more cases of that.

Continuing his survey of the Great Wall, Stein fell under his own horse and was severely bruised. He worried that the injury was worse but gradually he recovered. The expedition moved back to the Turfan depression. In a deadly combination of mist and 23 degrees of frost, Stein investigated cave temples visited before by the German archaeologists who had allowed the frescoes to be cut out very clumsily (and had then lost them to rats in their store at Berlin). He arranged for the collection of 60 cases of what was left. He also investigated a cemetery of the 7th century AD (dated by Byzantine coins) with the bodies, their silks (some apparently printed with portraits of the deceased) and other goods, including pastries, very well preserved. Continuing along the Silk Route's northern branch around the Taklamakan, he investigated cave shrines where he found early manuscripts.

The Afghans had by now decided to grant their archaeological concession to the French, so they refused to let Stein enter and the last part of his expedition had to skirt Afghanistan's northern border to Iran along the Silk

Route into Central Asia (where the Russians, checking his passport at the frontier with Sinkiang, were still allied to the British). At one stage his local porters had to build a road to carry the expedition across screes formed four years earlier by a massive earthquake. With local labourers, Stein investigated military posts that reminded him of Niya; making his way back to Pakistan he passed the carcasses of hundreds of camels, reminding him of 'the vast amount of suffering which that far more difficult route' in Sinkiang 'must have witnessed' 1,700 years ago.

At Koh-i-Khwaja, a distinctive and well known site in eastern Iran, he made a discovery that was like the last piece of a jigsaw puzzle. It was both a good instance of his sense for the distinctive character of particular places and another surprising illustration of the vast distances spanned by the Silk Road; and Stein's activity here pointed up the dilemma of collecting for science. 'The ruins were supposed to be Muhammadan,' he explained, 'but an instinctive reliance on the continuity of local worship ... drew me': behind a wall, he spotted a bit of fresco which turned out to be part of a large Buddhist scene. It complemented the Classical art at Miran. He exposed and took down the frescoes and sent them off to Pakistan just before the Iranian authorities protested about his infringement of their concession to the French and accused him of 'digging for treasure'.

In the 1920s, Stein's fieldwork was in Kashmir and Baluchistan (southwestern Pakistan). He visited the dig at Mohenjo-daro, where the true antiquity of the Harappan culture was being revealed; and then met Leonard Woolley on his dig at Ur in Iraq.

In 1930, Harvard University commissioned Stein to lead another expedition from Kashmir to Sinkiang, but it was a flop. Before he had accomplished much at all, he was driven out by Chinese resentment over his 'raid' on Dunhuang.

From 1931 to 1936 he reconnoitred new regions. The first survey was a search for the geography of Alexander the Great's campaign in the Punjab; and there followed a series of projects in Iran, the last of which he funded himself, but it all felt 'tame'. More exciting, because of the technology employed, was his last fieldwork. Inspired in part by the Frenchman, Father Poidebard, who had been flying over Syria, Stein carried out a survey of the

Roman frontier in Iraq using both motor vehicles and, notably, an aircraft. He was 75 and would die six years later in 1943. Aurel Stein stood little more than 160cm tall but was built very solidly. When he was in his 60s a young local soldier assigned to accompany him in the mountains of the North-West Frontier complained that 'Stein Sahib is ... supernatural ... he walked me off my legs'.

Stein's general expression was penetratingly alert. He had good friends in many places but he always remained a bachelor. By his own admission, he came to feel easiest out in the wilderness or at his beloved alpine camp in Kashmir. 'His work,' explained a friend, 'governed his life ... He planned well ahead and never allowed anything to interfere with ... his plans'; nor did he expect to discuss the details of them with anyone.

CHAPTER 10: THE ANCIENT MAYA

Two young men of good constitution, and who could ... spare five years,might succeed (JL Stephens, 1841)

The ruins of the ancient Maya are fascinating and romantic. They lie in Guatemala, Belize, El Salvador and western Honduras – the northern part of Central America – and neighbouring parts of Mexico. Their descendants still live there but today they are surrounded by other peoples, most of whose ancestors arrived in connection with the Spanish empire, which conquered the region in the mid 16th century.

The Maya have now been traced back almost 3,000 years but in the 19th century there was no idea of such antiquity. Nor did anyone recognize, at first, that the ruins belonged to the ancestors of the living Maya, though it was discovered that the ancient Maya had unique hieroglyphic writing; and then that the biggest of their cities succumbed to the jungles long before the Spanish Conquest. Each of these issues has fascinated scholars and explorers ever since.

Investigations of the ruins began in the later 18th and early 19th centuries with expeditions sent by the region's Spanish governors. The best documented was Guillermo Dupaix's in 1807, but he argued that Palenque and other monuments in Mexico were the work of Old World civilizations or even remains of 'Atlantis'. After the collapse of the Spanish Empire, Palenque was studied by a doughty French explorer, Frédéric de Waldeck, whose work was lively but wayward and who also investigated Uxmal in Yucatán. In 1836 Palenque, Copán and Utatlan were surveyed by Juan Galindo, a dashing Briton serving the Central American government. Five years later came John L Stephens's book, *Incidents of travel in Central America, Chiapas and Yucatán*, which combined accurate illustrated records of major monuments with an unput-downable tale of derring-do. Ever alert to commercial opportunity, Stephens carried out a second expedition and wrote it up in *Incidents of travel in Yucatán*; his books remain among the best in travel literature.

Two Frenchmen followed: Abbot Brasseur and Augustus le Plongeon. Brasseur concentrated on collecting manuscripts but he learned two Maya languages and studied the ruins near Rabinal in the mountains of Guatemala, convincing himself that this and other sites were remains of Atlantis. Le Plongeon settled in Yucatán, where he learned the region's Maya language. He held that the Maya were ancestral to the Egyptians and suggested that the Greek alphabet, 'alpha beta gamma delta', was the folk memory of a Maya hymn.

Galindo and Stephens made useful measurements but the first records of Maya monuments up to modern standards were achieved in the later 19th century by another Frenchman, Désiré Charnay, an Englishman, Alfred Maudslay, and a German, Teobert Maler. The last of the leading early explorers was an American, SG Morley, who travelled the region from 1906 to 1948. The stories that follow are those of Stephens (and his artist, Frederick Catherwood), Maudslay and the captivating Sylvanus Morley.

Stephens and Catherwood Break New Ground

'Our guide cleared a way with his machete, and we ... came to ... a structure ... so far as the trees would enable us to make it out, like ... a pyramid,' wrote John Lloyd Stephens (1805–52), and continued: 'we came upon a ... sculptured ... figure of a man curiously and richly dressed, ... the face ... solemn, stern, and well fitted to excite terror.' The only sound was monkeys overhead, 'mockeries of humanity ... like ... spirits ... guarding the ruins'. As he and his companion, Frederick Catherwood, found another 14 monuments and 'strove ... to penetrate the mystery', Stephens pondered on who might have created these buildings in Central America long ago: 'America, say historians, was peopled by savages; but savages never reared these structures, ... carved these stones. We asked the Indians who made them, and their dull answer was ... "who knows?".' This was a question that Stephens set out to answer.

It was 1839 and Stephens was in what had recently been the federation of Central American states to seek its government on behalf of the USA. Since the region was rapidly dissolving into civil war, he took the opportunity to pursue his interest in the ancient art and ruins of the region. By now 34 years old, he had started out as a lawyer in New York but had soon devoted himself to writing travel books about the Near East and eastern Europe. His venture into Central America would give him a chance to produce another travel book, or two, though ostensibly his aim was to flesh out the skimpy reports that had hitherto been published about the Maya ruins. Catherwood, the 40-year-old English illustrator who accompanied him, had studied Old World monuments in Italy, Greece Palestine and Egypt, and was intrigued by what he had heard about the jungle ruins of the New World.

They had landed first in Belize and then took a steamboat to Guatemala. Stephens recorded news of the politics and fighting, as he was bound to do for his government, but his first objective was Copán in Honduras – not just as an interesting site for ruins but also a safer destination, he assured himself, than the official one of Guatemala City since a rebel army lay athwart that route.

The travellers soon noticed ruined churches, abandoned villages and hastily filled graves. Food was scarce and they were often greeted with suspicion. The monsoon was still on, the trail was rough, their muleteer was unhelpful and in Guatemala they were briefly captured by a gang of ruffians led by a wicked-looking captain. It took them two days to reach Copán, where their initial welcome was cool but they soon gained a useful reputation. The wife of the owner of Copán's ruins had chronic rheumatism and, having advised her 'to take her feet out of a puddle in which she was standing', Stephens 'promised to consult Mr Catherwood, who was an even better medico'. The gods punished this charlatanry: the rains that afternoon were torrential and the pair got stuck in Copán's swollen river.

Stephens reflected that, had it been the dry season, the ideal technique for fieldwork would have been to burn off the vegetation. The explorers settled on cutting lanes through the trees, but their Spanish was limited and the mystified workers seemed lazy and were easily diverted. Then there was the wildlife to contend with: 'scorpions, and the bites of moschetoes and … ticks … which, in spite of … pantaloons tied tight over our boots and coats buttoned close to the throat … got under our clothes, and buried themselves in the flesh; at night, moreover, the hut … was alive with fleas'. To add to their discomfort, a posse sent by their captors in Guatemala arrived and was only deterred by the sights of the guns the two men carried.

Persistence revealed ruins stretching more than two miles. Their survey was a distinct improvement on that of Galindo and they mapped the main mass of ruins and the 'idols' (statues or stelae) and 'altars' found with some of them. With camera lucida and squared paper, Catherwood worked hard to draw several of these sculptures and he recorded some of the hieroglyphic inscriptions in detail. The designs were complicated and different from anything he had seen before – which would be a clue for those interested in the origins of Mayan hieroglyphics. They considered making plaster casts, a technique Catherwood had taught himself in Athens during the Turkish siege, but they lacked the materials. They worked for six days at Copán and then Stephens bought the ruins for fifty dollars.

The men pressed on with the original mission to Guatemala City, with Stephens mulling over the 'moral effect' of the monuments 'in the depths of a tropical forest ... strange in design, excellent in sculpture, rich in ornament, different from the works of any other people, their uses and purposes, their whole history so entirely unknown, with the hieroglyphics explaining all, but perfectly unintelligible'. They suggested to him a holy city, 'the Mecca or Jerusalem of an unknown people'.

Stephens commented on the political and economic turmoil in a landscape of mighty mountains and stunningly beautiful colours, and he clearly had little respect for the indigenous people, the Indians, who made up the majority of the population. Guatemala City was under strenuous martial law, but Stephens met the Central American Vice-President and tried to work out whether or not the federation still existed. Geography, though, excited him more than politics: he scaled an erupting volcano and witnessed and earthquake; and in Nicaragua he assessed the proposal for a canal from the Caribbean to the Pacific Ocean. He soon succumbed to malaria, which was rife along most of the coast from El Salvador to Costa Rica. Catherwood, still finishing off at Copán, also contracted malaria, but in the meantime he had followed rumours about ruins at Quirigua, where he found platforms and sculpture like Copán's.

By now Stephens had concluded that diplomacy was doomed by the disintegration of Central America and he decided to make for Palenque, in Mexico. The region through which he and Catherwood would have to pass was far from safe; it was rumoured that the local Indians saw white men as enemies. Along the journey they came to Utatlan, a citadel that had faced the Spaniards, and found a crop of corn being grown among the ruins by an Indian family claiming to be descended from 'the royal house' that had led the defence. They found layers of painted plaster on a pyramid at Utatlan and Stephens concluded that Utatlan had been built by the Indians but the absence of any of the features observed at Copán and Quirigua confirmed his view that the latter were 'cities of another race' and much older than Utatlan. The local priest told them of a mysterious cave and a ruined city to the north, and also of 'a living city, large and populous, occupied by Indians ... in the same state as before the discovery of America'. This presumably referred to the Peten, a district of refuge throughout the Colonial period and since, but Stephens and Catherwood resisted the temptation to change direction and continued to Quetzaltenango and thence through the great Cuchumatan moutains to reach the Mexican frontier.

Weary but relieved, the little party reached Mexican territory, but they soon heard news of an uprising around Palenque and in Yucatán and that the government had specifically forbidden foreigners at Palenque. Considering that the site was said to be remote, that the army was probably busy with counter-insurgency and that even one day's research at Palenque would be valuable, they decided to go on regardless.

On the way they were guided to the ruins of Tonina, where they were surprised to find a wooden lintel and intrigued to be shown what was said to be a tunnel to Palenque (a distance that today would be a 2-hour drive). They crawled into the stifling heat inside and Catherwood made a rough record of wall decorations in moulded plaster. It was not in fact a tunnel. Research has since confirmed that Tonina and Palenque were indeed connected 1,250 years ago – but by diplomacy and war, not a tunnel.

The final descent to Palenque, set among the foothills overlooking a plain that stretches to the Gulf of Mexico, was rough and exhausting. They came to the village and then struggled on through soggy forest until they reached the ancient ruins, where they were guided to *el palacio*. Here they found autographs of previous visitors – and a plague of mosquitoes and ticks. They surveyed the 'palace' and studied its reliefs, finding traces of colour on the plasterwork, and Catherwood took special care to record the hieroglyphs. Intrigued by the flattened forehead shown in some of the reliefs, Stephens compared it to a similar practice among the Choctaw and Flatheads in North America but surmised that the Maya pictures indicated 'a race now lost and unknown'.

More hieroglyphs were in what is now known as the Temple of the Inscriptions and they tried to make plastercasts of them by burning snails' shells from the river by the palace. Stephens again wanted to buy the site, but the law forbade foreigners from purchasing land unless married to a Mexican. He found that 'the oldest young lady was not more than fourteen' and that the prettiest was already married.

The Indians told the explorers that there were few other monuments to find at Palenque. Knowing that Cortés, the Spanish conqueror, had passed not far away without comment, Stephens deduced that 'this great and lovely city ... of a cultivated, polished ... people, who had passed through all the stages incident to the rise and fall of nations' was already abandoned by then without even 'a name to distinguish it'.

The next goal was the ruins at Uxmal. Stephens and Catherwood set off across the plain for Yucatán and on the first afternoon they found a 'large black animal with fiery eyes' roaring from a tree. Curious, Stephens shot it and blood poured down the trunk but the body was held fast by its long tail. A couple of days later, near the Gulf of Mexico, his gun was back in action amongst alligators. They sailed along the Gulf's east coast and then, riding or borne by litter, trekked through intense heat to Uxmal.

The site had recently been cleared and planted with corn (apparently the rubble of such ruins made excellent fertilizer) and so it was easy to study. They listened to the local Indians reciting the lore about the main buildings: the House of the Magician or Dwarf on its lofty pyramid, the Nunnery quadrangle and the House of the Governor – 'not unworthy,' opined Stephens, 'to stand side by side with the remains of Egyptian, Grecian and Roman art'.

All the lintels at Uxmal were of wood, or had been so; their decay, he deduced was what had allowed many of the buildings to collapse. Fascinated by the themes in Uxmal's intricate architectural ornamentation, he marvelled at the 'immense time, skill, and labour required ... and the wealth, power, and cultivation of the people who could command it'.

The explorers were tired and Catherwood was ill, as his last drawings seem to show. Regaining the coast, they found a ship, became becalmed and quite lost in the Gulf and their rations were exhausted before they were picked up by a brig bound for New York. They would return to Uxmal within two years.

This time they were accompanied by Samuel Cabot, a Boston doctor and or-nithologist, and on the way to Uxmal they rode out to visit the ruins of Mayapan (described by Stephens as an ancient city never visited before by archaeologists) but found their way challenged by impenetrable vegetation. They were pioneering a route across Yucatán from Mérida and Uxmal through Chichén Itzá to Tulum, a route still followed today by tourists from the world over. At Ticoh they glimpsed

the main pyramid at Mayapan from the church tower and then continued to
Uxmal, which had already been reclaimed by the bush. They cleared themselves
a patch at the House of the Governor and studied it in detail; they also described
the nearby House of Turtles, closely recorded the Nunnery quadrangle and its ornamentation (especially the twisting figures of rattlesnakes) and tested the ground
for the 'sculptured turtles' that Waldeck had reported as paving the court, but they
found none.

Puzzled by two parallel mounds near the Nunnery, Stephens instructed his crew
to cut into one of them but they found only solid stone. In the middle of the fac-
ing sides he found fragmentary stone rings. In his subsequent book he suggested to
his readers at this point in his tale that the two mounds were the sides of a sports
ground, not admitting that he had studied accounts of the Aztecs' sacred Ball
Game.

He dug the top of the Great Pyramid and discovered the zigzag 'greca' ornamentation that is now recognized as a hallmark throughout tropical Mexico a
thousand years ago. Convinced that he would find a tunnel into the middle of the
mound, he set his workmen to a frenetic but fruitless dig. he then collapsed with
malaria and retired to recuperate at Ticul. Four days later, Cabot arrived with the
same symptoms and then one of their assistants. Since Cabot's medicines had been
mislaid, he submitted to a local remedy of orange, cinnamon, lime and tamarind,
which healed him.

The local vicar, a typical amateur archaeologist of his day, showed Stephens
no fewer than 37 mounds nearby that had been steadily quarried for building
stone. Stephens asked the workers, their misgivings mollified only by the vicar's
participation, to dig a tomb, from which they took a pot and the skeleton ('They
are the bones of our kinsman,' he was told). Stephens wondered whether to collect
samples of skulls from local cemeteries, but was advised that it would have 'caused
an excitement among the Indians, and perhaps led to mischief'.

Stephens reconnoitred the district and examined other ruins, including those
at Siho and Tankuche and a cave system that, like the 'tunnel' at Tonina, turned
out to be the corridors of a building. He was gratified to be shown a ceiba (kapok)
tree aged just 23 years, because some visitors had argued for Copán and Palenque
that the great size of these trees measured the minimum age of the ruins from
which they sprang.

The expedition then traced a route to Kabah, Sayil and Labna. At Kabah,

Stephens and Catherwood noted the buildings' intense ornamentation and by now they could compare several sites. They noticed the little pillars typical of the region's 'Puuc' architectural style. Catherwood found a timber lintel carved in the same way as the masonry and they removed it for shipment to New York. Stephens compared with Kabah archway to Rome's triumphal arches.

Labna fascinated the explorers and they recorded the main pyramid and the archway. At the main range of buildings Stephens investigated the enigmatic pit in which, he was told by his trembling labourers, lived the lord of the place; Stephens found only a startled iguana. A few days later they were shown a *sakbe*, or 'white road'. These causeways are known in several parts of Yucatán, but Stephens and Catherwood had evidently missed the one across the middle of Labna and had not spotted in the undergrowth the *sakbe* that led back to Uxmal from the arch at Kabah.

At Santa Rosa Xtampak they found one of the region's biggest ancient buildings; at Dzibilnocac they found extensive ruins, but they were poorly preserved. At the little town of Mani, mounds amongst the yards showed that the place had been occupied since before the Conquest; and at Peto they were shown the copy of an old chronicle tracing more than a thousand years of local history.

It was in this district that they made one of their most famous discoveries, about the traditional management of water. The region's limestone allowed no rivers or lakes on the surface and, assuming that Uxmal had been a city, like Palenque, Stephens and Catherwood had puzzled about its water supply. Ignoring his workers' warnings of snakes, scorpions and hornets, Stephens explored the pits scattered about the site to see whether they were cisterns. The result was inconclusive but later, following hints from locals, they did discover that certain ponds were used as reservoirs, enhanced with tubes and pits to collect the water seeping from the rock and to trap rainwater during the dry season. At 'Nine Wells' the explorers were taken down a rickety ladder into a cave system more than 125m deep.

Their next destination was Chichén Itzá. It was well known compared with the other ruins, but it still lacked an accurate description. The principal ruins were comparatively easy to study in that the site was open, thanks to grazing (though the cattle did encourage ticks). Catherwood's survey marked all the largest or better preserved buildings and Stephens provided good, thoughtful general descriptions. He aptly compared the Great Ball Court and its two stone rings to the twin mounds at Uxmal (and it was here in his book that he mentioned the Aztec ball game). He also saw similarities between the wall paintings that they found at Chichén Itzá and Aztec arat, sowing an idea that has bedevilled Chichén Itzá ever since.

Catherwood's mapping did not stretch to the great sink hole (known as the Sacred Cenote) to the north of the main ruins, but Stephens pointed out that, as the only exposed water, this and a second smaller sink hole must explain Chichén Itzá's location. The Sacred Cenote was not a mere amenity; Stephens wrote that a 'mysterious influence seemed to pervade it, in unison with the historical account that ... human victims were thrown into it in sacrifice'.

Stephens and Catherwood then set out on the last part of their journey, making for the Caribbean coast. They heard about the ruins and a *sakbe* at Cobá but the report gave no sense of the site's immense scale and, being told that the forest was thick and lacked shelter, they decided to pass it by. On reaching the sea they took a cramped sailing-boat to the island of Cozumel, recently abandoned (its last inhabitant had been a pirate), and discovered some ancient ruins amidst the scrub. Their final investigation was at the spectacular cliff-top town of Tulum on the mainland; again it was thickly covered in scrub but they managed to make a useful survey.

Although Stephens had continually disparaged local ignorance or indifference about the monuments, he gradually became interested in the traditional way of life in Central America and his attitude to the Maya of Yucatán changed. He began to understand how reduced they had been by the Spaniards and he did at last consider them to be 'of the same great race' that had built the ancient cities.

As for the archaeology, Stephens noted Spanish descriptions of towns and buildings encountered during the conquest of Mexico and concluded that Tulum dated from not long before Cortés. He reflected that it was the work of 'the same people who created the great ruined cities over which, when we began our journey, hung a veil of ... mystery'. By then he had deduced that those other sites were ancient, though not as old as Dupaix had suggested on digging the Palace at Palenque in 1807. The Maya ruins were distinctive and not to be compared with Classical architecture or with anything that Stephens knew from Asia. Designs and hieroglyphs were not the same as Egypt's. What they had found was American, 'without models or masters, having a distinct, separate, independent existence; like the plants and fruits of the soil, indigenous'. Stephens thought again about that great city which the priest claimed to have espied in Guatemala.

Catherwood exhibited the finds that they had collected in New York, but all of them soon perished in a fire. Samuel Morton, an eminent anatomist, inspected the skull that Stephens had dug out at Ticul and pronounced that it was akin to others throughout the Americas, thus implying common origins for all Native Americans, and Stephens accept his deduction. So Stephens and Catherwood had not only produced good descriptive surveys of many Maya ruins (and told a rollicking good traveller's tale as well); they had also shown that the ancient race who had built them was the same indigenous race as the Indians that still lived in Central America and Yucatán and that their culture was American rather than imported from elsewhere.

After his explorations among the Maya, Stephens went into the shipping business and then, joined again by Catherwood, resumed his interest in linking the Pacific and the Caribbean by starting to lay a railway across Panama. Malaria finally killed him in 1852; and two years later Catherwood drowned as his liner sank off New England on the way from Liverpool to New York.

Alfred Maudslay Follows in Stephens' Footsteps

Alfred P Maudslay was born into a comfortable way of life a couple of years before Stephens died of malaria. Unlike Stephens, Maudslay was no journalist, but much more is now known about his adventures thanks to his biographer Ian Graham (whose own long career in the Maya forests has been as adventurous and illustrious as that of any of his predecessors). Maudslay had read Stephens's books and decided to follow his footsteps in Central America and Mexico; ultimately he would introduce a new standard of systematic accuracy in recording the ruins that had been visited by Stephens and Catherwood.

As a 22-year-old Cambridge University graduate, Maudslay had crossed Panama on the new railway (started by Stephens) and sailed up the Pacific coast. In those days his interest was not specifically archaeological; he travelled up to Lake Atitlan and Quetzaltenango and then toured the USA. He returned to Cambridge to study medicine but soon hankered for the tropics and went to Trinidad, where he was recruited to the staff of the Colonial Governor and accompanied him to Queensland before being sent to Fiji. He spent five years in the South Pacific, helping to negotiate among the interests stirred up by European imperialism, and then returned to England in 1880. He planned a three-month tour for the following year to gain a general impression of Guatemala's monuments – his first archaeological expedition. This new interest in ruins was probably partly inspired by an elder cousin who had carried out a dig in Jerusalem.

Packing his camera and Stephens's *Incidents of travel in Central America, Chiapas and Yucatan*, Maudslay duly set off in 1881 on his second visit to Guatemala and headed for Quirigua and Copán, thrilled to discover for himself what Stephens and Catherwood had seen and recorded. He had hoped to see the ancient sculptures at Santa Lucía Cotzumalhuapa but discovered that the best had been hacked up for export to the Berlin Museum. So he made his way to Tikal, which had been discovered barely ten years before, and here he was joined by Gorgonio López, who (sometimes accompanied by his brother) would become Maudslay's companionable mainstay, working with him on several future projects.

Maudslay had been assured that Tikal would be cleared of trees for his visit but the plan failed. Clambering up one of the pyramids on arrival, he spotted others poking through the forest but at ground level the trees obscured everything. He tried to clear three of the pyramids for photography but progress was slow because, as Stephens had found, the workers had to be watched. Maudslay's one source of cheer was a pair of eager curassow fledglings, orphaned when their mother had been shot; he put them in his pockets and made the trek back to Belize.

Back in Guatemala barely six months later, Maudslay gave himself a few days to enjoy the highlands before returning to Quirigua to make further observations of the sculpture and carry out a rough survey. Then, riding, paddling and hiking, he crossed Guatemala to the frontier with Mexico along the River Usumacinta, where, he had been told there was another ruined city with more sculpture – the site now known as Yaxchilan. He soon found the ruins and traces of resin which Indians had been burning with their prayers to the ancient gods. Over the next three days he found the enigmatic carved stone lintels now well known for the royal rites that they depict.

Amidst this work an envelope arrived containing a business card marked 'Franco-American Mission' and bearing the name Désiré Charnay. Having completed research in Central Mexico, Charnay was now exploring Maya country, funded by the French government and a leading tobacconist, Pierre Lorillard (whose company, founded in 1760, was the first to manufacture tobacco in the British colonies of North America). Charnay too had word of Yaxchilan – he wondered whether it was the ruined city that Stephens had heard about after visiting Utatlan – so he was most dismayed to discover that Maudslay had beaten him there. What followed seems to show something of the skills that Maudslay had learned as a diplomat.

His 'fair looks and elastic step', remarked Charnay, 'showed him to be an Englishman'. Maudslay assured Charnay that he knew him by name and sought to soothe his chagrin by describing himself as just an amateur: 'You can name the town,' he said – or so Charnay attests – 'and claim to have discovered it'. Charnay named it after the tobacconist. According to Maudslay's diary, Charnay had just recovered from his first attack of malaria. He shared his supply of food and, holding forth about his theory of the ruins, plied Maudslay with some of the wines that his porters had borne through the jungle. Ambitious for acclaim and academic eminence, reflected Maudslay, 'He is just my idea of a French traveller ... not ... a Scientific traveller of much class.' Yet he was very interested to watch Charnay's assistant making paper mouldings of the lintels – 'a very easy process'.

Finishing off at Yaxchilan, Maudslay selected one of the lintels to be taken back to England. It had already been trimmed by the man who had first mentioned the site to him and Maudslay had to reduce it twice more for carrying. He completed his tour with another week at Tikal, making large clearings for photography.

Maudslay returned in 1883 and started at Quirigua. Although he now had the previous year's survey to guide him, the work was hampered by mosquitoes, scorpions, snakes and the rains, which went on longer than expected and much of the site was flooded. Clearing the monuments of trees, moss and lichen to record them was hard work; and several of the carvings that he wanted to study had to be dug around the base but the excavations quickly filled with water. Many of his workers fell ill and then the healthy ones ran off.

This time, Maudslay had with him an assistant from London, Lorenzo Giuntini, an expert on moulding sculpture in plaster – a technique that works much better than moulding in paper for larger sculptures in deeper relief. Some of Quirigua's big complicated sculptures in the round had to be moulded in many pieces and Giuntini ended up with more than a thousand of them.

Maudslay's next expedition was in 1885. His first fieldwork was an
excursion to the ruins known as Pueblo Viejo (Old Town), probably one of
the sites raided by Cortés in 1524. Giuntini was delayed but when he arrived,
Maudslay listed the season's cargo: hand-tools and wheel barrows, survey
equipment, cameras and photographic supplies, along with a barrel of lime,
four tons of plaster and 500 lb of paper; and the plaster, bought in England for
£2.50, had cost him £50 by the time that it reached Copán.

The season went well but it was tough. The ticks were especially bad; and
smallpox broke out uncomfortably close; and then war erupted. Most of his
labourers conscripted and his supply of money was cut off but, tellingly, the
remaining villagers not only agreed to keep working for him but even offered
to lend him cash.

With peace restored, Copán was visited by a general. Showing him the
ruins, Maudslay must have emphasized the hieroglyphs, for, carefully copying
one text that he spotted, the general commented on how European the glyphs
looked – he had been studying a tourist's autograph.

The pyramids intrigued Maudslay. Although smaller, they seemed like
Tikal's great mounds, so he wondered whether they too had supported shrines
and was gratified to find on one of them the remains of a doorway that
confirmed his idea. He cut a section through one of the pyramids, recorded
evidence for a sequence of ceremonial deposits, and took samples of bone
and cinnabar for laboratory analysis. As late as 1899, Cyrus Thomas, the
leading US archaeologist, wrote admiringly of these digs, commenting of the
architecture exposed that 'it is difficult to realize ... that all this is the work of
native American artists, and not ... of the Orient'!

When Maudslay packed up after five months he had some 1,400 plaster
casts plus four sculptures and architectural ornaments that the President of
Honduras allowed him to take. The homeward journey started badly; the
mouldings got stranded on a reef off Florida; and Maudslay and Giuntini's
ship broke down off Yucatán, where it had to jettison its cargo of fast ripening
bananas like a yellow ribbon on the sea.

Maudslay returned to Guatemala again in 1887. He began by visiting and
surveying Utatlan and Iximche, in the highlands. Like Pueblo Viejo, these
were the ruins of local capitals on the eve of the Spanish Conquest. Utatlan
had been visited by Stephens and Catherwood and, like Stephens, Maudslay

reflected on how these sites lacked the impressive features of Copán and the other great ruins of the lowlands.

He then travelled across the middle of Guatemala to Belize. Parts of the route had rarely been used before, if ever. At one point, his carriers bridged a river by felling trees on opposite banks so that their branches tangled together safely in the middle. The wildlife was hazardous too: he lost one of his men to a snake bite; and there was a river full of alligators. Maudslay was adopted by another creature orphaned by one of his men, this time a mischievous howler monkey.

On reaching Belize, Maudslay sent part of his crew back to Tikal with instructions on taking moulds of some stelae that he had photographed before. Maudslay himself spent about a week carrying out a geographical survey in western Belize in order to report to the government on economic prospects.

Now Maudslay turned to Yucatán. On landing late in 1888, he was frustrated for a month, awaiting the arrival of both his supplies and the bureaucratic permissions for importing them. When his moulding paper at last arrived, half of it had been ruined by seawater. Then he learned that labour was scarce on account of an unexpected boom in the region's plantations.

His goal was Chichén Itzá, to test the idea that the ruins were a historical bridge between the ancient cities and late centres like Utatlan. Setting up camp at Chichén, he found that his workers all went home of an evening, so he paid one of them to stay with him 'but', explained Maudslay, the man spoke 'no Spanish ... and the way he ... silently ... followed my every movement with his eyes was worse than a nightmare'. As for excavation, Maudslay had been warned that 'the Indian's method ... was to scrape a little earth together with his hands and, in a leisurely way, to ladle it into ... plaited leaves or ... his ... hat. I must own', he conceded, 'that there was some difficulty in persuading' them 'that four men were not needed to take charge of one wheelbarrow'; and he 'did once see an Indian ... carry off the loaded barrow on ... his head' – but 'as soon as they found the wheels went round ... they always took kindly to wheelbarrows'. After some weeks, he was joined at Chichén by Henry Sweet, who had been working for his fellow New Englander, EH Thompson, at Labna. Like Stephens, Thompson had obtained a diplomatic post in order to study the Maya. So he was suspicious of Maudslay, and Sweet's defection made matters worse: 'It is not very pleasant', he complained about the 'competition', 'but ... Mr Maudslay is rich and generous [and] will not ... approach in value our work done'. Thompson did, indeed, stay in Yucatán, as we shall see.

Maudslay and Sweet got on very well. They discussed their discoveries and they enjoyed together the sights and sounds of the forest birds, the beauties of the rainy season evenings and the moonlight 'rippling' over the treetops. They both caught malaria 'but ... our attacks ... occurred on alternate days', Maudslay recorded dryly, so they helped each other.

Maudslay mapped Chichén Itzá and worked out the functions of some of the architectural features. He improved on Catherwood's survey and included the Sacred Cenote. Amidst felled trees, big buildings and heaps of rubble, the achievement was all the more remarkable considering the equipment – plane table, alidade and tape measures; and Maudslay's plan of the 'observatory' building was far more accurate than the one made a few years later by a Harvard University expedition. Sweet did most of the work on recording the highly ornamented lower 'temple' at the Great Ballcourt. It was gruelling, since the chamber faced the sun for most of the day and the walls were too hot for the moulding paper. They persisted until their stores ran out and noone else had any to sell.

Maudslay did not return to Mexico until 1891, probably partly for reasons of health. His new destination was Palenque and this time he brought a surveyor from England. After a difficult voyage along the Gulf coast, they sailed fitfully up the River Usumacinta. It took two weeks to assemble a team of porters. At last, a party of Indians returning to the mountains agreed to carry Maudslay's equipment to Palenque but they got 'hopelessly drunk' and the start, next morning, was late.

Then it proved impossible to hire workers locally and so Maudslay had to try 40 miles away. His muleteer was obstructive but their destination, when they reached it, was just girding up for Carnival, led by a blaring band. The party resumed the next night and, at four, the drunken muleteer reported for duty. When at last Maudslay was ready to leave, he found the laden mules wandering about. The muleteer grumpily threw Maudslay an insult that he could not interpret but the police chief heard it and gaoled him. Eventually, Maudslay secured his release but then his host insisted on providing a guide for the journey back to Palenque; and the guide was drunk and muttered unhappily about how 'It's always like this with the English: gallop, gallop!'.

Maudslay settled into the palace where Stephens and Catherwood had stayed. He was joined by Gorgonio López and they set about the laborious tasks of removing stalactites from the ornamented walls, making casts of the inscriptions and rigging the camera up on scaffolds. Scrambling across the trees between the buildings was exhausting; rain undid the mouldings; and the supply of workers was always uncertain.

The work at Palenque was the last of Maudslay's intensive field investigations. He travelled again widely in Guatemala and Mexico but then devoted himself to publishing his results and to literary research, notably on Bernal Díaz's famous 16th century history of the Spanish Conquest of Mexico.

What inspires or 'drives' such personalities? Unlike Stephens or Catherwood, who were 'self-made men', Maudslay lived largely on his family's business fortune. However, his biographer did have one big surprise, a chink in this impeccable English gentleman's image: a love affair that was only revealed in a posthumous bequest to his 'illegitimate child'.

Morley Finds History in the Hieroglyphics
Sylvanus ('Vay') Morley spent more than 40 years travelling in Maya country. He was on the short side of medium in height and very short sighted but he was immensely energetic – quite restless with it. He was confirmed by his eminent English follower, JES Thompson as 'a most lovable man'. The first stage of Morley's career was supported by a wealthy aunt; thereafter, he depended on appointments – and his infectious glee.

Morley became the leading figure in studies of the Maya during the second quarter of the 20th century. He was born in 1883 and went on to study at Harvard, where he was one of the three students enrolled in the university's first course on the Maya. He also heard EH Thompson lecturing on Yucatán and within months, set about learning Spanish (an art that he never really mastered), graduated, and sailed for Yucatán.

Morley was a vigorous tourist, photographing and measuring the ruins. At Chichén Itzá, he watched EH Thompson's dredging of the Sacred Cenote for treasures. On his way back to the USA he visited several of the main monuments of Mexico, studied the National Museum and looked up one of the capital city's leading archaeologists.

The following summer, he joined two other students to train under Edgar Hewett in New Mexico. One of them, AV (Ted) Kidder, quickly became a close colleague and recalled that Morley 'never let up': '... sunburn, thirst, saddle soreness, rock bruises, cactus stabs, nothing discouraged him ... whistling and singing as he stumbled about ... He was ... indefatigable'. Both the staff and the Native American labourers teased Morley for his enthusiasm. In 1912, he became excited about the architecture in Santa Fe and led a campaign to preserve it.

Kidder eventually made his reputation among the ruins and mounds of Pecos Pueblo, near Santa Fe, but Morley went back to Mexico. In 1909, Hewett sent him to measure the buildings at Chichén Itzá, Uxmal and Kabah, back in Yucatán. At Kabah, Morley caught malaria for the first time. The next year, Hewett took him digging at Quirigua and showed him Copán, where Morley immediately charmed the locals. He returned to Quirigua for two more seasons, by which time the site was owned by the United Fruit Company and in 1912 Morley had to arrange for a visit from the US Secretary of State. On a visit to Copán later that year, he succumbed to another bout of malaria and had to be borne off with feet tied under his mule; on recovering consciousness he immediately resumed scribbling in his note book before fainting again.

In 1913, Hewett sent Morley and a colleague to Yucatán to take photographs for the forthcoming California World Fair. Morley's plan was to visit Tulum, in the middle of rebel territory and they took the opportunity to join a negotiator treating with the last of the rebels still holding out from the uprising of 1847.

In 1912, Morley had got wind of a forthcoming job at the Carnegie Institution of Washington; and in the following year he was one of three candidates invited to propose a major project of research. Morley's idea was to investigate Chichén Itzá and its place in the history of the Maya. The competition was intense and even Morley was drawn into briefing against some of the opposition. Just as it looked as though his proposal was the favourite, it transpired that Hewett was lobbying against him.

By then Mexico had fallen into the bloodiest phase of its civil war, the Revolution, and the US Navy attacked the city of Veracruz. Tense but undeterred, Morley undertook a tour of monuments in northern Guatemala, mainly to collect inscribed dates. He travelled with HJ Spinden, a rising star of Maya studies who (as Morley's biographer, RL Brunhouse put it) 'had blue eyes and white hair, weighed over 200 pounds, liked to argue, and had a way of splashing into the news'. The going was no easier than it had been for their predecessors in the 19th century, and their plan for crossing the river to Yaxchilan, in Mexican territory, had to be abandoned on account of guerrillas. In the last phase Morley travelled alone in Belize, where he called at a plantation. Since the servant announced, 'He is a white man, sah,' the manager himself went to the door and later recalled that: 'there stood a short, little man in a huge poncho', who would not stop talking but 'looked very ill and'; 'the only dry thing about him was his notebook, ... carefully wrapped'.

Back in the USA, Morley finally secured the appointment in the Carnegie Institution. The war in Mexico prevented his return to Chichén Itzá, so he turned to Central America instead, to seek the evidence of history from the hieroglyphs.

He landed in Belize with a surveyor. Trekking into the interior, their guide wasted three days getting lost, but once they reached their destination Morley followed the gum tappers' paths through the bush and discovered how extensive the ancient settlements of the Maya could be. He returned to Copán, where he was welcomed as a friend and made several new discoveries; but he lost more time when a local informant led him on a wild goose chase in search of carved stones. By the end of this expedition, Morley calculated that he had covered 500 miles through forest and bush, including 100 miles with no trails.

He returned in 1916 with a team that included WH Holmes, an eminent old archaeologist who insisted on riding in a suit but quickly recovered from exhaustion with the aid of whisky. He also took a doctor whose skills with the villagers at Copán had the same benefit for archaeology as Catherwood's (and whose cures, presumably, lasted longer).

Moving across to the forest of northern Guatemala, Morley followed some obscure leads that yielded perhaps the biggest discovery of all: Uaxactun, where, on his first afternoon, he found a monument dated to AD 50, the earliest yet recorded. Some days later there was insurgency in the forest and, in an apparent case of mistaken identity, Morley lost two of his party in an ambush, including a US citizen.

The diplomatic consequences of this incident could have been disastrous for his project but that, in the following spring, the USA entered the World War. Morley enlisted in a fit of patriotism that persisted in his responses to Germans for years thereafter. Ordered to pose as a harmless archaeologist, he was sent back to Central America in order to find out whether they were plotting to hide submarines there. He visited San Salvador after the earthquake of 1917 and then he survived the 'quakes of 1917–8 in Guatemala City and pitched in to help with the relief effort. He managed to fit research of his own in at Quirigua and Copán and he visited the large site of Los Higos, to the east, and he found it easy to combine archaeology with espionage in Yucatán, where he returned to Tulum and found other ruins of the same kind. Travelling through old haunts to the west, he even used the end of his mission to visit Palenque.

From 1919 to 1922, Morley led expeditions to northern Guatemala. On the last of these trips, he was back in Tulum when he received a deputation of Maya asking him to remind Queen Victoria of her offer to protect them. A week later, another party arrived to announce their disapproval of the tree felling for Morley's photography; this awkward message was handled with cigarettes and brandy.

In 1923, all the different skills that Morley had developed were needed at once – how to manage locals and officials as well as diggers, how to survey and dig, how to write up his discoveries. For now, at last, almost everything was in place to begin digging in earnest with teams that he had picked by hand, including several survivors of Hewett's New Mexico. The final preparation demanded that Morley assure both the Carnegie and the Mexican authorities that his own project was appropriate. He also had to assure the Mexicans that the Carnegie Institution was very wealthy but not a museum, since EH Thompson, by then, stood accused of smuggling finds from the Sacred Cenote to Harvard.

It was a tall order, demanding attendance in both Yucatán and Mexico City, but Morley acquitted himself supremely. He flattered the city fathers of Mérida by assuring them (quite earnestly, no doubt) that the ancient Maya had been the most civilized people of the Americas. A mark of Morley's impact was that the state governor consulted him about how to manage his wife and his mistress when, in fact, he had just fallen in love with a journalist covering the Carnegie project for the *New York Times*.

At the eleventh hour, another *coup d'état* threw everything into doubt; but in 1924, at last, the digs began at both Uaxactun and Chichén Itzá. Morley concentrated on the latter but he was less concerned with the details now. He kept his crews and many guests entertained. Especially in the Great Ball Court, he developed a flair for combining 'son' – jazz or Sibelius and Beethoven – with the moon's natural '*lumière*'. In 1931, Leopold Stokowski came to investigate the Court's acoustic; and Morley brought the top brass of Mérida and dined them with a show of 'Maya' dances there. He also used the Ball Court to entertain an embassy of Maya rebels in trying to obtain permission for a colleague, Alfonso Villa Rojas, to work among them; visiting them in turn, Morley was fascinated by their blend of traditional worship and Christianity.

All the while, major finds were emerging at Chichén Itzá, especially from the so-called Warriors Temple; but in 1929 Morley had been eased out of the project's directorship in favour of Ted Kidder. Relieved of wider duties, he investigated the ruins at Piedras Negras and Yaxchilan. In 1931 the immense site of Calakmul was discovered and Morley hurried out to appraise it, finding 103 stones with texts, nearly half of which he proceeded to decipher at once – he was mainly interested in the dates they revealed. His assistant, Gustav Strömsvik, described him 'stumbling over creepers and ... logs and into holes'. 'We came after ... picking him up and cutting vines that entangled him .... torn and bleeding – "I never have time to look down", he cried.

Morley's later years were like Maudslay's. He did return to Mexico and Central America but devoted himself increasingly to writing. In 1946, he published a text book on the Maya which, repeatedly updated since, remains in print. He died in 1948. 'He was endowed with a greater power of personality than most,' concluded his biographer: 'He communicated his sincerity and friendship instantly'; 'his enthusiasm propelled him and his associates forward'.

Mitchell-Hedges and the Crystal Skull
Meanwhile, in 1924 (goes the tale), Thomas Gann was exploring the ancient

Maya ruins of Lubaantun, in southern Belize. Helping him was a British adventurer, 'Mike' FA Mitchell-Hedges, who was travelling with his wealthy companion, 'Mabs', Lady Richmond Brown. This much is true.

In 1943 or 1944, Mitchell-Hedges bought the sculpture of a skull made of quartz crystal and claimed that his daughter had found it back at Lubaantun in 1926. He also claimed that it had belonged to a traditional Maya priest; and that it was mortally dangerous. He never did explain how the priest left it around for little Miss Mitchell-Hedges to pick up; but, until her recent death, she exhibited the skull at her house in Canada. The story is plain fiction on one count; but, on others, it does ring somewhat true ...

Mitchell-Hedges's is one of five or six crystal skulls reputed to come from the land of the Maya. Of the others, the best known is at the British Museum. The Museum's was bought from Tiffany, the glass-makers of New York, in 1898, with the story that it had first been acquired by a Spaniard in Mexico, some 40 years before. In the 1930s, comparison of its skull with Mitchell-Hedges's showed that the dimensions of these two extraordinary carvings are very much alike; and, later, another study of the British Museum's revealed the traces of a jeweller's wheel. Since there is no independent evidence for such an instrument in the Americas before the European era, one suggestion is that both were copied from the same model in the 19th century.

How, though, did the Museum manage to see the second skull before Mitchell-Hedges bought it? Well, it was simply lent to the Museum by its owner. The results of the study were published in 1936.

Having abandoned a promising career as a stock broker in London, Mitchell-Hedges fell in with the flamboyant insurgent, Pancho Villa, during the Mexican Revolution. Surviving that with injuries, he went fishing in a dinghy in the Caribbean and hauled in a red snapper of more than 102lb, and then a sting ray, and then two sharks – one of the latter bulging with a recently swallowed girl. Soon afterward, he was in Beverly Hills, claiming to be at work on a screen play for Jean Harlow; and then – so the story goes – he threw a supper party at which Gen. Eisenhower and Richard M. Nixon did the dishes.

Why did the Mitchell-Hedges ever think their tale would be believed? Was it because it makes sense to imagine that the ancient Maya would have devoted such effort that would have gone into the skull? The crystal itself is a rare treasure, and the workmanship is extraordinary, even with the advantages of Victorian tools. The ancient Maya, like so many peoples past and present, valued the human head as a site of power. At Chichén Itzá's Great Ball Court, for instance, there are depictions of heads and beheadings.

But that assumes that Mitchell-Hedges's public knew about ancient Maya symbolism in particular. So is it just that we all know that many traditions around the world, ancient and modern, have invested the human head with symbolic values? Or is it that Mitchell-Hedges knew, however unlikely our earnest archaeologists find it, that his public would love the tale?

CHAPTER 11: MYSTERIES OF THE INCAS

When America was first discovered in its several regions, the Aborigines were found in two ... conditions. First were the Village Indians, ... in New Mexico and Central America, and ... the Andes. Second, were the Non-horticultural Indians ... of the valley of Columbia, of ... Canada, and of some other sections of America. Between these tribes ... were the Iroquois ... (LH Morgan, 1877)

The Native peoples of the Americas share common origins. Their histories and ways of life diverged and diversified from a common stock of Siberian immigrants who first began to colonize Canada roughly 20,000 years ago and then rapidly spread southward. Incas, Aztecs and the Maya were one with the ancestors of the Cherokees, the Sioux, the peoples of the Amazon and the hardy Indians of Patagonia.

Such is the consensus today, but there are academic minorities challenging it on various grounds. Nor was there agreement about the unity of Native America until the end of the 19th century: to many observers it was incredible that people like the Indians of their own day could have created the monuments revealed by explorers such as John Lloyd Stephens. Stephens himself was slow to admit the possibility; Lewis Henry Morgan struggled with the Paradox, yet everyone in Mexico or Peru knew about the empires that had confronted the Conquistadores in the 1500s. Public excitement about new archaeological evidence to match that common knowledge was what made the name of Hiram Bingham a century ago and Ephraim Squier, our next hero (or villain), tried to cash in on. With no such legends in the USA, the disparity between the great ancient earthworks of the Mid West or the South East of the country and the wretched condition of most Native Americans prompted various wild ideas about a race of 'Moundbuilders' already lost before the Europeans even arrived.

Squier, who was intrigued by so much neglected archaeology, tended to support that idea; soon after Stephens and Catherwood returned to New York, he rapidly set about gathering and publishing an enormous amount of archaeological evidence about the ancient mounds and other earthworks in the USA. It was not until research by Cyrus Thomas in the 1880s and early 1890s that the connection between past and present became undeniable here – and with it, in the plight of the Native Americans, came a chilling lesson about the frailty of 'civilization'.

Ephraim Squier: from New York to Peru

Ephraim Squier declared early that he wanted to leave 'a NAME in the world'. He was born in 1821 in upstate New York and in due course, after a couple of false starts, he took up as a campaigning journalist. In 1845 he moved to Chillicothe in southern Ohio, where he was fascinated at once by the ancient mounds and all the more as he discovered local people's ignorance about them. He met Edwin H Davis, a doctor who shared his curiosity and who had entered correspondence with the anthropologists of the day, including the anatomist, Samuel Morton (whom Stephens had consulted). Morton was collecting data on skulls from throughout the Americas in an effort to prove that Native Americans did indeed comprise a distinct race, albeit divided in two main families.

Although Davis found Squier 'so enthusiastic ... that he goes off half-cocked sometimes', they agreed to work together. Squier's fellow journalists soon found him unreliable, distracted not only by archaeology but also, in late 1846, by joining the state House of Representatives. Ranging as far as West Virginia ('most infernal country'), Davis and Squier investigated scores of sites. One hesitates to imagine the technique of excavation but their surveys of earthworks, if often inaccurate and too interpretive, were later to prove useful.

Davis and Squier soon compiled a very large report and began to negotiate with the Smithsonian Institution to publish it. Collating their information with that of others, amounting to nearly 100 surveys of earthworks and almost 150 digs from Wisconsin to Louisiana and Georgia, it was heavily illustrated with very striking plans of earthworks, archaeological sections through mounds, simple plans of burials, finds recovered from the digs, rock art and other observations. The interpretive discussions are thoughtful but, Squier's disapproval of local ignorance notwithstanding, they share the prevalent assumption of the day that the Moundbuilders were not ancestral to the contemporary Native Americans of the north but had been related to 'the gorgeous semi-civilization of Mexico and Peru'.

Two problems sprang up. Firstly, Squier was asked to forge some of the correspondence in order to avoid the impression that the Smithsonian would accept unsolicited submissions; this he evidently agreed to. Secondly, an argument blew up once Davis heard that authorship of their report was to be printed in reverse alphabetic order – 'Squier and Davis'. To make matters worse, Squier then summed up the results in an article with barely a mention either of his colleague or of others who had shared data with them. The scandal was aired in the *Cincinnati Gazette*. Squier dug his heels in, remarking to the geographer GP Marsh that Davis had done no more than could 'any boy in the country'. (There was also the suspicion that Squier forged a report from the American Ethnological Society to the Smithsonian in order to aggrandize himself.) The two colleagues then argued acrimoniously about ownership of some of their finds. Once the reviews of their book started to appear, Davis erupted incandescently – correctly detecting Squier's own hand in the suppression of references to Davis himself.

Squier then left Ohio and undertook a weatherbeaten season of archaeological survey in his home state, where he deduced that the most prominent archaeological sites were the work of people ancestral to the Iroquois. He corresponded with LH Morgan, the great expert on Iroquois social anthropology

Squier yearned for grander monuments. With the election of President Taylor in 1848, he lobbied to be posted as a diplomat to Central or South America. The idea may well have been prompted by Stephens's experience. Supported by Stephens himself and the celebrated historian of Peru, WH Prescott, as well as by Morton, Marsh and the Smithsonian, Squier was duly sent to Guatemala; but he was recalled on the President's untimely death.

Blandishing as many eminent supporters as he could, Squier tried to persuade the Smithsonian to create a museum but by then the Institution seems to have been wary of him. Next, he tried unsuccessfully to cash in on the plans for linking the Caribbean Sea to the Pacific Ocean by a railway across Central America. Eventually, he returned to journalism.

In his second book, Squier described this period as defeating his 'hopes and aspirations'; but he was seconded to the State Department in 1863 for a mission to Peru; and on completing that he awarded himself two years to explore the country. His avowed inspiration was Prescott's account of the Spanish Conquest of the Incas; but much of his writing and even the book's title (*Peru: incidents of travel and exploration*), betrayed again the example of Stephens. Although the prose is wooden and much less concise, *Peru* combines accounts of the country at that time with useful observations that helped to define several issues that archaeologists only began to take up properly well into the 20th century. At first, perhaps, Squier had wanted to emulate Stephens, especially his literary success, but genuine archaeological research interests set in as he discerned telling differences between monuments in different districts. He became interested in identifying the archaeology of the Incas and in recognizing the traces of other civilization in the same regions.

Once arrived in Lima, Squier's first excursion was to Pachacamac, which had been the most powerful shrine in the Central Andes before the Conquest. He described the ruins with helpful sketches and a couple of plans roughly measured; and he reported briefly on digging one of the many tombs with their mummies wrapped in textiles and accompanied by goods for the hereafter. He also explained how he took a shot at a condor that was eyeing him up for a snack but only managed to knock off a feather, which was 70cm long.

Squier visited several other sites near Lima. He experimented with photography – and claims to have made the first picture taken during an earth tremor (the result blurred). His drawings, though simple, show certain details that help to distinguish Inca remains from earlier ones. He was especially engrossed among the extensive ruins of Cajamarquilla when he surprised some bandits. Cordiality was established soon enough and Squier's assistant delivered some wine to them the next day; but coming back he was late and much the worse for wear since the bandits' leader made him sample the gift before accepting it. A month later, the army killed the brigand and exhibited his rotting body in Lima.

Then Squier prepared to visit the great ruins on Peru's North Coast. He explained that he hired a photographer, 'Mr P___'. This was that energetic and imaginative Augustus le Plongeon (later to move to Yucatán), who had arrived in Peru the previous year and whose local contacts would several times prove useful.

The journey was made by coaster, with frequent stops, some of which allowed Squier to visit local ruins. On arrival Squier introduced himself to the local prefect, whom he had met in Lima but who now received him coolly.

Squier visited Chan Chan, the capital of the ancient Chimú people, deserted since the Incas conquest in the 1460s. He provided a very useful description both of the ruins and their history and of the marvellous pottery, though he did not distinguish the later black wares of Chan Chan from the earlier coloured pottery of Moche, which he visited too (nor does he mention the 'pornographic' pots of Moche, now a favourite draw for tourists).

Returning southwards, Squier visited the Nepeña valley, where he made rough surveys of several well built Inca and Chimú ruins. Observantly, he distinguished them from other remains built less regularly. Ironically, he commented too on the accuracy of other archaeologists and the pitfalls of copying others' work uncritically. He also pointed out how his investigations were watched and followed up by local people searching for treasures from ruins – a tradition enshrined in a popular Peruvian song.

From Tacna, in the far south, Squier turned inland for the long and arduous climb up into the Andes mountains. Both men and animals suffered from the altitude and drinking water was scarce.

At last the expedition reached the great basin of Lake Titicaca, where Squier crossed into Bolivian territory and made for the ruins of Tiwanaku (Tiahuanaco). He described the monuments, including a row of stones that he dubbed 'The American Stonehenge' and the famous 'Gate of the Sun'. He speculated on how the massive stones were brought to Tiwanaku; and, considering the difficulty of growing food at such altitude, he wondered whether it was only a ceremonial site rather than a town (modern research has shown that, in fact, there were the farms to support a big population).

The expedition moved on to visit the great shrine of Our Lady at Copacabana and then the Inca complex on the island in the lake, which they reached on a hazardous and very uncomfortable raft like 'a mammoth cigar'. Squier surveyed the buildings of the Inca 'palace', and also investigated the ancient shrine of Coati.

Now they turned north for the long journey to Cuzco and the Inca heartland. Squier had grown sceptical about local informants and ignored a number of leads about other monuments 'a little' off his route; but on arriving at the great Inca temple at Rakchi he was amazed that the ruin remained scarcely known. Nearing Cuzco, he visited some of the ancient remains at Pikillakta but he scarcely recognized the evidence for its long and complicated history.

Cuzco was capital of the Inca empire and Squier was especially interested in the survival of Inca streets and masonry. He remarked on the political significance of how the Dominican friary was built on top of the great walls of the ancient Sun Temple. Then he studied the great ceremonial precinct of Sacsahuaman overlooking Cuzco, marvelling at the precision of its massive stonework. He described it as a citadel but criticized the old idea that it was modelled on the 'fortress' at Tiwanaku.

From Cuzco, he trekked across to the Urubamba valley and described the Inca remains now so well known. At Ollantaytambo, having found that the governor depended, for his knowledge of the archaeology, on Prescott's book (Prescott never went to Peru) Squier spent two weeks studying and surveying the ruins there. The party then moved up the valley to Pisac, where he was intrigued by the distinctive the Sun Stone and thought carefully about what it showed of Inca astronomy. He also noted the rock-cut tombs at both Pisac and Ollantaytambo.

The last part of the great expedition was the long journey back to Lima and Squier was disappointed to find few traces of the Incas' roads. It was another tough journey, through mountains, over great empty plains and across several rope bridges. One of his companions baulked at the 'bridge' over the River Apurimac but lost his clothes as he swam it and was then stoned as a savage when he was spotted naked.

Squier lived until 1888 and his troubles did not diminish. Delegated to attend an archaeology congress in Paris in 1867, he took his wife and sailed to Liverpool with Frank Leslie, a fellow journalist and 'friend'. The latter wired British creditors from the Central American railway fiasco so that, on landing, Squier was imprisoned and his wife went off to enjoy the lights of London with Leslie who then produced the bail that he had brought from New York and the threesome cheerfully proceeded to Paris. Six years later Mrs Squier arranged for her husband to get drunk at a party with another woman having previously commissioned Leslie's artists to document the scene; she divorced him and married the 'friend'. In 1874, Squier was declared insane.

Peru was published in New York in 1877, and to boost sales Squier published a popular article, as he had for 'Squier and Davis'. It included unattributed photographs by le Plongeon, who accused him of 'unscrupulous and superficial ... plagiarism'. Commenting on his earlier treatment of Davis, the eminent anthropologist, HC Schoolcraft, described Squier as a 'reptile'.

Hiram Bingham and the Mountain City

Bingham's name is inseparable from that most spectacular of the world's monuments, Machu Picchu, which he 'discovered' in 1911. Like Squier, le Plongeon, Charnay and Stephens, Bingham sought success. Machu Picchu – or his exciting writings about it – yielded that.

Hiram Bingham III was born in 1875 in Hawaii, where his grandfather had led the Christian missionary effort there. Bingham married an heiress in 1900; in 1905 he was awarded a doctorate in South American history at Harvard University and then obtained for himself a new post in his subject. The following year he undertook a trek in the footsteps of the South American liberator, Bolívar, and wrote a book about it.

In 1908 Bingham persuaded the US Secretary of State to send him to a conference in Chile, an assignment that enabled him to trek across the Andes from Buenos Aires to Lima and gave him his first experience of Andean archaeology as he followed leads to the Inca ruin of Choqquequirau, near Cuzco. The climbing was arduous and more than once Bingham or his mules nearly slipped down precipices. Choqquequirau ('Cradle of Gold') was fabled to be rich in treasure and Bingham found the buildings comparatively easy to explore since a previous project had cleared the heaviest vegetation in search of it. He admitted that, 'inexperienced and unacquainted' with the techniques for recording remains, he depended on the Royal Geographical Society's 'Hints for Travellers', although where the Society recommended photography, Bingham was hampered by cloud, mist and rain – it was the rainy season and that year's rains, everyone assured him, were the worst in a generation.

Soon captivated by the sights and scenes that Squier had visited, Bingham wrote about them with much more excitement and grace. He was probably quicker than Squier to learn about local sensitivities, not least the prejudice that, while it was deemed reasonable to hunt for treasure, to measure the bones from burials was weird.

Bingham's next expedition was in 1911 and would make his name. Funding eluded him until he inspired the Yale Club, in an after-dinner speech, to support a multi-disciplinary project. In the event, of course, archaeology took the limelight.

The romantic idea that a site like Choqquequirau was the Incas' last redoubt had been kindled by the historian, Sir Clements Markham, who had shown, on the basis of contemporary accounts, that, quite unlike the Conquest of Mexico, the Spanish Conquest of Peru took all of 40 years and that the Incas had made a final stand deep in the mountains west of Cuzco. To find their 'last capital' was the goal that Bingham set himself.

The team began with some digging near Cuzco. They then set off along Squier's route to the Urubamba, passing 'romantic Ollantaytambo', and came to the fort at Patallakta where they surveyed the remains above it. Bingham speculated as to whether these sites were of Inca date or earlier – an idea finally settled in the 1980s by the British historian, Ann Kendall. Further on, Bingham was told of a site like Ollantaytambo that promised to be a lost city. A week was spent on opening a trail, only to find that, although the ruin was, indeed, Inca, it comprised one solitary house. Bingham was at a loss to understand the comparison with Ollantaytambo.

The expedition moved on into the Vilcabamba valley. The district was being opened to the outside world for the fist time by a small trail. Antonio Raimondi had been here but reported only one small ruin. As for local 'leads', Squier had been sceptical but, with a specific goal in a country never visited by archaeologists before, what option was there but to seek and follow such clues? Bingham found that although the Kechwas (the Incas' descendants) were indifferent to archaeological remains, they did, 'remember' any number of them when directed by local officials or landowners and in return offered rewards or wages.

With a method like Stephens and Maudslay in Guatemala and Mexico, Bingham had studied the Spanish sources. On the basis of their descriptions of both buildings and their settings, he interpreted quite exactly some of the ruins that he was shown. Thus following an account of the headquarters of one of the Incas' last leaders at Vitcos, he was convinced that he could recognize it at the site now called Rosaspata, a place-name that mixes Spanish and Kechwa most appropriately. Test pits yielded a mix of Inca domestic artefacts along with horseshoe nails, scissors and three jews' harps that matched just the kind of exchange between the Incas and the Spaniards to be expected of the period of Conquest. Yet Rosaspata's location did not quite match the accounts of the Incas' final stronghold.

Their next lead took the expedition into 1,500 unmapped square miles. The Indians were rumoured to be hostile and led by a strongman in a palace with 'fifty savage servants'. Bingham's guide led the party to a homestead where the women obligingly served coffee, killed four or five scampering guinea pigs and roasted them then and there. The chat over lunch was about how the village had lost a pony to a cougar the night before.

From there the trek was along a ridge too narrow and slippery to ride mules. Mist and rain all but blocked the view of the canyons below. The following day brought the team well below the cloud but still on slopes so steep that Bingham and his naturalist colleague had to cut a terrace to pitch their tent. Then, at last, they met the district's dreaded 'boss' in his modest thatched hut, attended by a single 'wild-eyed maid-of-all-work'. The visitors were welcomed happily and shown various Inca finds that the man had turned up on his plantation. Exploring over the next couple of days, they found an Indian hut with Inca pots in daily use; and they revealed the remains of an Inca settlement that reminded Bingham of the Spanish report of a 'University of Idolatry where lived ... wizards'.

Moving on, the expedition camped wearily at a jungly riverbank. Although the neighbourhood was notorious for vipers, the naturalist decided to look for butterflies and Bingham's other colleague voted to deal with laundry and stitching. Ruins, they reminded him, were Bingham's responsibility. Their sole neighbour, in his thatched hut, had confirmed that there were ruins – on top of the opposite mountain – but it was raining so hard that he refused to guide anyone for less than three or four times the daily wage.

It was agreed. They crossed a roaring stream on logs spliced together by vines and clambered up the mountainside in hot and humid conditions. They passed some terraces of the kind that the Incas had built so extensively. Then Bingham noticed ashlar walls – very big, of white granite, the masonry assembled more beautifully, he thought, than anything in Cuzco itself. 'Dimly, I began to realize,' he says, that this was 'as fine as the finest stonework in the world.' Visibility was good, since local farmers had cleared parts of the site and planted it. 'Suddenly we found ourselves standing in front of the ruins of two of the finest and most interesting structures in ancient America ... The sight held me spellbound.' It was Machu Picchu. Bingham clambered back to the camp and gradually revealed what he had seen. He set about assembling a crew to clear the site to map it; and of course they had to build a new bridge.

It was no easier to collect workers here than for Maudslay among the Maya and it is fairly clear from Bingham's account that, although he did not know it, he recruited the labour according to the custom of 'mita' (work by rota or corvée) which dates from the Inca period and probably far earlier. As well as wages, Bingham had to give his workers coca leaves (which, he grumbled, they took 40 minutes a day to prepare); and he added 'trinkets ... from Mr Woolworth's emporium'.

The work was hard. Despite the weather, Bingham's engineer set fire to the undergrowth and, fleeing, fell over a cliff, saved only by sturdy vegetation. Shortly afterward, following another tip about ruins, he was injured in scaling the peak, Wayna Picchu. When Bingham climbed its companion peak with his camera, vertigo made him lie down there with workers holding his legs.

The idea of clearing the rest of the vegetation from Machu Picchu was inspired by WH Holmes (the elderly archaeologist later taken trekking by SG Morley), whom Bingham had met at the conference in Chile and who described how Maudslay prepared Maya ruins for photography. Like Maudslay, Bingham found it difficult to avoid damaging buildings in which the trees had rooted; but he 'even cleaned the moss off the walls'.

Bingham's book, *Lost city of the Incas*, accounted for the ruins with the clear, measured and orderly description to be expected of a professor. Summing up the results of his survey, he explained what he took to be defences, alleys, the supply of water, gardens and 'the sacred plaza'; and he offered an interesting sociological interpretation of the housing. He pointed out how extraordinary it was that massive stones were obtained and manhandled in this unlikely ridge-top situation. He also summed up the results of the four months of digging that followed, with special attention to the scores of burials that his workers found for him down the surrounding slopes. The clearing of the site continued in the following year, including dispersal of the farmers who had been using the ruins. Bingham did not mention that his team found a stone recording in charcoal the visit of a local man in 1902. It transpired that a French explorer had heard about the site in 1870 but decided, like Squier, that a visit would lead him too far off his route.

Like the Romans, one of the most famous things about the Incas is their roads. So, leaving some of his colleagues to the digging, Bingham organized a survey to find out how Machu Picchu was linked to its hinterland. Landslides both ancient and recent made it very hazardous as well as making it difficult to discover a pattern. Bingham left some of the toughest work to his engineer who, once his feet began to suffer, took to riding by mule (rather against his own better judgement). When the animal almost fell over a precipice, he saved them both but was trampled all over by the desperate beast.

Bingham's detailed survey succeeded in defining a pattern of routes replete with some of the wayside features typical of the Incas' systematic management of long-distance travel; and it transpired that the solitary house near Patallakta was one of them – perhaps, after all, Bingham's guide had a telling point in mind when he related that building to Ollantaytambo.

The team found another ruin at Espíritu Santo, but Bingham left assistants to measure it while he climbed the region's highest mountain. Much later, it transpired that Espíritu Santo was probably that final Inca retreat that he had set out to find in the first place.

Bingham returned three times more. His last survey, in 1915, began to show how Machu Picchu fitted into the pattern of other settlements around it as well as the roads.

Two years later, on the USA's entry to the World War, he joined the Air Service and rose to a senior command. He entered politics in 1920 with flair and served as a Senator from 1925 to 1933. He died in 1956.

Hiram Bingham was both bold and brainy. Like Charles Lindbergh and Colonel Glenn later, he was a 'celebrity'. In his day, fiction had little need to create an archaeologist hero.

EPILOGUE

… good archaeologists … live and plan adventurously for the future.
(M Wheeler, 1955)

Archaeology's Heroic age: is it over?

Was Hiram Bingham the last of archaeology's heroes? Does the scientific design of projects now suppress personal inspiration or has technical specialization restricted the scope for creativity by requiring complicated teams of experts in which no one leader's vision prevails? Even Schliemann began to adapt his methods and interpretations to the recommendations of specialist colleagues.

Do ethical standards now prevent 'raiders'? Aurel Stein's last difficulties in Sinkiang showed the growing suspicion of foreign or 'imperialist' interventions; and by 1980 it began to look as though such sensitivies by ethnic minorities in the USA and Australia would jeopardize the feasibility of much archaeology in those countries.

In large part, archaeology has now 'grown up' enough to regulate itself as a discipline with codes of practice. It has become a profession. Most archaeologists are employed as part of public provision for mitigating the impacts of 'development' – new roads, reservoirs, housing and so forth. Have the bureaucratic and technical procedures for this work curtailed imaginative genius and robbed archaeology of its colour?

The career of Augustus Lane-Fox, in England, is the exception to prove all such hindrances to the romance. He was a Victorian general who inherited Cranborne Chase in Dorset on the condition that he adopted the surname Pitt-Rivers. On this land he found prehistoric, Roman and medieval sites and to these he applied military thoroughness and order in developing techniques and precision in excavation and recording that put the barrow diggers before him to shame.

Pitt-Rivers's principles were taken up by Mortimer Wheeler (1890–1976), whose career marked the transition to archaeological professionalism. Among other technical accomplishments, Wheeler's principal contribution to the development of archaeology was training.

A striking feature of nearly all the adventurers described in the previous chapters is that, more or less diligently and effectively, they taught themselves to dig as they went. Catherwood, and Schliemann's assistant, Dörpfeld, it is true, were trained in the survey of buildings. Other pioneers were engineers with similar skills even better suited for the less regular outlines and positions of many monuments – Cunningham and Beglar in India, and one of Maudslay's assistants, and Bingham's, for instance; and one of Pitt-Rivers's strengths was the military experience of measuring the ground in detail, a technique more appropriate for ancient earthworks than architectural survey. For digging, however, there were very few prior examples to follow.

Wheeler was not the first to see a need for training. Morley, after all, was one of the School of American Research's first students (in New Mexico in 1907); but Wheeler would hardly have approved of their fearsome teacher's method. Hewett's first instructions were in survey: he took Morley, Ted Kidder and another student out for a day in southwestern Colorado and then, waving across the view, told them to find and record the remains for him to assess their results after three weeks. Their companion turned into a poet; but Morley and Kidder flourished. 'Well,' remarked Hewett of Morley, 'it may be possible to live down a Harvard education.' He sent them next to measure the cliffside ruins at Mesa Verde; and then to dig the site at Puyé, near Santa Fe – 'very good for us,' recalled Kidder, 'although it might have been hard on the ruin'. In Mexico too there was provision for training, beginning in 1906, but this scheme fell foul of the Revolution there. Forty years later, Kidder started training in excavation at Mayapan.

Wheeler's story shows that glory could still be created in the mid 20th century even while developing professional standards. Wheeler grew up in a family of middling means. It was not until finishing studying at a London University that he took an interest in archaeology, with the university's first scholarship in the subject awarded by a committee that included Sir Arthur Evans. In 1913, he joined a survey of the older buildings and monuments north-east of London. On his first outing, he was shown how to start a frosty morning with a double measure or two of whisky – 'I just simply can't stand the pace,' he groaned that evening.

He must have coped, though, for he was given responsibility for the district's Roman remains, notably at Colchester; but war broke out and he joined the army. He was assigned to training gunners, then brought into the Battle of Passchendaele. Writing from there, he explained that only the mud prevented higher casualties from shrapnel. In 1918, Wheeler was decorated for a feat like Alexander Cunningham's at Gwalior, capturing German artillery which he then used for lobbing 'gas-shells back to their rightful owners'.

After the war Wheeler returned to the historical survey. Shown Colchester Castle's 'dungeon', he spotted that the vaults were Roman. 'Dungeons be damned,' he retorted, soon working out that they belonged to the temple of victory so pointedly and savagely destroyed in Boudicca's rebellion of AD 60. There is little sign of this confident attitude in his work for the survey before the war.

In 1920, Wheeler was given responsibility for archaeology at the National Museum of Wales. This job offered an opportunity for more creative work and he took his cue from Pitt-Rivers's great reports on Dorset, which, published privately in 1887, had attracted little notice. He decided to demonstrate Pitt-Rivers's principles by digging the Roman fort at Caernarvon and an additional principle of his own on this project was to train students at the same time.

If it was not naïve, to have pulled off this double feat is a mark of extraordinary confidence, clarity and managerial skill. It was Wheeler, after all, whose dictum that digging destroys the evidence itself, archaeologists still invoke today to remind each other to work with care; but he went in with very little experience of digging. Yet it would not be quite right to say that Caernarvon was his turning point: on the next dig, explained one of his students, 'He would begin the day by directing ... what we were to find, and ... then disappear, suitably equipped, in the direction of the river. In the evening he would return, not always overburdened with trophies' and explain to them what they had found. One summer, Flinders Petrie came by to measure ancient stone circles – with a pea stick, a business card (for right angles) and a logarithm table.

Along with his principle about recording on the dig, Wheeler insisted on prompt publication. His own technical reports were both. During this same period, he began to show his skill as a lecturer and as a popular writer; but he drew criticism for accepting a national newspaper's sponsorship in return for the rights to report his third dig, on the Roman fortress at Caerleon.

Wheeler was frustrated by what he felt was Wales's provinciality. He turned down an invitation to take up heraldry as Bluemantle Pursuivant (that *is* the title of a job); but in 1926 he accepted the directorship of the London Museum. From there, he ran digs in western England and on the Roman town of St Albans before turning his attention to the massive earthen defences of Dorset's Maiden Castle, where he found evidence of a Roman attack during the conquest, and then to related fortifications in northern France. At Maiden Castle, Wheeler developed a technique for digging larger areas by leaving 'baulks' of unexcavated layers as controls for the site's historical sequence: a grid of 'boxes' is cut into the site.

By now, Wheeler had become flamboyant and charismatic. His biographer, herself very striking, pointed out that (presumably during the war) he had become a truly heroic figure, admirable and awesome. She wrote about him at length as an energetic lover too. Some other commentators remarked that his field projects were notable for a high proportion of young women; but during the season in France he lost his wife to another man.

In 1937, Wheeler's principle of professional training came to life with the foundation of a London University institute for teaching archaeology. He had been mulling over the idea for more than ten years: there was 'need for systematic training in a discipline ... emerging from the chrysalis stage and ... now in the public eye'; there were more students and more jobs; the art of excavation was 'a hidden mystery' so 'something had to be done about it, and, ... in my war-depleted generation, I could see no one but myself to do it'. His determination was reinforced by a tour of the Near East in which he found that (Petrie's example notwithstanding – see chapter eight) the study of successive layers, '*stratification*, ... was almost non-existent. And the work ... carried out upon a lavish and proportionately destructive scale'. The contribution of Petrie's own collections to the new institute was a fillip. The London Institute of Archaeology has been Britain's largest university department of archaeology ever since, 'a workshop' (as Wheeler once put it) with a distinctively happy atmosphere redolent of 'interesting finds' and muddy boots.

On the fresh outbreak of war in 1939, Wheeler was commissioned again to train gunners. He was sent to the Battle of El Alamein, and, promoted to brigadier, took part in the invasion of Italy. One of his contributions was to

ensure respect for archaeological sites: at the time, they included the vast
Roman ruins of Lepcis Magna, in Libya, where the Royal Air Force had plans
for a large radar.

In 1943, Wheeler was appointed to head the Archaeological Survey
of India that Cunningham had first run in 1870. Leonard Woolley,
commissioned to review Indian archaeology after the depression years of
the 1930s, had recommended the appointment of 'a European Adviser' to
rectify a 'detrimental' policy for museums, inept conservation and haphazard
unscientific digging 'by men anxious ... to do well but not sufficiently trained
and experienced to know what good work is'.

Wheeler described first arriving at his new office. 'I stepped over the
recumbent forms of peons, past ... little clusters of idle clerks and hangers-on'
where 'only a wavering murmur like the distant drone of bees indicated the
presence of drowsy human organisms': he 'emitted a bull-like roar, and the
place leapt to anxious life'; 'within an hour the purge was complete'. Prof. DK
Chakrabarti pointed out that this particular image of "mad sahib" set among
the natives to stampede them into ... activity' was over-done; but he allowed
that, in his five years in India, Wheeler helped to modernize archaeology.

Wheeler then set out to inspect his new domain, starting with the territory
that is now Pakistan. His first discovery was that the ruins at Charsada were
being quarried for fertilizer. Next he inspected Taxila, Harappa and Mohenjo-
daro. For the newly recognized Indus civilization revealed at the latter two
sites, the view was that it had been that 'Elysian' rarity, a way of life at peace;
but at Harappa, ignoring the advice that work should respect the heat by
stopping at eight, Wheeler kept his assistants scraping the bricks until noon,
by which time they had revealed what he took to be a defensive wall which
disposed of notions about peace; and he obtained the same result at Mohenjo-
daro. He completed his tour by visiting the east coast, where he was as shocked
as Cunningham at Khajuraho by the 'smut' adorning the mighty temple
of Konark.

Six months after arriving, Wheeler opened his first training dig at Taxila.
The students converged from every part of India and he enjoyed insisting
that they should see themselves as 'Indian archaeologists' foremost: Hindus,
Muslims, Sikhs and Parsees were expected to dine together. Wheeler once
remarked that where in England the sign of a dig well run is silence, in India

it is happy chatter. The students were taught how to dig and record in the trench and learned at least the rudiments of survey, drawing, photography and project management. Wheeler considered that they gained no more than a 'general knowledge of the standards aimed at', but, dispersing, they bore his message back to their regions and Wheeler's principles remained a byword in India, Pakistan and Bangladesh until surprisingly recent calls to shake off the British influence ('boxes' are still being dug by his students' students even where hardly necessary). At the same time he aroused the universities' interest in archaeology, urging that they should coordinate research with geologists, botanists and other scientists.

Wheeler was amazed to discover that there were Roman finds at Arikamedu, near the sleepy little French colony of Pondicherry, south of Chennai (Madras). He assembled another group of students and, after two weeks' slog in a protracted monsoon, the expected finds emerged. They soon helped to date evidence from other parts of southern India, as he then showed in 1947.

The progress stopped that year with national Independence and the bloody Partition between India and Pakistan. Wheeler himself witnessed some of the horrors; and the accompanying political malice soon engulfed the Archaeological Survey. In 1949–50 the Pakistanis brought him back to set up a National Museum, and he conducted a training dig at Mohenjo-daro. One highlight was a couple of public excursions from Karachi: Wheeler struggled to explain their ancient heritage to vast crowds, including 'a peculiarly repulsive small boy ... in the forefront ... with revolver and a fully charged bandolier' and 'a bushy-bearded frontiersman girt waggishly with a revolver in a bright pink ... case, with cartridge-belt to match'; at one point there was 'a bang immediately behind me and a mangled dove fell into our midst'.

On returning to London, Wheeler devoted most of his time to writing up and administration, although he did undertake a dig in Afghanistan and then went back to excavate Charsada. In the 1950s and 1960s, his dashing appearances on television programmes made him a household name and helped to boost the popular appeal of archaeology. He was knighted in 1952.

Is Wheeler's professional heritage disappointingly remote from the dirt, sweat and gold of yore? One consequence of today's standards for valid and legitimate archaeology is a clearer notion of uncontrolled excavation or vandalism and looting. The Turkish and Greek concerns about Schliemann were among the first expressions of it. Yet, partly thanks to an international market in 'antiquities', it still has to be repeated today that, without records of where and how they were found, finds are valueless. Recent years have seen improvement among museums in the USA, for instance, but some of the authorities in western Europe are almost certainly still colluding with cynical auctioneers.

Looters, are not the only ones still enjoying archaeology's excitements. Amidst their more mundane duties, today's archaeologists do from time to time experience the thrill of some discovery, whether optimistically anticipated or quite unexpected. Most still work as persistent and sometimes perceptive and ingenious detectives. As Wheeler knew, their best stories will always be worth hearing – for the tingle of exploration.

Bibliography

Belzoni, GB 2007 *Travels in Egypt and Nubia*, White Star Publishing, Vercelli, Italy

Bernal, I 1980 *A History of Mexican Archaeology: the Vanished Civilizations of Middle America*, Thames & Hudson

Bingham, H 1951 *Lost City of the Incas: the Story of Machu Picchu and its Builders*, Phoenix House

Bingham, H 2002 *Lost City of the Incas: the Story of Machu Picchu and its Builders*, (2nd ed.; H Thomson, Editor) Weidenfeld & Nicolson

British Museum, www.britishmuseum.org

Brunhouse, RL 1971 *Sylvanus G Morley and the World of the Ancient Mayas*, University of Oklahoma Press

Burckhardt, JL 1819 *Travels in Nubia*, John Murray

Burckhardt, JL 1822 *Travels in Syria and the Holy Land*, John Murray

Cadbury, D 2000 *The Dinosaur Hunters: A True Story of Scientific Rivalry and the Discovery of the Prehistoric World*, 4th Estate

Ceram, CW 1966 *The World of Archaeology*, Thames & Hudson

Chakrabarti, DK 1988 *A History of Indian archaeology from the beginning to 1947* Munshiram Manoharlal

Colbert, EH 1968 *Men and Dinosaurs: The Search in Field and Laboratory*, Evans

Cottrell, L 1984 *The Bull of Minos* (4th ed.), Bell & Hyman

Deuel, L 1978 *Memoirs of Heinrich Schliemann: a Documentary Portrait Drawn from his Autobiographical Writings, Letters, and Excavation Reports*, Hutchinson

Evans, J 1943 *Time and Chance: the Story of Arthur Evans and his Forebears*, Longman Green

Fidler, K 1972 *Diggers of Lost Treasure*, Epworth Press

Gaimster, D et al. (eds) 2007 *Making History: Antiquaries in Britain 1707–2007*, Royal Academy of Arts

Graham, I 2002 *Alfred Maudslay and the Ancient Maya: a Biography*, British Museum Press

Hawkes, J 1982 *Mortimer Wheeler, Adventurer in Archaeology*, Weidenfeld & Nicolson

Hopkirk, P 1980 *Foreign Devils on the Silk Road: the Search for the Lost Cities and Treasures of Chinese Central Asia*, John Murray

Layard, AH 1852 *A Popular Account of Discoveries at Nineveh*, John Murray

Layard, AH 1903 *Autobiography*, John Murray

McGowan, C 2001 *The Dragon Seekers: The Discoverers of Dinosaurs During the Prelude to Darwin*, Little, Brown

Meltzer, D 1998 'Introduction' *Ancient monuments of the Mississippi Valley*, by EG Squier & EH Davis, Smithsonian Institution Press

Mirsky, J 1977 *Sir Aurel Stein, Archaeological Explorer*, University of Chicago Press

Mitchell, TC 2004 *The Bible in the British Museum*.

British Museum Press

Moorehead, C 1994 *The Lost Treasures of Troy*, Weidenfeld & Nicolson

Morant, GM 1936 *A Morphological Comparison of Two Crystal Skulls* Man, 36 pp. 105–7 (comments and reply on pp. 107–9)

Morell, V 1995 *Ancestral Passions: The Leakey Family and the Quest for Humankind's Beginnings*, Touchstone

Norman, D 1987 *Footsteps*, BBC Books

Novacek, M 2002 *Time Traveller: In Search of dinosaurs and Ancient Mammals from Montana to Mongolia*, Farrar, Straus and Giroux, New York

Palmer, D 2000 *Neanderthal*, Channel 4 Books

Palmer, D 2003. *Fossil Revolution: the Finds that Changed our View of the Past*, Collins

Palmer, D 2005 *Seven Million Years: The Story of Human Evolution*, Weidenfeld & Nicolson

Palmer, D 2007 *The Origins of Man: an Illustrated history of Human Evolution*, New Holland

Palmer, D, Bahn, P and Tyldesley, J 2005 *Unearthing the Past: the Great Discoveries of Archaeology from Around the World*, Mitchell Beazley

Rich, CJ 1818 *Memoir on the Ruins of Babylon*, Longman & John Murray

Shipman, P 2001 *The Man Who Found The Missing Link: Eugene Dubois and His Lifelong Quest to Prove Darwin Right*, Simon & Schuster

Singh, U 2004 *The Discovery of Early India: Early Archaeologists and the Beginnings of Archaeology*, Permanent Black

Squier, EG 1878 [1877] *Peru: Incidents of Travel and Exploration in the Land of the Incas* Macmillan

Stein, A 1987 *Ruins of Desert Cathay: Personal Narrative of Explorations in Central Asia and Westernmost China*, Dover Publications

Stephens, JL 1962 *Incidents of Travel in Yucatan* (VW von Hagen, Editor), University of Oklahoma Press

Stephens, JL 1969 *Incidents of Travel in Central America, Chiapas and Yucatan*, Dover Publications

Theunissen, B 1985 *Eugene Dubois and the Ape-Man from Java: the History of the First 'Missing Link' and Its Discoverer*, Kluwer

Thiede, CP & D'Ancona, M 2000 *The Quest for the True Cross*, Phoenix

Traill, DA 1995 *Schliemann of Troy: Treasure and Deceit*, John Murray

Tyldesley, J, 2005 *Egypt: How a Lost Civilization was Rediscovered*, BBC Books

Van de Mieroop, M 2007 *A History of the Ancient Near East*, Blackwell Publishing

Vyse, Col. H 1840 *Operations Carried on at the Pyramids of Gizeh in 1837*, James Fraser

Walker, A 1995 *Aurel Stein, Pioneer of the Silk Road*, John Murray

Wheeler, M 1955 *Still Digging: Interleaves from an Antiquary's Notebook*, Michael Joseph

Index

Picture Credits